PUSHING FORWARD

PUSHING FORWARD

A Memoir

Lynne Barber Vigesaa

Publishing support provided by
Ignite Press
55 Shaw Ave. Suite 204
Clovis, CA 93612
www.IgnitePress.us

ISBN: 979-8-9937294-0-4
ISBN: 979-8-9937294-2-8 (Hardcover)
ISBN: 979-8-9937294-1-1 (E-book)

For bulk purchases and for booking, contact:

Lynne Barber Vigesaa
lynnevigesaa@me.com

Library of Congress Control Number: 2025928189

Cover design by Hassan Ullah khan
Edited by Nikola Stojkovic
Interior design by Jetlaunch

FIRST EDITION

I would like to dedicate this book to my incredible grandson,
Soren In-Woo Vigesaa. He is 16 years old now and the light of my life.
When he wishes to, he can read this book and learn
about his grandmother's life.

I would also like to dedicate this book to my brave and courageous son,
Kell Barber Vigesaa, who lost his life battling intractable depression,
unresponsive to any treatment. Kell is sorely missed every day.

Acknowledgments

To my husband, Joe Beck, who has been steadfastly beside me with love and encouragement during these past several years while writing this book. He has been persistent and patient, and I will be forever grateful.

To my daughter-in-law, Kye Soon Hong, for taking the time to read what I had written and giving me honest and important feedback, as well as encouragement.

To my long-time good friend, Christine Hill, for seriously suggesting to me years ago that I had an unusual and interesting life and I needed to write a book. After persistent suggestions, she then offered to help me. She was instrumental in doing some first important editing and getting me on my way to finishing it.

To my editor, Claudia Volkman, for taking my book of close to 219,000 words and carefully cutting it down to 84,000 in order to have a book that could be published and still not lose the important content and message. I can appreciate now that it was a monumental task of careful study and work. I could never have done it by myself.

Table of Contents

Preface

I have been married to Joe Beck for 14 years. He is my fourth husband, and the absolute best of the four. It took years of persistent energy to find this man, and I marvel at how I could be so fortunate. For some time, Joe has been encouraging me to write about the adventures and accomplishments of my life. "Write it all down now before you are too old to remember it," he says.

At the age of 79, I think now is the time to start.

I have written a lot about my life over the years. I have all the letters I exchanged with my parents throughout my life. I have letters from friends, old boyfriends, and my sister Jacquey. I have my daily diaries from ages 13 to 18, and those that I've kept as an adult. In this memoir, I'll pull all of these pieces together, along with my memories, offering information as accurately as I am able.

My sister Jacquey, who is nearly ten years younger than I am, and I share a passion for genealogy. For me, it started in the summer of 1976 when I flew to the East Coast with my two-year-old son, Eric. My dad, Eric, and I drove to the town of Canton in upstate New York, where my dad grew up. Many of the Barbers on my dad's side of the family are buried near there. A whole world opened up for me as I thought of all the

Barbers who had lived before me. I thought of all the questions I never asked my grandmother, Nellie Belle Morrell Barber, my father's mother. She died when I was 12 years old, and all the answers to my questions died with her. That passion of wanting to know everything about my past relatives and their lives is still very much with me. I want to be sure that members of my family, present and future, will know the truth of what has happened in my own life.

During that same visit to Canton, we learned that there was another cemetery "full of Barbers" about five miles out of town at a crossroads called Eddy (formerly Jerusalem Corners). From an article in the *Canton Commercial Advertiser* on July 24, 1934, when my dad would have been nine years old:

> Those old days of the Jerusalem Corners are recalled every day on the street when the Wilson boys pass—Rollin and George—Jerusalem, now Eddy, was some little place on the map in those days. . . . Barbers were there in, it seemed to the small boy, countless numbers. . . . How many Barber families were in and around Jerusalem Corners would require considerable figuring. . . .There were Barbers on every highway, and their farms were found everywhere.

We drove on a country road to Jerusalem Cemetery in Eddy. We explored it and discovered among the trees literally hundreds and hundreds of graves with the name of Barber. Who were these Barbers? What were their stories? Someone had to know, and I had to find out.

With little Eric on my left hip, I walked across the road from the cemetery to a white-painted farmhouse situated alone in a large meadow. I knocked at the screen door on the side of the house. A thin, spry, elderly woman, with frizzy white hair tied up in a knot at the back of her head and wire-rimmed glasses, appeared and opened the door.

"My name is Lynne Barber and my father and grandfather used to live in Canton." I said.

She smiled widely, her eyes sparkled, and she exclaimed with enthusiasm, "Well, nice to meet you! I am Verna Barber, and I was born right here!"

She told me about one of her cousins, Elon Barber, who lived in Jamestown, New York, and also had an interest in Barber genealogy. Over the next few years, I corresponded with Elon Barber until he died in 1980. It turns out that both Verna Barber and Elon Barber are my third cousins once removed. My passion for exploring the Barber family had taken off.

I'm not sure if any of my future descendants will be interested in my life, but my incredible grandson, Soren—Eric's son—is already express-ing interest and has lots of questions for me about my past. Will it be important to document what life was like for a girl or woman living in the second half of the 20th century in the United States? My goal in writing is to document some of the adventures I have had so that my life will live on for others to learn about.

CHAPTER 1

———◆•◆———

Early Life

AUGUST 13, 1946, Chicago, Illinois—I was one of the first baby boomers born after World War II. My mother, Emma Lou Orth Barber, was a rebellious, headstrong 21-year-old. She was reportedly quite the hell-raiser in her junior year at the University of Chicago, the year she met my father at the University Tavern. She wrote to her brother, my Uncle Joe, that she was "on probation" at her dormitory, Gates Hall, primarily for staying out late partying and breaking curfew.

My dad, Carl Henry Barber, was ten years older, a handsome and charismatic traveling chemical salesman, soon to be drafted into the United States Navy. He had taught high school calculus and physics for seven years before leaving that occupation because teachers' salaries were so low.

It was obvious even then that my parents had very different values. When they met, my mother had been dating Roy Nakagawa, a fellow university student. Years later, when we kids were growing up, my dad would make racist remarks about him. My mother was politically very liberal. She and her friends once picketed the Armor Company in Chicago for some perceived or real injustice. My dad joked that my mother could not articulate exactly why she was picketing the Armor Company. Despite this, my parents had a real chemistry between them, at least in the beginning.

My parents were married in June 1945, four months after they met. My dad had been traveling on business when he received his draft notice. He had not been drafted before then because he was the sole supporter of his mother and sister. When his sister graduated from college, a draft notice was promptly sent to him. Dad then sent my mother a telegram, "Got my draft notice. Let's get married."

After the wedding, my mother, who was just finishing her junior year at the University of Chicago, dropped out for reasons I have never really understood. It was quite a privilege in 1945 to be a young woman nearly at the point of graduating from one of the finest universities in the country. My mother did not see it that way then, but this was during World War II, and decisions sometimes had to be made quickly without considering the ramifications. I don't think either one of my parents thought with any depth about what the decision to get married would mean for the two of them in the long run.

The wedding was quickly planned. The only relative to attend was my mother's mother, Frieda Amanda Busboom Orth. Grandma Orth was a kind, loving, and very proper woman who was a practicing Christian Scientist. Grandma Orth was to arrive in Chicago by a combination of bus and train from her home in Des Moines, Iowa. For some reason, she arrived much earlier than expected. My parents, who were staying in a rooming house for young women, were sound asleep that morning when there was a knock at the door. My dad, half asleep, in his underwear briefs and shirtless, stumbled to the door and opened it. There stood his mother-in-law to be. He had never met her before, but suddenly realized who she was. My dad just stood there for a moment in silence looking at her, and then closed the door on her. After several seconds, he realized he had to open the door. He did, smiling, and said, "Well, Mrs. Orth, nice to meet you."

My grandmother never said a word about it to anyone.

After a small wedding service at the university chapel, my mother continued to live in the rooming house, and my dad, who was now an active duty sailor at Great Lakes Naval Base, would join her when he could. He told me years later that he could never get into the solitary bathroom at that rooming house in a timely manner with so many young females all trying to use it. He had to resort to keeping a beer bottle in their room to pee in. My mother became pregnant with me about four months after the wedding.

In 1937, when Dad was a senior at St. Lawrence University in Canton, New York, his father, Roscoe, died of a heart attack at age 57. That same year, the family lost the beautiful, big Adirondack home in Canton that my dad's grandfather, Lyman Barber, had built for them, because they could no longer pay the property taxes. My dad then became the sole supporter of his mother and 14-year-old sister, Genevieve (Genny). His mother, Nellie Belle Morrell Barber, had no marketable skills and had never worked outside the home. My dad earned the money to send Genny to the Eastman School of Music in Rochester, New York, and supported her until she graduated in 1945.

This was all unknown to my mother before their wedding. When she found out, she was very resentful about it for many years. My mother told me on numerous occasions, "I married your father, but I did not know that she came with him."

Grandma Nellie had a small monthly pension from her husband's service in World War I and no other assets of her own. She also had a well-known, serious drinking problem. Grandma Nellie lived mostly with our family until she died in 1959.

When World War II ended, my parents moved into an apartment on the south side of Chicago, and my dad went back to his job as a traveling chemical salesman. My mother did not work outside the home after they were married.

As a new father, my dad was very focused on me. His nickname for me was "Boop-Boop-A-Doop." I have a postcard from him written in late 1946 from the Hotel Lincoln Douglas in Quincy, Illinois. His message starts with, "Dearest Boopie."

My dad and I just after I was born

My mother didn't think a woman could get pregnant while still breast-feeding, and my brother, John, arrived 18 months after I was born. Years later, when she talked about this time in her life, I got the clear impression that she missed those carefree days at the University of Chicago and regretted dropping out.

We lived in an apartment on Harper Avenue on the south side of Chicago until I was two years old. My dad's work involved a lot of travel, so my mom had her hands full.

———◆•◆———

When I was two or three years old, my parents moved to Park Forest, Illinois. This was a new, self-governing community in Chicago's south suburbs that had grown out of the new prosperity after World War II. The village of Park Forest was partly designed in the tradition of the planned communities cropping up around the nation to provide housing for veterans returning from World War II. We lived in a two-bedroom, apartment-like condo attached to other apartments situated around a circular driveway. There was a small play area with swings and a climbing structure in the center.

When I turned four years old, my sister Carol was born. My mother told me years later that Carol was the only one of her four children who was actually planned.

My mother came home from the hospital with Carol just a few days after my fourth birthday. My mother let me hold her on top of a pillow on my lap. She was a pink baby with chubby cheeks, and I held her on the pillow so carefully.

Mother, John, and I just after Carol was born

Some of the happy memories of this time in Park Forest were a few trips we took as a family to the Indiana Dunes on Lake Michigan. There, my dad and I would walk on the sand out to where the waves began. When a wave came, I would squeal and laugh as Dad lifted me up by my hands and the water washed over me.

In those days, my mother must have been exhausted. I remember her being angry and resentful, often announcing in the middle of the day that it was "time to sleep." I was too frightened of her anger to object. She would tie me to my bed with a rope, attaching the other end to herself. She would then try to sleep. I remember how angry and short-tempered she was, and I felt bored and depressed lying in bed wide awake, with a rope tied around me.

In early 1951, when I was four and a half years old, my parents bought a little Cape Cod house in Western Springs, a small suburb of Chicago. I went to kindergarten and first grade at Andrew Laidlaw School, which was close enough to our house that I could walk there and back.

I had a friend at school named Melinda Armour. I have a picture of the two of us dressed up in our mothers' clothes and holding candy cigarettes to our lips, trying to look very glamorous. Candy cigarettes for kids were "the thing" in those days. Melinda's father was a lifeguard at a local private outdoor swimming pool. One day, Melinda invited me to spend the day with her there. My mother packed lunch for me. Unlike Melinda, I couldn't swim—but I didn't know that yet.

After we arrived, Melinda's father went down to the locker rooms and Melinda and I were left on the deck of the pool before it had actually opened. I had no concept of deep water. I remember Melinda jumping off the diving board and paddling to the side of the pool. She encouraged me to jump off too. I still remember standing on the end of the diving board, jumping, and then going down, down, down into the water. I came up splashing and gasping and went down again. I'm not sure how many times this went on. Finally, while I was underwater, I felt a hand grab my arm and pull me up and out. It was Melinda's father, who had finally emerged from the locker room. My parents never knew about that close call.

———◆•◆———

Near the end of our time in Western Springs, my parents started the tradition of taking a two-week summer family vacation. The first year, we went to Lake Ozonia in the Adirondacks, where my dad vacationed as a boy. It was there that I finally learned to swim. I had a little old-fashioned life preserver vest composed of balsa wood pieces. I would wear the vest and paddle in the water around the rowboat while my dad rowed. He would take the balsa wood pieces out of the vest one by one as I swam around the boat. When he took the last piece out, I panicked and started crying.

My dad yelled, "SWIM!"

And I did.

Lake Ozonia was pristine and beautiful, with its cold, clear water, and green fir and deciduous trees surrounding it on all sides. The first time we went to Lake Ozonia, I was seven, John was five, and Carol was three. My parents rented a house on the lake with no electricity and no running water. We got our drinking water from a fresh spring in the nearby woods. That first year, we had an outhouse and got blocks of ice from a country store for the refrigerator. As we had no electricity, we used kerosene lamps for light in the evenings. After dinner, we played a family card game called "Pig" around the dining room table. Our bedrooms were on the second floor. Under our beds were shallow ceramic chamber pots we could pee in rather than going to the outhouse in the dark.

One night, while we were playing Pig, Carol had to go to the bathroom and went upstairs to use the chamber pot under our bed. Somehow, she either missed the chamber pot or accidentally spilled it. So there we all were, with playing cards in our hands, when suddenly, from the rafters above, a yellow stream of urine came down, dribbling across the table and spattering all over us. Although we were all upset at the time, it became a favorite funny family memory for years to come.

All of us loved our vacation at Lake Ozonia—except for my mother.

She frequently would say angrily, "This is no vacation for me. I just do the same goddamn thing every day that I do at home, only it's harder. The only difference is a new scene out the kitchen window!"

When I think of having no running water or electricity, an outhouse, and three small children, I can understand her feelings now.

We went to Lake Ozonia one other time four years later, when I was 11 years old and Jacquey was just a year old. This time, we rented a different cottage with electricity, a bathroom, and running water.

My mother exclaimed excitedly to me just before the trip, "Lynne, we are going first-class this time, and we are taking disposable diapers for Jacquey!"

Many years later, in 1976, when my oldest son, Eric, was two years old, my dad, Eric, and I visited Lake Ozonia once again. We went to the last cabin we had rented. The cabin was called "Ferndale," and it was just as I remembered it. It had a homey, comfortable sun porch with wicker furniture. I had an exhilarating swim off of the wooden dock in that crystal-clear, cold water. It hadn't changed a bit from my memory so many years before. And the spring where we got our water was still there! The visit brought back such great memories of my childhood at Lake Ozonia.

———◆•◆———

When I was six years old, my dad was transferred from Chicago to New York City for his job as sales manager at International Minerals and Chemical Corporation. My parents sold our little house in Western Springs and we moved to Mountain Lakes, a bedroom community about 30 miles west of Manhattan, in New Jersey.

Mountain Lakes was–and still is–a beautiful town with woods, hills, and five lakes. There was no industry in the town, with the exception of a little family grocery store, and it's pretty much the same today. Many of the men in the town worked in New York City and commuted back and forth by train, but my dad drove his car back and forth every day. In 1951, the car commute was about 45 minutes through the Lincoln Tunnel and into Manhattan, and 45 minutes back home. When we left Mountain Lakes in 1964, the commute was two hours into the city and two hours out. My dad still drove to work every day.

A product of the 20th century, Mountain Lakes was established in the winter of 1910-1911 by Mountain Lakes, Inc. Herbert Hapgood, the president of the corporation, converted this beautiful wooded area into a residential community. He was particularly influenced by the arts and crafts movement, which was at the height of its popularity in 1910. He built many large, three-story stucco houses during this time, which became known as "Hapgoods."

In 1952, my parents bought one of these Hapgood homes, situated on three-quarters of an acre, on a scenic canal that ran from two of the five lakes in town. It had a full basement, a coal furnace (which was upgraded to oil before we moved in), a large dining room, a large kitchen with an informal eating area, and a 32-foot-long living room with a huge fireplace. The second floor had four bedrooms and a bathroom, and the third floor had another three bedrooms and a bathroom. There was a covered sun porch on the first floor and a large deck on the second floor. The grounds were beautiful, with a large number of huge, very tall white and black oak trees. There was also an unattached two-car garage at the back of the property. On the canal, we had our own boat dock, rowboat, and canoe. It was a gorgeous place to live.

We moved into a rented house while waiting for our new house to be ready. One day, my Grandma Nellie fell down the stairs from the second floor. She rolled all the way down, her body bumping on each step. I remember being terrified and crying, seeing her lying flat on her back and moaning in pain at the bottom of the stairs. The ambulance soon arrived and took her away for several days. Years later, I found out she had lost her balance and fallen because she was drunk.

My mother was famous for sleeping in as long as she could. When she finally got up, she was usually in a foul mood. She was unhappy much of the time in those days. Unlike my mother, my dad was at his best in the mornings. He was always fun to be with. I would get up and make pancakes and donuts in the kitchen with him. However, as the years went on and he abused more alcohol, he slowly became scarier and less fun.

I have had a degree of anxiety all my life, always fearful of things that might happen. My mother didn't allow us to see certain scary movies, which made sense for me. But in 1958, when I was 12 years old, *The Horror of Dracula* came out. I was with some girlfriends at one of their houses for the evening. Everyone wanted to see the movie, so we all went to the Boonton Theatre. As the movie progressed and Dracula, with fangs out, started stalking his female victims, I became so terrified that I ran to the women's bathroom and just stood there shaking in fear. I stayed there alone for some time before I finally came out, but I still couldn't take the terror on the screen and ran back to the bathroom again.

Back at home, I didn't sleep well for days. I would wake up in the middle of the night and check my neck for fang marks. At that time, I had piano lessons before school with an elderly piano teacher, Mr. Max Drittler. I was never quite sure that Mr. Drittler wasn't really a vampire in disguise. I wore a large gold cross on a chain around my neck, clearly visible to him, just in case. As we sat on the piano bench together, I watched him closely for any signs of danger or sudden moves. Fortunately, my terror of vampires gradually became less of an issue over the years.

My mother continued to be very hard on me. She frequently hit me. I never knew when her hits would come. When she hit me again during one of her emotional explosions, my dad would sometimes say, "Emmy, don't break her spirit!" His words at those times gave me some emotional strength.

When I was 11 or 12, I finally spoke up.

One time, after she hit me for not eating breakfast before school, I yelled, "Every day you hit me!"

She looked up with her red, clenched face and said, "I do not!" She didn't hit me again for a very long time.

My mother resented us children. Her infamous expression, which we heard quite frequently, was, "You goddamn kids, I am so sick of you!"

But in fairness to my mother, after Jacquey was born, she "grew up." Jacquey rarely experienced the raw fury that John and I did. Jacquey didn't have it easy growing up either, though, because my dad's drinking grew worse as time went on. He became more and more out of control after I left home for college in 1964. I know Jacquey experienced some terrible things stemming from our dad's alcohol abuse.

In 2009, I visited my mother one week before she died of lung cancer at the age of 83. She was living alone in Berkeley, California, and I had flown down from Seattle. She told me the biggest regret she had regarding her children had to do with me. I was shocked by her admission. Why me more than my other three siblings? She said she had no regrets about Jacquey and thought she had done very well raising her. But she regretted always making excuses for John rather than letting him succeed or fail on his own, and she regretted not protecting Carol from my dad. Her biggest regret was about me because I was always such a dutiful child. At the time, she thought that if I was well-behaved and achieved well, people would see that she was a good mother.

In my mother's own words that day, she said, "I set the bar very high for you. As a little girl, you tried so very hard to please. Then, when you reached the bar I set for you, I just raised it higher."

I have fond memories of our house on Barton Road in Mountain Lakes. We had three-quarters of an acre, and more than ten huge oak trees in the yard. When the leaves fell in the fall, we raked them into huge piles and jumped in them. The leaves were so numerous that we were never able to rake them all before the snow fell in the late fall. We also had a full badminton/volleyball court on one side of our house. My mother was instrumental in putting it up. She discovered that the court size in badminton and volleyball is the same, and only the net is at different heights. She had posts put in cement, and hooks on the posts to raise and lower the net depending on whether you were playing badminton or volleyball. We really loved playing on that court.

As a child, I spent a lot of time in our yard. We had a big tire swing. I remember my mother climbing one of our huge white oak trees to attach the tire on a long rope, with my dad watching and yelling, "Watch yourself, Emmy!"

She had placed a big extension ladder against the trunk of the tree, and then at the top of the ladder, she launched herself onto a large branch to attach the tire swing. My mother was quite athletic and daring when she was younger.

Despite living in the affluent community of Mountain Lakes, money was not always easy to come by. During the years our family lived there, my dad was the only breadwinner. My mother worried a lot about finances, and I can still see her late at night, trying to pay the bills once a month, with piles of papers stacked over the dining room table, visibly stressed.

At one time, there were three of us taking music lessons: my brother on the trumpet, and my sister Carol and I on the piano. My mother decided she could only afford to have two of us taking music lessons. She told me I would have to stop because I was the "least talented." That hurt my feelings at the time, but it was most likely true.

I took school very seriously right from the beginning. One of the qualities I have always had is that I am a hard worker. I was never a straight-A student, never appointed to the National Honor Society, but I worked hard and had very good grades. The academic competition was high in Mountain Lakes High School. I am not exaggerating when I say that I had a minimum of two to three hours of homework every weeknight during my four years in high school. Most of my sleep deprivation during those high school years was due to staying up late doing homework.

One of the foremost events of my life was the birth of my sister Jacquey on June 2, 1956, shortly before my tenth birthday. From the moment she came home from the hospital, I had such an overwhelming feeling of wanting to be with her and take care of her. I would take her on long walks in her big black baby carriage. My parents allowed me to babysit her by myself for several hours in the evening or during the day. I gave her baths, dressed her, and held her close.

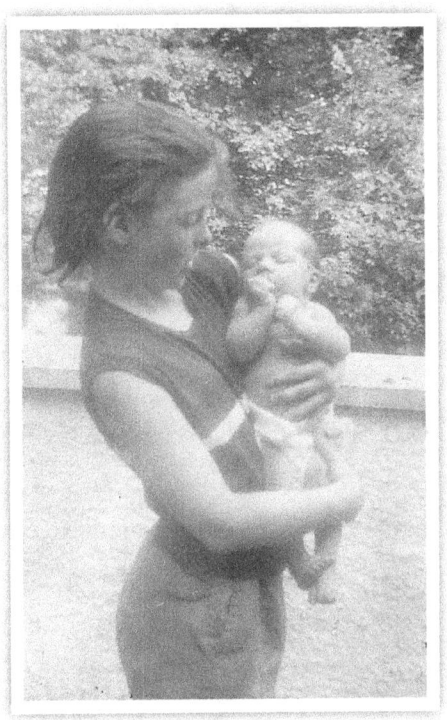

Jacquey and I a few days after her birth

After Jacquey's birth, my Grandma Nellie realized that not one of her four grandchildren had been baptized. Baptism was not a big deal in the Christian Science Church my mother had been raised in, and my dad didn't care one way or another. But suddenly the four of us had to be baptized because Grandma Nellie thought it was important.

I didn't want to be baptized. I thought it was silly and embarrassing. Didn't it matter what I thought? This was about me and what I wanted for myself, or so I reasoned. My mother had the minister of the Mountain Lakes Community Church give me a stern talk. After much arguing, I finally realized that I had no real choice in the matter. The baptism ceremony was anticlimactic. Fortunately, it was held Saturday afternoon, and not in front of the whole congregation. I don't remember if Grandma Nellie even attended the ceremony.

Grandma Nellie had white, wrinkled, thin skin and completely white hair with a bluish tinge. She was short and plump and wore loose house dresses and a big, mid-calf length fur coat when she went outside. She wore thick, sturdy shoes with nylon stockings rolled up around her ankles. She never helped with any housework or babysat any of us. For the last year or so of her life, she just stayed in her bedroom.

My mother's mother, Frieda Amanda Busboom Orth, was in sharp contrast to Grandma Nellie. She lived in Iowa and later in Colorado and visited us no more than once a year, sometimes less. She would stay with us for a week. She was kind and nurturing—the antithesis of my own mother. As soon as we would pull into our driveway and get out of the car, she would take a deep breath of fresh air and say, "Listen!" She loved hearing the birds chirping and the breeze rustling in the trees.

<hr>

Just before I turned 13, Grandma Nellie became weaker and sicker because of liver cirrhosis and gastrointestinal bleeding. She was only 73, but she looked and acted much older. Her doctor made it clear to my parents that there was not much more he could do for her, and that we should care for her at home.

During the summer of 1959, I eagerly took over the role of my grandmother's caretaker. Grandma Nellie refused to eat. I spent hours spoon feeding her, saying, "Just one more bite, Grandma . . ." To me, it didn't feel like work; it felt like a job with a purpose. I can't say it was fun, but somehow I really liked taking care of her. I looked forward to it every day; it was my responsibility.

That summer was the beginning of my interest in healthcare and my desire to become a nurse. I loved being the one "in charge," helping Grandma Nellie, figuring out ways of encouraging her to eat and making her feel better. I wanted to do the best I could to help her.

The next year, at age 13, I decided to volunteer at St. Clare's Hospital, where Grandma Nellie died. I wanted to be around people who were sick and needed help. I became a "Clare Cadet," similar to a candy striper in other hospitals. I had a uniform: a white blouse and a pink jumper. I was at the hospital most weekends. My parents would drop me off in the morning and pick me up in the late afternoon.

I just loved the atmosphere of the hospital. It filled me with interest and excitement. I loved visiting the patients and doing errands for them. I would bring them their mail or flowers, or just talk with them. I would also push the big laundry cart and fold laundry. I remember visiting an older Catholic nun who had a private room. There were crucifixes hanging from the bed rails. She was very ill, semiconscious, and breathing heavily. She remained in that state for a long time. I visited often just to talk to her quietly.

A recurrent theme in my diaries was a desire to go to developing countries and work with Dr. Tom Dooley and other health professionals. However, neither of my parents gave me any encouragement to pursue a career in healthcare or any other profession. I was expected to go to college, like everyone else in Mountain Lakes, but there were no other verbalized expectations.

I kept diaries from age ten until I graduated from high school. I would get a new diary each Christmas. Each diary had a zipper around it and a lock. I faithfully recorded daily entries. There are multiple entries about wanting to go to Africa and join the doctors and nurses there. After high school, I stopped keeping a diary, but I kept all my past diaries at my parent's home while I was in college. After college, when I was packing for my move to Seattle for my first job, I discovered that my sister Carol had destroyed all the locks and zippers and had opened every one of my diaries. Luckily, she did not destroy the actual diaries, and I still have all of them.

In my diaries, I wrote about rereading *Jane Eyre* and *Wuthering Heights* over and over again, and about always trying to clean up my room. I was passionately affected by the movie *The Snake Pit* with Olivia de Havilland, which further intensified my focus on a career in the health field.

I was an incurable romantic. I had lists of beloved movie and television stars in my diaries, such as Pernell Roberts, who played Adam on the television western, *Bonanza*. I had a crush on my Latin teacher, Mr. Yanni, and I had multiple silent crushes on older boys in my school. I wrote a lot about wishing I had a boyfriend. There are many entries expressing confusion about how to deal with boys and about not understanding them. In high school, I did not really know what sex was. For me, it was all about a belief in true love.

I wrote about my fears regarding the escalating fighting between my parents. I know now that much of it was related to my dad's alcohol consumption. I wrote about my dad's cruelty in making fun of my mother's relatives, and my mother crying in response. The older he got and the more he drank, the harder it became for him to maintain a sense of control and reason. I often felt caught in the middle trying to please both of my parents.

Instead of encouraging me to pursue a career, when I was about 16 years old, my mother took me aside and told me, "Men have two decisions to make in life: the career they choose and the woman they marry. But you have only one decision to make: a man to marry."

I was stunned into silence after that statement. My mind was in a fog, trying to figure out exactly what that meant for my life.

In 1964, at the time of my high school graduation, 40 percent of the boys in my class were accepted to Princeton University, although many of them went on to other schools. Others went on to get PhDs or become doctors, dentists, and lawyers. We were a high-achieving group of kids. The valedictorian of our high school class was a girl, and she went on to become an accountant. There were unspoken lower expectations for girls.

Despite the fact that my mother was unhappy and angry much of the time, she became the stabilizing force in my life then. Though her behavior was frequently angry and unpleasant, I knew more or less what she was going to do. I never knew for sure what my dad was going to do.

In Mountain Lakes, although we had so many beautiful freshwater lakes to swim in, for two summers we went on family vacations to the Jersey Shore on Long Beach Island. That's where I developed a deep love for the ocean. At age 12, I would get up early in the morning at low tide and collect shells and rocks. I still have all those shells and rocks, and they're now displayed in my library at our home.

When I was about 13 years old, my school friend, Tish Hopkins, invited me and three other girls to her parent's vacation house on the Jersey Shore for four days. Tish was the youngest of four children and had three older brothers. Her family was quite wealthy; her father was a vice president of the Chase Manhattan Bank in New York City. My parents innocently let me go without any questions. Once I got there, I realized that there was no adult supervision. Her father wasn't home, and her mother was a serious alcoholic who spent the days drunk in her bedroom. We never even saw her. My bathing suit had torn and I had to borrow one from one of the other girls. The new bathing suit exposed a three-inch-wide area on my back that had previously not been exposed to the sun. While swimming in the ocean, I got a severe second-degree burn on my back with significant blistering that left skin discoloration for years. I couldn't sleep for three nights due to the pain.

Some boys saw us on the beach and followed us back to the house. I was terrified. The other girls went for a ride in a big convertible one of the boys drove. Tish's oldest brother, Edgar, was there at the house for the long weekend. He was probably in his early 20s. He was so kind to me in a very genuine way. When the other girls were out partying, I just stayed back at the house and hung out and watched television with Edgar.

My parents also took us on vacations to Cape Cod. To this day, just thinking about Cape Cod makes me hold my breath a bit. My mind goes right back to that glorious, cold salt water that comes gleaming over your head as the wave crashes over you when swimming in the surf. Swimming in the cold, refreshing surf along Cape Cod prepared me to swim in the ice-cold mountain lakes in the Cascade and Olympic Mountains of Washington, and in the surf of the Pacific Ocean. Swimming in that frigid ocean water still gives me a thrill.

In August 1962, after finishing my sophomore year of high school, friends of my parents, Dana and John Munro, asked me to come to Cape Cod with them for three weeks and take care of their three school-aged children, along with two children of their friends. I jumped at the chance to go back to Cape Cod, especially when I discovered that the Munros had rented the same house as my family when we vacationed there.

I have saved all my letters written to my parents during this time. In a letter to them dated August 31, 1962, I wrote about John Munro trying to "sing serenades to me in the kitchen" while I prepared dinner for them. "Every time he goes past me in the kitchen, he always hits me on the arm or the stomach. When I tell him to stop and that it hurts, he laughs and calls me a sissy," I wrote. Interactions with John Munro were always unsettling and uncomfortable. When I reread this letter, I can clearly see why. There was no response from either one of my parents, written or verbal, to his inappropriate interactions with me.

A year or so later, we were at Cape Cod again. This time I was with my parents, and the Munros were visiting. We were all playing volleyball on the beach. The adults were doing their usual amount of fairly heavy drinking. My sister Carol was around 15 and had a generous, womanly figure. John Munro would repeatedly tackle her on the sand during the volleyball games. Volleyball is not a contact sport. It made me so uncomfortable and then really angry. My parents were there and saw it all. Not one adult objected. Finally, I couldn't stand it anymore.

I yelled out, "Stop tackling my sister, you dirty old man!"

John Munro abruptly stood up and stopped tackling Carol. There was a long, uncomfortable silence. Years later, my mother told me how glad she was that I had said something to him about his behavior. I asked why she hadn't said something at the time. She had no answer and just shook her head.

When I was a high school freshman, I tried out for a part in the high school musical, *The Boy Friend*. I landed the small part of a girl named Nancy, and had a wonderful experience in that play. In my diary at that time, I wrote about my fears of not being good enough and feeling uncomfortable with the upperclassmen in the play at the same time. But I felt good about my performance in the end.

Years later, when I was an adult, I ran into Mr. Harrison, the English teacher who directed The *Boy Friend*. He told me how terrible I had been in the audition. He said he was surprised I had "the guts" to try out at all, and for that reason he gave me the small part of Nancy. In retrospect, I had to agree with his assessment. I was long on enthusiasm, hard work, and dreams—and quite short on talent.

In ninth grade, I longed to become a cheerleader. Although we had a Girls Athletic Association in our high school, there were no sports for girls, so being a cheerleader was a prestigious thing. We had to try out, and were voted on by the entire high school body. In our day, cheerleading was not just shaking pompoms; it was an athletic sport. We did cartwheels, round-offs, handsprings, and the splits. It was so scary trying out in front of the whole school, but I was voted in and spent three years in high school on the cheerleading team. I was thrilled to be elected co-captain of the varsity cheerleading team in my senior year.

In my junior year I found my first real boyfriend, Bob Bowden. He was a senior, a year older than me. Even in retrospect, he was really a wonderful guy. Unfortunately, Bob left for Bates College in Maine at the beginning of my senior year. We tried to keep it together despite the long distance. When our relationship ended in the spring, I was heartsick.

Aside from physical education classes in high school, in which we played field hockey in the fall and half-court basketball in the winter, there were no other sports activities for us girls. But we still had the Mountain Lakes High School Girls Athletic Association. Virtually every girl in the school signed up for it. The GAA, as it was best known, consisted of two teams: The Orange Team and The Blue Team. Orange and Blue were the Mountain Lakes High School colors.

In my senior year, I was voted captain of The Orange Team, consisting of 140 girls, freshmen through seniors. There were some sporting events between the teams, but the biggest event was the GAA Show every April. Both teams spent the entire school year preparing for this. Each team picked a theme and a story. The events were tumbling, marching, Danish exercise, tap dance, and modern dance. There were large painted backdrops, costumes, dance routines, and original songs around the chosen theme. Preparation and planning for the GAA Show were part of our everyday existence.

As the captain, I had a co-captain, and each event had a captain–chosen by me–as well as participants. The entire team reported to me through these captains, and I was responsible for everyone. It was a thrilling experience, although there was a tremendous amount of work and responsibility. I found I could utilize my cheerleading skills—I would stand up on a chair in the large gymnasium in front of all 140 girls and give them a loud and dynamic pep talk.

"You can do this!" I'd say. "We are The Orange Team!"

At the end of the year, one of the physical education teachers, Miss Nancy Walsh, took me aside and complimented me on my enthusiasm and leadership qualities. I think that, without knowing it, I brought some of these skills to my future professional life as a nurse practitioner.

———◆•◆———

At the beginning of my senior year in high school, my dad, after years of working in New York City, was transferred to Skokie, Illinois, outside of Chicago. My dad knew how important it was for me to spend my senior year at Mountain Lakes High School, so he made the decision to commute every week to Chicago. For my entire senior year, he left on an airplane on Sunday night and would come back late on Friday night. I will never forget the sacrifice he made. Then, immediately after my high school graduation in June 1964, our family moved from Mountain Lakes to Winnetka, Illinois.

I wanted to go to college on the East Coast like most of my friends, but my mother decided I could only go to college as far east as Ohio. It was a ridiculous decision, and I should have pushed back, but once again, I was a very compliant daughter. I was accepted at Western Reserve University (now known as Case Western Reserve University) in Cleveland, Ohio.

Right after my high school graduation, two huge moving trucks arrived, loaded up all our possessions and furniture, and moved us to Winnetka, Illinois. I was brokenhearted to leave the only home I had known since age six and move 800 miles away. I lived with my parents in Winnetka for about two months and then started my freshman year at Western Reserve University in September 1964.

Except for the summers of 1965 and 1966, I never lived at home with my parents and siblings again.

CHAPTER 2

College Life: 1964–1968

M Y FRESHMAN YEAR at Western Reserve University was extraordinarily difficult for me. I didn't know anyone there. The home I had left in Mountain Lakes was gone; I had lost my roots. I felt isolated and depressed, and this depression lasted nearly the entire school year.

Certain "traditions" at Western Reserve University made me uncomfortable. There were about 100 girls in our dormitory. At the beginning of the fall semester, we all had to memorize a fraternity song from each of the dozen or so fraternities on campus. Then, on a certain night, we all walked to each of the fraternities and sang their song on their front lawn. All the fraternity members were gathered on the porch to hear us sing. After we finished, the president of each fraternity would choose one of us and then come over and plant a big kiss on the "lucky" girl. The girl had no choice in the matter.

In those days, there were no sports for girls in college, but there was cheerleading. I tried out for the Western Reserve cheerleading squad. They only had two positions open, and I was chosen to be on the squad.

I don't remember it being a very positive experience, and I didn't really connect with the other cheerleaders. In retrospect, I was too engulfed in feeling out of place, depressed, and empty.

On that first Thanksgiving in November 1964, I flew home from Cleveland to Chicago. My parents met me at the airport. I had gained about 15 pounds since I left home in September, which was a lot of weight on my five-foot-four-inch frame. I tried to hide it all under a large winter coat.

When I got off the airplane, my mother took one look at me and, with a look of puzzlement and disapproval, said, "What happened to you?"

Those were dark times. I remember wondering if I would ever be happy again. I never really talked about how badly I felt, and no one asked me. I just forced myself out of bed every morning and pushed through every day.

In April 1965, at the end of my freshman year, I met Rich Spivak at a party and began a romantic relationship with him. I was so depressed and lonely, and he was nice and friendly and liked me. It was a relief from the misery I lived with every day that first year in college. It also spoke to a large part of me that has always succumbed to romance. A good woman friend once told me that there is no such thing as true romantic love, only close companionship and friendship. But I still believe in true romantic love. I actually have it now with my husband, Joe. Joe and I have been married for 14 years. Love and romance is very much alive with us. But that longing for love and romance has gotten me into big trouble in the past.

I took biology classes at Western Reserve University in a huge auditorium of more than 200 people. Every one of the premed students taking that biology class was male. Years later, in 1971, the University of Washington School of Medicine told me they did not want nurses in medical school because nurses didn't take the same biology and chemistry classes as the premed students. Clearly, they were in error, which I told them at the time.

I survived my freshman year at Western Reserve University in part due to my friendship with my soon-to-be roommate, Joni Foster, but also largely due to my new boyfriend, Rich. Rich was a freshman at Case Institute of Technology, majoring in astrophysics. He wanted to be an astronomer, but he had lots of problems applying himself and was not doing well academically. Unfortunately, none of those important facts caught my attention then. I had been so unhappy, and my relationship with him had temporarily alleviated so much of that unhappiness.

When I returned to Western Reserve University in the fall for my sophomore year, I was determined to apply to the School of Nursing at the end of the school year. My goal was a bachelor's degree in nursing.

Whenever my dad was in Cleveland on business, we would go out to dinner together, and those times were so much fun. He would choose the restaurant, which was fine with me. It would be a place he knew, and where the people working there also knew him well. But one time, Rich went with us. Rich had heard about an Italian restaurant in town, and he wanted to go there. I told my dad we would like to try the restaurant Rich had suggested. I knew my dad didn't approve of Rich because he was Jewish, but I did not anticipate the scene that would occur.

As the dinner progressed, my dad had his third "beefeater martini on the rocks with a twist," and started making vague, mean-spirited comments. At first, his angry insults didn't sound as if they were directed toward Rich, but I knew that they really were. Then, he started complaining about our orders—steaks with special Italian roasted vegetables heaped on top, which was what the restaurant was famous for. He started yelling at the waiter, and then the manager arrived, bowing and apologizing. By this time, I was crying.

"Please, Dad, stop . . ." But he never listened. Broiled rare steaks without the roasted vegetables appeared as Dad demanded. The rest of the night was a blur to me.

During my sophomore year at Western Reserve University, Billy Wilder was filming a new movie called *The Fortune Cookie*, featuring the Cleveland Browns. The Cleveland Browns didn't have any cheerleaders, so the Western Reserve cheerleaders were recruited for the film. We spent one cold day in Cleveland Stadium being filmed jumping up and down on the field and watching Jack Lemmon do the injury scene over and over. If you watch the film now, you can see 30 seconds of us cheerleaders jumping up and down.

I was significantly happier during my sophomore year than I had been during my freshman year. I had a new roommate, Joni Foster, and we became good friends.

My relationship with Rich became more intense. He pressured me constantly for sex. I didn't know how to handle it. I felt at that time that if I ever got pregnant, it would be an unforgivable sin, and I would never be able to go home to my parents. That may sound melodramatic, but I knew there was no tolerance in my family for any mistakes, especially one so egregious as a pregnancy outside of marriage.

During the fall semester, I took an anthropology class. A group of us in the class would study together in the evenings at the school main library.

One of the students was a 28-year-old woman who lived in an apartment in Cleveland. She was divorced and was working toward a degree. She seemed so old and wise to me, so I anxiously confided my dilemma to her. She gave me the name and address of Dr. Lavin in Cleveland, who could prescribe birth control pills, which were just brand new on the market then. Together with Rich, I went to three pharmacies in the university area before I could get the prescription filled. The first two pharmacies refused to fill it. I was an unmarried young female student and should not need birth control pills.

In the mid-1960s, it was considered a sin to live with a man who was not your husband. It was unthinkable. You had to break off the relationship or get married; there was no in-between. Rich and I both wanted to get married. I was self-conscious about being on birth control and not married, and Rich wanted a more formal commitment.

In retrospect, I am not sure why we were so intent on getting married. Rich was Jewish, and my dad was strongly antisemitic. Rich's parents wanted him to marry a Jew. There was so much conflict, but we thought we were in love.

In the spring of 1966, I was thrilled to be accepted into the Western Reserve University School of Nursing, and then Rich surprised me with a diamond engagement ring. I was overjoyed, but frightened to tell my parents. I called them to tell them the news, and, just as I knew, my dad was furious.

My mother told me, "If you get pregnant, you will never be able to finish college. *He* will finish college. *You* will have to give up going to college. The man always has preference when it comes to education."

In June 1966, after finishing my sophomore year, I arrived in Winnetka at a very tense and unhappy time because my parents disapproved of my engagement. I was very proud of my diamond ring, and I was determined to quietly follow my own direction in life without making them too unhappy.

At that time, there was a small, private psychiatric hospital called North Shore Hospital, situated right on the shores of Lake Michigan in Winnetka, very close to my parents' home. Years later, it was torn down to make room for some grand, expensive mansions, but that summer I worked there as a nurse's aide. There were three floors in the hospital, and I worked on the locked third floor with the most seriously ill patients. What an experience it was! The nurses wore white uniforms and caps. It seemed to me that they spent little, if any, time with the patients, and the time they did spend was mostly just to "keep them in line." After a week, I finally figured out that these "nurses" were not nurses at all, but women with no professional education who called themselves nurses.

Despite this, I liked helping to care for the patients, who had a wide variety of serious psychiatric illnesses. There was very little instruction or orientation for me, but I found it fun and interesting nonetheless.

At the beginning of the summer, I flew to Rich's home on Long Island, where his parents planned to host an engagement party for us.

I stayed in the guest room, and Rich's mother sternly told us both, "All four of your feet need to be on the floor at all times." Just another reminder that sex outside of marriage was forbidden during those days.

The party guests were primarily Rich's parents' friends and relatives, and we received lots of presents.

But the big disappointment was Rich. He had not done well in his last semester at Case, and was taking summer classes at the University of New York at Stony Brook. He was still not at all focused on his responsibilities. The worst part was that he had suddenly bought a little sports car, an MGB, for $2,500. That was half of his bar mitzvah money, which was what we were going to live on after we were married while still in school. I was incredulous at his irresponsible action. He never even asked me about buying the car.

After the engagement party weekend, I flew back to my parent's home and continued working at Northshore Hospital, where I met Dick Vigesaa. He had just started working on the third floor, where I worked. He was three years older than me and attending Garrett Theological Seminary in Evanston. Garrett Theological Seminary had some funds for educating students who, while not committed to it, might consider joining the ministry. Working at North Shore Hospital was a summer job for him too.

I was immediately wildly impressed and totally smitten with Dick. He spoke about literature, movies, and books in a scholarly and learned way. He made wonderful eye contact. He majored in philosophy in college and thought that it was one of the only things worth studying in life. He seemed so mature, so intelligent, and so interesting.

Dick was the first man in my entire life who asked me what I thought about anything and was actually interested in the answer. Dick Vigesaa was very different from Rich Spivak.

Dick knew I was engaged when he saw my engagement ring. One day at work, he mentioned that a new movie, *Who's Afraid of Virginia Woolf?*, was playing, and I said I would like to see the movie sometime myself.

"Do you want to go?" Dick asked.

"Yes," I immediately said. I told myself I would pay for my own theatre ticket so it wouldn't be a real date.

After seeing the movie, we walked out of the theatre and Dick grabbed my hand. And there it was. I was totally taken with him and his smooth philosophical talk.

The next day, we went out again. My mother reminded me that I was engaged and should not be going out with other men on dates. Something clicked in my head, and I took the engagement ring off, never to wear it again. I called Rich and said I wanted to break off our engagement. He was furious. The next day, he drove his new MGB sports car all the way from Long Island, New York, to Winnetka, Illinois. He stayed the night at my parents' house, spending two days alternating between tears and outrage. He wouldn't take the engagement ring back. After two days, he drove back to Long Island. A month later, I sent the engagement ring back to his parents.

For the next two months, I was totally emotionally involved in my new romance with Dick Vigesaa. We were inseparable. He talked about ideas and books. He seemed so mature. Rich continued to call me, sometimes with a threatening, angry tone, and sometimes with declarations of love.

Dick was from Minnesota. His parents were both deaf, and he was the oldest of four children. His years growing up were marked by poverty and not much in the way of any expectation. While in high school, he impressed some of his teachers with his intellectual abilities. With the support of his high school teachers, Dick received scholarships to Morningside College in Sioux City, Iowa. He was at Morningside

College for four years working toward a bachelor's degree in philosophy. He wanted to get a PhD in philosophy and teach it at a university, but he was missing one course in order to graduate. He just had to write one paper on some aspect of religion to complete that course. He never finished the paper or the required course, and hence did not graduate from Morningside College.

Dick never really had a good reason for not finishing the paper. I couldn't understand it because I had put so much energy toward a specific goal in my own life. I did all I could think of to motivate him to finish the paper. I explained to him how to do it. I told him it was a matter of breaking the task down into parts and then completing one part after another. Week after week, he did not finish the paper, but despite this, for some reason, I had confidence that this wonderful new man in my life would come through.

I didn't want to go back to Cleveland and be confronted by Rich Spivak again. In August, I started looking into transferring to another university with a nursing school. I knew that Columbia University in New York City had an excellent nursing school, so I wrote to them and sent them all my grades from Western Reserve University. On September 6, 1966, I received a telegram stating that the admissions committee had approved my application for acceptance to the Columbia University School of Nursing, beginning September 11, 1966.

Receiving that acceptance gave me a new lease on life. My future looked so bright. I was headed to New York City to get a bachelor's degree in nursing from Columbia University! What was not clear was what Dick Vigesaa was going to do with his life. But unfortunately, I did not think of that at the time.

I moved into a room on the tenth floor of Maxwell Hall, the student nurses' residence, which was part of the Columbia Presbyterian Medical Center at 168th Street and Broadway. My tiny room had a sink in one corner, a single bed pushed against the wall, and one window just to the right of the bed. If I looked out the window and turned my head sharply to the right, I could see the George Washington Bridge and the little red lighthouse sitting just below it.

As I had been admitted later than the other students, I arrived early for an orientation. I met with the dean of the School of Nursing, who took me on a tour of the six-hospital Columbia Presbyterian Medical Center. As the dean and I were ascending the stairs back to Maxwell Hall, Rich Spivak suddenly appeared. He told the dean that he needed to talk with me. She told him that we had just finished, and went off to another meeting.

Rich looked at me angrily, with a clenched jaw, raw emotion dripping, and repeated, "I need to talk to you."

I was angry and said, "What can you possibly say to me that you haven't already said?"

I tried to leave and walk around him, but he grabbed my purse. I pulled back, but he held on. I realized he was too strong, so I let go, ran down the stairs, and told him to leave the purse at the front desk. He then threw the purse down the stairs at me, the contents spraying all over the stairwell—lipstick, combs, wallet, keys, all bouncing and clanking down two flights of stairs. I gathered everything together as quickly as I could. I was mortified and hoped no one had seen what happened.

"I love you!" Rich shouted from the top of the stairs, and then he was gone. It was quite melodramatic in retrospect. I didn't see him again for 17 years.

I felt strong and filled with excitement to be in New York City, starting my junior year at Columbia University. I had just turned 20 years old. It felt so different from my freshman year at Western Reserve University, when I was lonely and depressed for the entire year. Now I was where I wanted to be. I was moving forward in my life. Rereading letters to my parents, I wrote about wanting to be the best nurse I could possibly be and how I loved the academic atmosphere at Columbia. I felt some real happiness and stability for the first time since high school.

The history of the Columbia University School of Nursing goes back a long way. In the mid-19th century, the population of New York City was about one million people and growing rapidly. The result was overcrowded living conditions with increasing problems of illness and accidents. Much of the population was poor and lacked access to healthcare. In 1868, a group of citizens who understood the gravity of the situation drew up a plan for a hospital to care for the people in need. In 1872, the Presbyterian Hospital opened. A polished granite tablet inscribed in bronze letters was installed that read:

PRESBYTERIAN HOSPITAL
For the Poor of New York
without regard to
RACE, CREED OR COLOR
supported by
VOLUNTARY CONTRIBUTION

When I was at the Columbia Presbyterian Medical Center in the 1960s, that spirit of delivering quality healthcare to all patients, no matter their situation, was a very serious business. Everyone who worked there felt that responsibility.

The first nurses to work at the new Presbyterian Hospital were sent from the training school at New York Post-Graduate Hospital in 1885. But before long, in 1892, the Presbyterian Hospital founded its own School of Nursing.

In 1921, The Presbyterian Hospital and Columbia University established an affiliation primarily for physicians. Columbia University's College of Physicians and Surgeons had been founded in 1754 as King's College, and later became incorporated into the new Columbia University in 1807. By 1921, it was agreed that medical students needed more direct contact with patients on the wards of a hospital, and so the close affiliation between Presbyterian Hospital and Columbia University began.

In 1937, with the increasing complexity of delivering quality healthcare, a baccalaureate program in nursing at Columbia University was established. All practical education and training for nurses was to occur at the Columbia Presbyterian Medical Center. This was a time in the United States where there were few, if any, nurses who were educated in a university setting. Schools of nursing were owned and operated by hospitals that provided the students with the clinical experience considered necessary for the education of a nurse. The hospitals depended economically on the patient care that was provided by these students. While in the program, students carried out the majority of patient care offered by the hospital, receiving only limited classroom education in the form of lectures on patient care and related subjects. At the end of the educational program, students received a diploma and were eligible to seek work as a trained nurse.

In those early years, there were courageous, energetic nursing leaders, such as Miss Helen Young and Miss Anna Maxwell at the new Columbia University School of Nursing, who worked tirelessly to establish a professional nursing education. They stressed the human approach to patients as well as the highest standards of science-based healthcare. Even though these nursing leaders had long since left the School of Nursing and the Columbia Presbyterian Medical Center by the time I arrived, their philosophy of exceptional nursing care was still very much alive. I felt that strongly from the first year there.

The Columbia Presbyterian Medical Center had expanded over the years to include six hospitals: Presbyterian Hospital, the Neurological Institute, the New York State Psychiatric Institute, Babies Hospital, Harkness Pavilion, and Sloan Maternity Hospital. They were all connected underground by wide walking tunnels, which were also connected with the student nurses' residence, Maxwell Hall. You did not have to go outside, but could walk from Maxwell Hall to any of the hospitals through the underground tunnels. The tunnels were also wide enough for pushing large laundry carts, which would squish giant cockroaches under their wheels. We nursing students got accustomed to always passing a large number of cockroach bodies on our way back and forth to the hospitals.

The nursing baccalaureate program was a total of five years: two years of undergraduate work, which I had already completed at Western Reserve University, and three years in the School of Nursing at Columbia University. The last three years were actually completed in two years, as the school year was extended all year long, including summers, for six semesters. In the first week, we were given four uniforms, which were washed daily in the laundry at Maxwell Hall. The blue-and-white-striped uniform was essentially unchanged from the uniforms that had been worn by the members of the first class of student nurses in 1892. The only difference was the hem: rather than hanging down to the floor as it did in 1892, the length hit the middle of my calf. There was a gathering of material at the waist in the back of the dress to accommodate the "bustle" worn in the old days. The gathering was still present in my uniforms, but of course we had no "bustle." The dress had long sleeves, with ten buttons running from elbow to wrist on each sleeve. It was covered with a starched white apron, which tied in the back. We wore white stockings and white oxford shoes. We were not allowed to roll up the sleeves of the uniform, even in hot weather. I had to wear my watch over the lower part of the sleeve, near the wrist, as I was not allowed to fold the sleeve over. The hospitals were not air-conditioned in those days. With so much starch and so many buttons, it took me nearly 15 minutes to get into the uniform every morning. The student nurses stayed in their uniforms all day and evening, even when studying in the medical library. It was just too hard to get in and out of them.

The nursing cap, known as the Presbyterian cap, was considered an essential part of the uniform. The cap was made of linen and hand-sewn in the sewing room of the student nurses' residence. The Presbyterian cap was selected by Miss Anna C. Maxwell in 1892. Our dormitory, Maxwell Hall, was named after her. The cap had to be worn at all times when in uniform, and it identified the school from which a nurse graduated.

My energy in taking care of patients was boundless at the Columbia Presbyterian Medical Center. There was so much to learn, so much excitement. I loved being in the hospital. I spent time in all six hospitals, but mostly in the 14-story Presbyterian Hospital. There were 16 bed units, with eight beds on each side of the room and a curtain around each bed. The attending physicians, wearing long white coats, would sweep from the elevators into the large room, a passel of medical students in short white coats trailing behind them. The nurses were attentive to the needs of the physicians as well as the patients. The window shades in the large room were all set at the same level during physician rounds. Nursing students were there in our striped uniforms and caps, and the nurses were there in their white uniforms and caps. Virtually all the physicians and medical students were men, and all the nursing students and graduate nurses were women. No one ever questioned that gender divide at the time.

I met a good friend my first year, Pat Smyth. She and I became very close throughout all our years at the School of Nursing. She had come from Mt. Holyoke College, and we had a similar passion for striving to be the best nurses we could possibly be. We had single rooms at Maxwell Hall and spent time together in the evenings talking about our aspirations for our new careers. Those years at the Columbia Presbyterian Medical Center, and sharing ideas with Pat, cemented my strong connection to the nursing profession.

Meanwhile, I continued a long-distance romantic relationship with Dick Vigesaa. He was still trying to finish the one paper he needed to complete his baccalaureate degree in philosophy. I was so sure he would do it. How hard could it be? It was just one paper. For some reason, I felt the commitment we had to each other was unbreakable, and I could not see a future without him. It seems hard to believe now.

In addition to not finishing the paper, I also saw that Dick was not doing other things either. He should have been filling out graduate school applications. So why wasn't he? I started filling them out for him. This was on the premise that he would finish his religion paper and finally get his BA in philosophy.

Long distance communication was difficult in those days. It was mainly by letter. Telephone calls were expensive. Our phone conversations became more and more unsatisfactory. It seemed impossible to get basic information. What was Dick doing with his time anyway?

To make enough money to visit Dick in Chicago for a secret long week-end, I sold a pint of my blood for 20 dollars. In those days, I could fly student-standby for $22.95 from New York to Chicago. I could donate a pint of blood every eight weeks. I remember going to the blood bank, which was in the Columbia Presbyterian Medical Center, to give my pint of blood and collect my 20 dollars. The blood bank was staffed by medical students and residents, all of whom were men. I was so naive in those days. When they said they had to take off my blouse and do a full heart and lung examination before I could give blood, I did not understand what was really going on. To this day, it makes me angry to think about it.

The next year, I did my public health nursing rotation in Mott Haven in the South Bronx. Regulations required me to get a complete blood count before the rotation. Due to giving blood every eight weeks, I had worked myself into a significant anemia and had to stop selling my blood. It took a few months, but my blood count finally returned to normal. That was the last time in my life I ever gave blood.

The Vietnam War was raging, and Dick received his draft notice. He was supposed to report for his physical examination near his hometown in Faribault, Minnesota, where he was staying with his parents. But a huge snowstorm hit the night before the draft appointment, and everything was completely shut down. By the time they rescheduled, he had slipped back to Garrett Theological Seminary in Evanston, Illinois. If you were studying to be a minister, you were able to get a 4D deferment, which was even better than the 2S student deferment. Anything to avoid going to Vietnam. But Dick never wanted to be a minister either.

In retrospect, I can't explain why I couldn't see the danger signs about Dick Vigesaa. In November 1966, my mother wrote to me, "You are cutting yourself off—hadn't you learned from past experience?" I was defensive. I still believed in Dick's potential. Even more significantly, I had already developed a sexual relationship with him, which at the time, in my mind, was an unbreakable commitment. You only had sex with someone you were going to marry.

Living in New York City was quite an experience. It was significantly different from Cleveland. It was a rough city; I don't think a day would go by without someone yelling at me or saying something mean. It might be the man issuing subway tokens or a woman at a little food market. I got used to it. After a while, it did not bother me.

In New York City at the time, you had to be vigilant just walking down the street. If someone made eye contact with you, it was nearly always a sign of trouble. If someone tried to talk to you, it was a sign of danger 100 percent of the time. You avoided eye contact if you wanted to feel safe. One time, I was coming back on the subway unusually late. The train was nearly empty. I sat down on a seat facing the other side of the car. There was a young, heavy-set man with dirty, disheveled clothes sitting opposite me. He started staring at me licentiously while grabbing his crotch and rubbing it. I was frightened and stood up and walked to the next car, holding on as the train was moving fast. He followed me. I went on to the next car, and he was still right behind me. When I entered the third car, there was a policeman. I immediately went up to him, telling him about the man following right behind me. When the man entered the car, the policeman grabbed him and threw him off the train at the next stop. I was so relieved. My destination was still a few stops away, and the policeman struck up a conversation with me. Where was I going? Where did I live? I told him I was a nursing student at Columbia.

"Ah," he said, "I knew a few nurses once. We had some great parties together. You and I could have some fun too." My subway stop could not come too quickly.

In the meantime, my dad was very concerned about my relationship with Dick Vigesaa, a man he thought had come from nothing and was going nowhere. In June 1967, he wrote me a long letter that expressed his point of view. Here is a short excerpt:

> [Dick] comes from nothing. Where he and his family go in life will be 100 percent up to his efforts. . . . Dick is going to have to be better than average to attain a place on the side of the tracks I think you both will want to live on. At this writing, I haven't seen enough kindling to start a fire in the fireplace. If there is and I am wrong, I hope I am big enough to admit it. Possibly my words had something to do with his decision to enroll once again at Garrett. It would seem to me that he should have done this last summer. . . . I hope you take this letter in a constructive manner. Sometimes it is difficult to write exactly how one feels. I do not dislike Dick as one might gather. On the other hand, I do not especially like him. We are by nature quite different, Dick and I, but this can apply to most of us.

During the summer of 1967, after I had been at Columbia for three semesters, Dick moved to New York City just for that summer. He rented a room at 116th Street, across from the main campus of Columbia University. He got a job in a bookstore on 5th Avenue. He still hadn't finished his religion paper. All the applications that I had filled out for him were rejected when it was discovered that he did not have a bachelor's degree in philosophy. But then an amazing thing occurred: he was accepted at the University of Washington in Seattle as an "unclassified student," meaning he could take classes without having them applied to a degree. At the end of the summer, he intended to move to Seattle to start at the University of Washington.

About this time, I was home on a school vacation. My whole family was having a big Sunday dinner in Winnetka, and Dick was invited. As I write this, I can still hardly believe what happened, except that I was there. We were all eating, but the atmosphere was tense and uncomfortable, and I could feel my dad's anger percolating.

Suddenly, my dad stood up from the dinner table, red-faced, and said, "Dick, you are no better than Cassius Clay—you are a draft dodger, and I think I can take you now . . ." He removed his glasses and turned toward Dick, ready to fight him.

My mother stood up and yelled, "Run, Dick, run!"

Dick quickly left the table and ran from the house. All hell broke loose after that.

For days afterward, everyone was mad at my dad. My mother even moved out of their bedroom for several days. But my dad's behavior didn't change.

In September 1967, when I had just one more year of school at Columbia University, Dick borrowed my brother John's student ID and flew to Seattle at half fare to start classes at the University of Washington. I have to give Dick credit for at least surviving. He arrived with no money and no place to stay. While walking up University Way NE with his one suitcase, he passed The Wesley House, near the University of Washington campus, and went in. The Wesley House is connected to the Methodist Church, which had some connection to Garrett Theological Seminary, where Dick had taken classes. The Methodist minister, Dr. George Jordan, gave him a room in return for cleaning the bathrooms. There was a common kitchen at The Wesley House where one could prepare a meal.

Back in New York, I was about to start my third and final year. Graduation from Columbia University was to be June 1968, and my last semester at the School of Nursing ended in August 1968. It was time to think seriously about the next phase of my life.

I was determined to continue my relationship with Dick Vigesaa. I believed in him. There was no logical reason to think he would succeed after all his failures, but I was also afraid to be alone. He was at the University of Washington, so after graduation I decided I would need to find a job in Seattle.

During spring break in April 1968, I flew from New York to Seattle. I just about fainted when I saw Mt. Rainier—this gigantic volcano of snow and glacier glistening in the sun, with green forests surrounding it. I had never imagined there was something so majestic, so beautiful, so enticing to explore right here in Washington State.

But then I saw Dick at the Wesley House. He was profoundly depressed. He wasn't working. He was living on leftover instant mashed potatoes he found in the kitchen. I was not sure what he was doing in school.

So, what did I do? I gave him a pep talk and told him what he had to do to meet his goals. Honestly, when I think about all of this, I'm not sure why I kept on trying to make this relationship work. Part of it is my philosophy: if you want something bad enough, you have to work hard for it. That's one thing I knew how to do—work hard. I just didn't know how to cut my losses and give up.

I had four job interviews in Seattle: University Hospital, Group Health, Virginia Mason, and Swedish Hospital. I received job offers from all four. I chose University Hospital, and was to start my job on September 3, 1968, after graduating from Columbia University in June, and finishing at the School of Nursing and the Medical Center in August.

While in Seattle, I bought a big poster of the University of Washington. When I got back to New York, I taped that poster right above my bed. I would look at it every day and dream about my upcoming new life in Seattle at the University of Washington's University Hospital.

Meanwhile, although I was so worried about Dick and his inability to get on with his life, I wrote a rosy picture of how he was doing to my parents. It was a total fabrication on my part. I was frightened of revealing the truth to them. I had hoped the truth would change for the better before they found out what was really happening. In my mind, I had made an intractable commitment to Dick and our relationship. I was determined to do everything I could to see it through.

My dad wrote me a long letter concerning my decision to move to Seattle and marry Dick. He ended by saying, "Your mother advises me that in August you will be 22. Doesn't seem possible. Therefore, it is time I give up advising you and Dick and leave your future plans strictly up to the both of you. This I plan to do from here on in."

My formal graduation from Columbia University was on June 4, 1968. It seemed premature in my mind, only because I still had classes and had to be in the hospital until August 16. The ceremony took place on the main campus at 116th Street and Broadway, exactly the same place where students had taken over five administration buildings the previous April. The atmosphere was thankfully more calm, but people were still riled up about the Vietnam War. We were all in our caps and gowns, many hundreds of us, sitting on seats assembled in the large open area, with the huge granite buildings with giant Corinthian columns standing high above us. On the flat tops of our caps we all had the peace sign drawn in thick white marker. If one walked up the steps of the huge surrounding buildings with their columns, they would be able to clearly see those hundreds and hundreds of caps with the peace signs. It was our statement.

My parents, John, Carol, and Jacquey all came to my graduation. I was so glad they were there. They flew to New York together, and my dad rented a big convertible to take everyone around New York City. Dad took us all out to one of his favorite restaurants in Manhattan, Chris Cella's. Besides great steak and seafood, they had the most wonderful, fresh tomatoes and excellent roquefort salad dressing.

After the main ceremony, the student nurses had a second, separate graduation at the School of Nursing. My whole family was there as well. At the graduation, I received The Margaret Eliot Prize, considered the highest student achievement award at the Columbia School of Nursing.

It was awarded to the senior nursing student "who most nearly combines professional competence, capacity for leadership, and wholehearted compassion for patients." I had no idea I would get that award until the day of graduation. It was a complete surprise, and a very happy one.

The following is one of my last student evaluations from one of my nursing professors, Mrs. Britten:

> Lynne Barber has more enthusiasm than any student I have ever taught. She has a very questioning mind. The one thing that baffles me is how she is able to discuss patient problems and desired actions to be taken on the floor without threatening the graduate nurses. They should be threatened, because she is talking about suggestions and ideas she wants to accomplish which should have been done by them a long time ago. But somehow, her manner doesn't put them on the defensive, and they are less likely to become hostile and apply barriers to change.

I had so much respect for Mrs. Britten, considered by most at the school to be one of the best nursing instructors at Columbia University. Her final evaluation gave me hope that I would someday be successful in becoming a very good nurse. I was on the brink of joining the nursing profession and hoped I would make a positive difference.

Back home in Winnetka, my dad reserved a sleeping car on a passenger train for me. On August 22, 1968, I left Chicago with 20 large cardboard boxes containing everything I owned. Included were all my rocks and shells from Cape Cod. I arrived in Seattle two nights and three days later.

I will always remember the train trip from Chicago to Seattle. After leaving Chicago, the train headed west, and eventually night fell. I had dinner in the dining car, and then went to sleep in my private sleeping car by pulling a bed down from the wall. When I woke up in the morning, we were in Wyoming. The train stopped for a short time in Cheyenne. I had never seen territory like that. That day, the train rode endlessly through huge rock formations, mesas, prairies, and plains. I felt like I was in a John Wayne movie. I was glued to the window in my sleeping compartment, mesmerized by the strange and very beautiful scenery.

When I arrived in Seattle, Dick met me at the train station. He had a friend with him who had a car, and after several trips, all 20 of my boxes were safely in my new studio apartment. I was beginning a new life in Seattle.

CHAPTER 3

———◆•◆———

Life in Seattle: 1968-1972

M Y NEW STUDIO apartment was walking distance from University
Hospital, one mile away. Dick and his roommate, Dave Apple,
shared a one-bedroom apartment on the upper level in the same apartment complex. Of course, as soon as I arrived there, I was in Dick's
apartment, and he was in mine.

I'm not sure why I felt my only option was marrying Dick. I could have
insisted that we live separately until he got his act together, but I was
also lonely, unsure of myself, and frightened about life after college. The
idea of marriage felt much more secure. It didn't register that he was
working part-time for minimum wage at a bookstore down the street
while I was making many more times his income at my job as a registered
nurse at University Hospital. It was he who needed economic security,
not me, but I didn't see it that way at the time. In my mind, marriage was
really the only real option I had, and the sooner the better.

But first, I had to start my job as a registered nurse at University Hospital.
It began with an orientation program. The head nursing administrator

pointed out the Cascade Mountains to us from a big picture window facing east, but also mentioned that her favorite mountains were the Olympics to the west. Were there really multiple exciting mountain ranges here in Washington for me to explore?

One of the new nurses at my orientation was Cynthia Walsh, who became a good friend. Cynthia had just graduated from the School of Nursing at Stanford University, and had married her husband, Bud, two months prior. Bud was entering law school at the University of Washington. She told me there was no way she would have been able to move in with Bud if they hadn't been married before they arrived. Her word at the time: *unthinkable*. I was completely aware of that.

My new job involved working primarily with patients with spinal cord injuries, many with quadriplegia. There were also a variety of other patients with different injuries requiring rehabilitation, and also patients with chronic pain issues.

What a shock Seattle's University Hospital was after working at the Columbia Presbyterian Medical Center. I was amazed at the modern construction of the building itself. No more 16-bed units; instead, there were single-bed and double-bed units arranged around a huge oval, with the nurses' station in the center. There was so much privacy for the patients, and also easy, quick access to each patient from the nurses' station. Long gone, too, was the cumbersome, starched student nurses' uniform. Now, I was wearing a light, white cotton dress along with my Columbia Presbyterian cap.

One of the real shockers for me was what we nurses were expected to do at University Hospital. At the Columbia Presbyterian Hospital complex, female nurses (and there were only female nurses) were not allowed to attend to, or really even look at, the genitalia of men. I know that sounds ridiculous, but it was true at that time. If a man had to be catheterized, a male orderly was called to do it. If we were giving a male patient a bed bath, we were told to offer the man the washcloth so he could "finish" the bath himself. If the male patient could not manage to do that, the male orderly was called to finish the job. But here, a female nurse could deliver any care that a male patient needed.

Dick and I decided to get married as soon as we could. We asked George Jordan, the Methodist minister who had given Dick a room at the Wesley House, to perform the ceremony at the chapel of the University Methodist Church. The date was set for November 9, 1968. I tried to keep the whole thing as inexpensive as possible.

I wasn't sure if anyone in my family would come to our wedding. In October, my dad wrote to me informing me that he would not attend. He wrote that he was so proud of me and wrote "to take good care of yourself and always remember I love you more than anything." My mother couldn't decide whether to come or not. She finally arrived the day before the wedding and left just after it. She seemed sad and emotionally distant.

I recently reread the letters my mother had sent me during this time. They are filled with anger, frustration, and despair over what she was facing at home. There is virtually nothing positive in any of the letters. There are vivid details of my dad's abusive drinking episodes and having to "make tracks" by leaving the house, sometimes with Jacquey and sometimes alone, to avoid the verbal abuse. Jacquey told me years later that when our mother left the house without her, she would hide among the cobwebs in the basement to avoid our father. My mother also wrote about the disappointment and frustration she felt toward my brother,

John, who had poor grades at Lea College in Minnesota. My sister Carol was going through destructive behavior with drugs, shoplifting, and arrests, and my mother detailed all that too. Understandably, my mother was far too engulfed with her own problems to have any interest in my new life in Seattle.

Jacquey made a wedding present for Dick and me: 25 plaster of paris Christmas ornaments that she hand-painted. She was 12 years old. To this day, and for the last 57 consecutive Christmases, her ornaments are the first ones to go on our Christmas tree every year.

The nurses on 6 North were kind and supportive. One was my bridesmaid, and the others poured tea and coffee and served cake at the small reception we had at the chapel. With the friends I had made at the hospital and other friends that Dick had made, there were about 30 people at our wedding.

Since we didn't own a car, a friend of Dick's loaned us hers so we could drive to a restaurant for dinner and then back to our apartment. Dick's roommate, Dave Apple, had moved out, and I moved in, giving up my little studio apartment. I didn't take any time off, but continued working the 3:00 p.m. to 11:30 p.m. shift. I could have taken a bus, but I loved the relaxing walk back home after work.

Dick finally managed to finish his paper on religion and was awarded a BA in philosophy from Morningside College. Then, a most unexpected thing happened. The University of Washington Graduate Philosophy Department granted him admission. We thought there must have been some clerical error, as he never actually applied to the graduate school. Looking back, I believe it was a very fortunate clerical error. All he had to do was complete his coursework there, and he would have a master's degree in philosophy. It was a great opportunity for him. I was so excited and so hopeful, and I fully believed in his ability to do it.

But that isn't what happened. Instead, Dick was unable to complete his coursework. A pattern of behavior reappeared. I would watch each day for his progress, but nothing was happening. Day after day, as the deadlines came closer and closer, he would do little, if any, work. I tried to be encouraging and gently explain how serious it was not to complete his assignments. Finally, when the due date came and his assignments were not completed, I would get totally upset.

"Why can't you do this? How can you let this happen?"

Dick would blame me. He couldn't write because I put too much pressure on him. It was all my fault.

I had health insurance, and Dick was on my plan, which enabled him to see a psychiatrist, first at the University and then in private practice. Despite a lot of individual therapy from two different psychiatrists, there were no positive changes.

Throughout this time, I gave a completely different picture of my life to my parents. I wrote about how great married life was. Dick was a wonderful husband, working hard in graduate school, and I was so happy. I felt that I had to put up a good front.

About a month after our wedding, my dad came to Seattle on business with an associate, Mike O'Connor, better known by all as just "O'Connor." Dad said he wanted to take Dick and me out to dinner. We reluctantly agreed to meet him at a restaurant he suggested. The dinner turned out to be an absolute nightmare. The longer it went on and the more Beefeater martinis my dad drank, the more abusive he became. Finally, all hell broke loose and he totally lost it.

He leaned over the table toward Dick, teeth clenched, eyes bloodshot and narrowed, and shouted, "You had better turn out good or I will kill you!"

I was sobbing and terrified.

I think by now it should have been completely obvious to anyone who knew the real story of Dick's failures that my marriage to him was a total mistake. But I still felt that Dick was my husband and needed me to believe in him. I also knew I could not allow my dad to be abusive to my husband again.

One month later, after we had been married two months, I received a postcard from my dad saying he was coming to Seattle again on business and would like to take Dick and me out to dinner. The fear and dread started again. I felt we could not have dinner again on my dad's territory: a restaurant of his choosing, where he would be paying. So, I made a plan. I replied that we would prefer to have him over for dinner at our apartment. I would make his favorite meal: grilled New York steak, baked potato with butter and sour cream, a salad with roquefort dressing, and chocolate cream pie for dessert. I would have one six-pack of beer, but there would be no "Beefeater martinis on the rocks with a twist." I wrote that I hoped we would all be able to be civil to one another at this dinner. After Dad received my letter, he called me.

"What the hell are you trying to tell me?"

"Dad, we just need to get along," I said.

His voice crescendoed on the telephone. "I am 53 years old! What the hell are you trying to tell me?"

I finally said, "Dad, you can't insult my husband anymore."

He just hung up.

A week later, I received another postcard from him telling me of his upcoming arrival in Seattle. I wrote back that we would be happy to have him at our house for dinner, and I set a time. I was convinced it would be a terrifying evening.

My dad arrived for dinner that night and stayed three hours. He ate all his favorite foods and drank his six beers. He never made one insult—not even a subtle one. Not one single insult during that entire evening, and he maintained that insult-free behavior for the next 14 years—until I called him and said, "I'm getting a divorce from Dick."

Dad replied, "That worthless guy. It's about time. How are you doing?"

After that, Dad called me every day for a month to check on me.

The next day after that fateful dinner, Dad picked me up and we drove up and over Snoqualmie Pass for the first time. Dad noticed his rental car had chains in the trunk.

"What are these chains for?" he asked.

We still thought of Seattle as wet and rainy, but then we ascended Snoqualmie Pass. The snow! Multiple feet of beautiful, white, gorgeous snow! We watched some men shovel several feet of the previous night's snowfall off the roofs of the buildings at the top of Snoqualmie Pass. We both went wild over the snow-covered, gigantic red cedar and Douglas fir trees growing en masse in all directions. Snow-covered mountains with rocky faces were all around us. Those views ignited my love for the Pacific Northwest.

That winter, a group of nurses on 6 North were planning a snowshoeing trip in the Cascade Mountains. Did I want to go? Of course! They offered to rent snowshoes for me at REI, and I borrowed long winter underwear from Dick's old roommate, Dave Apple. I had my winter coat, scarf, and ear muffs from New York City. At the trailhead, it was snowing gently but consistently. I put my snowshoes on, and away we went through the snowy woods. I just loved it. I couldn't wait to go again.

Life for my parents and siblings was becoming fraught with more problems. My dad had a heart attack, and during this same period, my sister Carol was having serious mental and emotional problems and getting professional help. My mother was in counseling, trying to deal with it all. Being far away in Seattle, I could only listen and offer advice over the phone.

In February 1969, I accepted the position of head nurse on the evening shift. I was feeling more comfortable and more skilled at my job. However, I was not fond of the evening shift, which also involved working many weekends. But that was the life of a hospital nurse at that time.

Meanwhile, I was saving money to buy a car. Dick, in addition to going to graduate school, was working weekends at the Washington Bookstore. His boss had a used Volkswagen Bug and sold it to us for $1,000: $300 down and $100 per month until it was paid for. Wow, a car of our own, and we could travel!

The first thing we did was drive to Paradise at 5,400 feet elevation on the south side of Mt. Rainier. There was snow everywhere—30 feet deep in some places. The 14,410-foot snow- and glacier-covered Mt. Rainier towered above us, gleaming and beautiful. It was thrilling. I had never experienced anything like it before. The very next day, we went to REI and bought hiking boots, backpacks, and a two-person backpacking tent. I just couldn't wait to get out on the trail. I couldn't get enough of the wilderness of the Pacific Northwest.

At the same time, I longed to get out of the hospital routine and thought about a job as a public health nurse. It would be weekdays only, during the day, and the salary was better. The idea of seeing patients in their homes and the independence this would offer me was very appealing.

I applied and got a job as a public health nurse at the Seattle King County Department of Public Health. I left the hospital and joined the other public health nurses at the Central West Office on Queen Anne Hill. My service area was Capitol Hill, Beacon Hill, the International District (known at that time as Chinatown), Pioneer Square, and Downtown Seattle. Now that I had weekends free, I was dying to start backpacking and camping in the mountains.

As Seattle outdoor enthusiasts know, there is a large snowpack in the Cascades and Olympics in the winter, but during the spring it gradually melts off, exposing more and more glorious hiking trails. Hikers start with lower-elevation hikes in the early spring and then, as the snow melts, hike higher and higher in the mountains. But early in the season, if you are an eager hiker like me, you think, *I can get up there even with some snow.* You start following a beloved trail in the woods and just can't wait to get up to the meadows and more expansive views. You breathe in the cold, crisp air. But then you hit snow partially covering the trail. As you hike on, you look ahead for trail markers or familiar topography as your boots crunch through the deepening snowpack. The snow gradually obscures most of the trail. The melting snow destabilizes the snowpack, which collapses underneath you, and you lose your balance and fall. You stand, brush yourself off, look around, and realize that you need to come back in a few weeks. I was an eager hiker, but had to face the reality of the seasons in the mountains.

I cannot adequately express the thrill of hiking in the Cascades and Olympics. I think I bought every hiking book ever published in order to discover what was out there to explore. I still have them all. Somehow, I can't bring myself to get rid of any of them, even the old editions. They hold a special place in my heart for introducing me to a world that became a big part of my life.

Dick seemed excited about the mountains as well. We would spend every Monday unpacking from the previous weekend's backpacking trip. On Tuesday and Wednesday, we would decide where we were going the next weekend. On Thursday, we would pack up all our gear, and then on Friday, we would drive to the trailhead and throw our sleeping bags on the ground so we could get an early start on Saturday morning. After hiking for several miles with our gear on our backs, we would pitch our tent beside the mountain meadows and do some exploring. Then on Sunday, we would hike back out to the trailhead. The thrill of being there! The beauty! The physicality of moving your body forward with all your belongings on your back! To this day, I have never gotten over my love of hiking, backpacking, and climbing in the mountains.

During the spring, summer, and fall of 1969, we became more and more adventurous on our hikes. We hiked to the Lena Lakes in the Olympic Mountains on the Olympic Peninsula. We hiked and camped in Olympic

National Park along the Pacific Ocean at Cape Alava and Third Beach. We hiked through the rain forest and then along the beautiful, sandy seashore of the Pacific Ocean. I swam and dodged the waves in the ice-cold surf. Swimming at Cape Cod as a child made me comfortable in cold ocean water. We hiked the trails all around Mt. Rainier: Klapatche Park, Eunice Lake and Tolmie Peak, Spray Park, Moraine Park, and Mystic Lake. In the Cascades, we hiked and camped at Tonga Ridge and Fisher Lake, the Foss Lakes, Lake Serene, Rachel Lake, and Annette Lake. We explored the Goat Rocks Wilderness with hikes and backpacking trips to Snowgrass Flats and Goat Ridge. The more we hiked and backpacked, the better physical shape we were in, and the further and higher we wanted to go.

In September of 1970, we climbed to the top of Mt. Adams at 12,307 feet. It wasn't a technical climb, and we didn't need a rope or other climbing gear. It was a long snow climb—one foot in front of the other in a rhythmic cadence. As we climbed higher and higher, we saw spectacular views of the surrounding peaks: Mt. St. Helens (before it blew in 1980), Mt. Hood in Oregon, and Mt. Rainier. It was a monumental experience for me. It made me want to learn how to really climb mountains and explore even higher.

My job as a public health nurse was new and exciting. In the morning, we would get our assignments telling us who in the community needed our help. With my nurse's bag in hand, I would get into my car and drive to the homes of my patients. The Seattle-King County Department of Health was a "combined agency," meaning that we saw well patients who needed health guidance as well as sick patients who needed evaluation and home care.

I saw new mothers and babies who the hospital felt needed extra help and guidance. I remember one first-time young mother newly arrived from Japan. She was living with her husband in a tiny apartment in Chinatown. My task was to evaluate her home situation, examine her new baby, demonstrate a proper baby bath, and anything else I felt she needed. I was greeted at the door by her mother-in-law, wearing a kimono. No one spoke English, and I spoke no Japanese. All went well until I attempted to demonstrate the baby bath in the usual little, shallow plastic bathtub I brought with me. The mother-in-law was aghast at the size of my plastic bathtub. She immediately took over and insisted that the bathwater level be nearly two feet deep, and produced a larger bathtub from the other room. All communication was done by hand signals. I saw no harm in the deep water level and the large tub, as long as she had a firm hold on the baby, which she did. At the end of the visit, I was served tea and pastries in the living room with the father. The mother, mother-in-law, and baby were hidden away in the kitchen, and only the mother-in-law came out to serve us.

Another patient was an elderly sea captain living in an old hotel in downtown Seattle. The manager of the hotel had called the health department because the sea captain couldn't get out of bed anymore and had no family to call. I climbed the rickety steps to his room. On entering, a foul smell hit my nose. It was the odor of urine, feces, and a human body that had not been washed in many weeks. Thin and pale, with a grizzled white beard, he was lying in bed, covered in blankets and surrounded by empty food containers. I suddenly became aware of dozens of small cockroaches climbing over his sheets and blankets. I was horrified. I hadn't seen a cockroach since New York City, and never crawling in a patient's bed. His mind was clear, but he was weak and tired and hadn't had any healthcare for years. I called an ambulance, and he was transported to

Harborview Medical Center. The next day, I visited him there. He died a few days after that.

I had several patients at the old Frye Hotel, which was gorgeous once. I didn't use the elevator so I could walk up the beautiful marble staircases and see the crystal chandeliers, even though many of them were broken. There was a strong smell of urine on the landings and some garbage on the stairwells, but the beauty and majesty of the hotel always spoke to me.

Many of my patients had some degree of mental illness. My job was to check on them, talk with them, encourage them, make sure they knew how to take their medications correctly, and coax them to make use of the social services available at that time.

As a public health nurse, I worked closely with the Maternal and Infant Care Program at Harborview Medical Center. I visited high-risk mothers and babies in their homes and communicated with the nurses, social workers, and pediatricians in the outpatient clinics at Harborview. I became friends with one of the social workers, Arlene Hinckley. Later that summer, in 1971, Dick and I climbed Mt. Hood, the 11,250-foot snow-covered volcano in Oregon, with Arlene and her husband, Tom. I loved long, steady snow climbs, ascending slowly higher and higher, with the views of other mountains everywhere you look.

I loved my job working as a public health nurse, but as time went on, there were frustrations. The biggest were for me the limitations on collaborating about the care of my patients. When I tried to talk with one of the doctors, either in private practice or at Harborview Medical Center, I often got no response from them. Most would not return a telephone call. I rarely got a response from any physician in regard to an idea I had about a change in my patient's care.

I thought about going to medical school. I wondered why I'd never considered it before. I called the School of Medicine at the University of Washington and talked with an intake person about applying. I told her I was a registered nurse with a baccalaureate degree and had graduated from the School of Nursing at Columbia University. She immediately told me that the School of Medicine did not want nurses applying to medical school. When I asked why, she said the biology and chemistry classes I took were not the same caliber as those that premed students took. Of course, this was absolutely not true. There had been lots of premed students (all men) in my biology and chemistry classes at Western Reserve University. Feeling embarrassed and angry, I quickly thanked her and hung up.

Dick had just failed his graduate coursework at the University of Washington and could not go back. He hadn't completed most of the work required to graduate. The schoolwork he *had* done might have been great, but much of it was unfinished. My fears kept flashing before me. If he failed to attain a career, what would happen to our marriage? It seemed to me at the time that I had to work as hard as I could to get him on some path to success.

Dick had a friend, Jerry Anderson, who taught in the philosophy department at the University of Vermont. Jerry told Dick that he thought he could get him admitted to the philosophy department, and Dick could then work toward his master's degree. If he could succeed there, he could go on to get his PhD and get a job teaching philosophy at a college. There was hope.

In the spring of 1971, Dick and I took a mountain climbing course sponsored by the University of Washington. It was a wonderfully fun and exciting experience. As part of the class, we climbed Mt. Washington in the Olympics, the class 4 rock route of The Tooth in the Cascade Mountains, and Mt. Baker at 10,778 feet in the North Cascades. We also practiced crevice-rescue techniques on the Nisqually Glacier. Dick and I obtained more skills and knowledge about the mountains, which made our outdoor trips safer and even more fun.

I wanted to move out of our tiny one-bedroom apartment, so we found a wonderful older home and rented the bottom half of it. I loved that house; it had character. I made curtains for the kitchen and had lots of fun doing it. It was also right on Green Lake, a beloved city lake with a three-mile shoreline and a running path along it. I started running almost daily after work to stay in aerobic shape for weekend hiking and climbing.

We were saving money, but then we decided to take a trip to Europe in the summer of 1971. With all the uncertainty around Dick's career, I now wonder why we chose to do this. I don't think I wanted to face the problems in our lives—problems that were becoming more prominent and more difficult to avoid. At the time, Dick told me he thought the trip to Europe was a needed vacation before he started school again somewhere. I took a leave of absence from my job, and off we went.

We spent nearly two months in Europe that summer. It was a wonderfully exciting trip. With no major responsibilities to deal with, Dick and I functioned very well together. He was always great on a vacation. We decided to buy a Volkswagen Bug and pick it up in Wolfsburg, Germany. We initially flew to Amsterdam and took a train to Wolfsburg. I'll never forget visiting Anne Frank's hiding place behind the bookcase in the perfume factory in Amsterdam. I'm still haunted by her pictures and mementoes pinned up on the wall of her little room.

After we picked up our new car, we had no specific plans and just started driving. We had a lovely time along the Rhine River in Germany, then drove to Denmark, and finally to Norway. Dick had always wanted to visit Norway. At first, we thought it was too far to go, but then we just headed north, taking the ferry from Hirtshals, Denmark, to Kristiansand, Norway. We arrived in Kristiansand late at night and discovered there was absolutely no place to stay. We ended up sleeping on the side of the road in the Volkswagen Bug—Dick was in the back seat and I was in the front seat. I actually don't know how it was physically possible, but we did it somehow. We were young then.

Dick's grandparents were born in Vikesa, Norway, a little village on a fjord just south of Stavanger. We stopped there, went to the first little cottage we saw, and knocked on the door. A friendly woman answered, and Dick announced he was a Vigesaa and his grandparents had been born there. We were immediately taken in as long-lost relatives. No one spoke English except for a relative from a distant village who was immediately summoned to help translate. It was a memorable, once-in-a-lifetime experience.

Norway was quite expensive, so we drove back down to mainland Europe and spent about a month in Austria. There, we climbed a few mountains and swam in very cold mountain lakes. We loved the food, the mountains, and the people there.

When we returned from Europe, I knew we could not continue the way we had been going. Dick could not keep making minimum wage at the Washington Bookstore. Something had to be done. I was overwhelmed with worry over what would happen if Dick never worked hard enough to achieve any of his career goals.

Gretchen Schodde, a public health nurse with whom I worked, and I became friends. Gretchen had the same concerns about our nursing profession that I did. We wanted more authority and responsibility. Gretchen had gone to the University of Washington School of Nursing and had connections with some of the professors there. Then as now, the School of Nursing at the University of Washington was considered one of the best nursing schools in the country. Some of the professors there wanted to find a way to change Washington's Nurse Practice Act. Their belief was that registered nurses were already successfully performing many tasks and procedures and making decisions that were beyond the scope of nursing practice as defined by Washington State law. The law was not keeping up with modern nursing practice and the future of nursing.

The Vietnam War was winding down, and many servicemen with skills in delivering healthcare—usually emergency care—were leaving military service but could not legally use their new skills. In 1969, the University of Washington School of Medicine developed the second program in the United States for educating former military men who had learned medical skills in the armed forces. The Medex Program was a three-quarter certification program. After finishing the program, students could be hired by a physician as a physician assistant (PA). These new physician assistants could not practice independently; they were "the arm" of the physician and had no legal authority of their own. Any professional or legal responsibility for what the physician assistants did actually belonged to the physician who hired them.

The physicians involved in the University of Washington's Medex program wanted to recruit nurses to be trained as physician assistants. Physicians would maintain employment and essential control of the nurses. The School of Medicine approached some of the professors at the School of Nursing and proposed this idea. It was soundly rejected by the nursing leaders.

They said, "We are neither physician assistants nor arms of the physicians. We are registered nurses and have our own scope of practice."

That concept was not understood by the physicians. That didn't matter to the nursing professors at the University of Washington, though. They wanted to find a way to change the Nurse Practice Act in the State of Washington to legally allow nurses to perform in expanded practices and roles. But how?

Citizens living in a small rural town in western Washington were instrumental in helping to create a new, advanced, and specialized level of nursing practice, as well as bringing about the advent of nurse practitioners. The story began in Darrington, a town about 80 miles northeast of Seattle, in the foothills of the Cascade Mountains. The nearest town to Darrington is Arlington, 50 miles north of Seattle. In 1971, there was no public transportation to or from Darrington. The population of Darrington was about 1,200 people—4,000 if including residents from local outlying areas.

In the early years, the people of Darrington received healthcare from Bayard Taylor Blake, "Doc Blake," as people called him. Doc Blake came west to Darrington in 1906, straight from medical school at the University of Vermont, and was the first healthcare professional in the town. No one knows why he chose Darrington, but he loved the land

and the people, and never left. He saw patients in their homes, arriving by horseback, buggy, or on foot.

In 1916, Doc Blake acquired some land from the US Mill and converted the cookhouse into a hospital—a one-story whitewashed house with a few rooms for patients to spend several hours or days in. Doc Blake was short, very plump, loved to drink, and took care of his patients 24 hours a day, seven days a week. In later years, his drinking consumed him, and he was gradually unable to continue caring for his patients.

In 1929, Norman C. Riddle, "Doc Riddle," came to Darrington to help Doc Blake. Like many of the people of Darrington, he came from North Carolina. He bought the hospital from Doc Blake and built a house for his family next door. Doc Riddle was much loved and respected by the people of Darrington. While living and working there, I heard many colorful stories about him.

As the years went by, Doc Riddle slowly went blind. But even blind, he continued to treat patients very skillfully. I heard stories of him reducing and setting fractured bones with just his touch, skill, and experience. As time went by, Doc Riddle's blindness became more of an impediment to him, and he couldn't treat patients anymore. Darrington no longer had any medical professional delivering medical care. That's when the citizens of Darrington sprang into action. A group of primarily women made it their mission to attract a doctor to Darrington. If they could build a real medical clinic, then maybe a doctor would come.

In 1958, through a grant from the Sears Foundation, this group of Darrington citizens sold bonds to raise money to build a clinic. The Sears Foundation matched their funds, and in 1959, the Darrington Clinic was built. It was a one-story building with a waiting room, a reception area, two offices, four examination rooms, a large treatment room, an X-ray area, and a bathroom. This is the same medical clinic where I practiced in 1972.

The Darrington Clinic succeeded in attracting a doctor. In 1960, Dr. Robert Koop, a general practitioner, came to Darrington to live and stayed there treating patients until 1967. When he left, the Darrington Clinic was empty. A group of citizens jumped into action again. They formed a "Doctor Procurement Committee" and interviewed many medical interns and residents. They erected a huge 20-foot sign on the right side of the main road entering Darrington that read, "This Town Needs a Doctor." For three years, there was no response to the sign.

Finally, the group of citizens, now known as The Darrington Clinic Board, began looking for another solution. In 1970, they heard about the Washington Alaska Regional Medical Program (Washington Alaska RMP). This program no longer exists, but it was formed under the Reagan Administration to get medical resources to rural areas of the country. The Clinic Board finally realized that hiring a physician was not an economically viable solution. They decided to look into the new Physician Assistant Program at the University of Washington instead. But the Washington State Board of Medical Examiners required that any physician who had hired a PA be on the premises of the Darrington Clinic at least 50 percent of the time. There was no physician in the nearest town, Arlington, who was willing to do this.

Next, Washington Alaska RMP approached the professors at the University of Washington School of Nursing. The timing was exactly right. The professors at the School of Nursing were already searching for a way to amend the Nurse Practice Act by establishing a nurse practitioner practice in Washington State. Would a nurse practitioner clinic help convince the legislature to legitimize advanced and specialized levels of nursing practice, something nurses had already been successfully doing for years (albeit not legally)? The nursing professors believed that registered nurses with special educational and practical preparation could deliver quality primary healthcare independently to the people of Darrington.

In the early 1970s, there was an increased awareness of a growing primary healthcare crisis in the United States, especially in rural areas. This led to an expanded utilization of registered nurses and their skills. This was greatly influenced by the nursing faculty. The dean of the School of Nursing, Madeleine Leininger, RN, PhD; Delores "Deo" Little, RN, MN; and Marguerite Cobb, RN, MN; were savvy, smart, forward-thinking women. They recognized that there continued to be a significant professional role for nurses in primary care. There were already examples of this, such as in public health nurses and flight nurses practicing independently in Alaska and nurse midwives delivering babies in New York City. At the time, there were about 800,000 registered nurses in the United States. This was the largest, best-prepared reservoir of healthcare professionals to help extend the availability and access to healthcare services.

Additionally, people in the United States were beginning to see healthcare as more of a right than a privilege. A need for more accessible, less fragmented, and better quality healthcare for all people was being recognized.

Nursing professors at the University of Washington and representatives from Washington Alaska RMP met with the Darrington Clinic Board. They convinced them that nurse practitioners could potentially meet the needs of the town by delivering quality healthcare. At this same time, my public health nurse colleague Gretchen was in contact with some of the professors at the School of Nursing. When she first told me about the possibility of being a part of a new movement to expand the practice of nursing, I was beyond excited. This was the opportunity I was looking for. Gretchen was keenly interested as well. They would be hiring two nurses to work together to establish the Darrington Nurse Practitioner Clinic. Gretchen and I decided we would apply together.

At first, Dick was very negative about the idea. What did I know about rural America? Didn't I know that people who lived there were poorly educated and not interesting to talk to? And what was there for him to do in Darrington? Additionally, he had just been accepted into the philosophy department at the University of Vermont as a graduate student, thanks to his friend Jerry Anderson.

So, Dick and I developed a plan in case I got the job in Darrington. We would both move to Darrington, and Dick would leave for Burlington, Vermont the following September and spend the academic year there. That was as far as our plan went.

Gretchen and I had interviews scheduled with the Darrington Clinic Board. Off we went, driving 50 miles north on Interstate 5 near Arlington, and then 30 miles east on a country road toward the Cascade Mountains. To this day, I love the 30-mile ride from Arlington to Darrington. I have bicycled it several times in my later years. After a few miles, a gushing waterfall pouring into the North Fork of the Stillaquamish River appeared on the right. We crossed a scenic wood-and-metal bridge over the river and another little bridge over Deer Creek as it flowed into the Stillaquamish. The road meandered among fields, forests, and small farmhouses. After that, beautiful snowy mountains appeared and rose up from the valley—Three Fingers, Mount Pugh, and White Chuck, all snow-covered and gorgeous in the distance. About four miles outside of Darrington, White Horse Mountain appeared, with its beautiful cascading glacier rising above the town. The view just took our breath away.

When I lived in Darrington, swimming in the glorious, clear, cold water of the North Fork of the Stillaquamish River was something I looked forward to each summer. It is one of the thrilling experiences I have had in my life. I was able to get through the painful labor with my oldest son, Eric, by reliving that exhilarating swimming experience in my mind between uterine contractions.

When Gretchen and I arrived at the Darrington Clinic, we met with about 15 members of the Darrington Clinic Board, primarily women. I had no idea what to expect. We sat in the waiting room of the clinic with the board members sitting right in front of us. They didn't seem to have any particular agenda during the interview. I asked questions about their major health needs and problems as they saw them. They talked about logging accidents in the woods and how there was no one there to help them. I asked how the board members were elected or chosen, and it seemed there were no actual rules—just citizens of the town who saw a need and wanted to help. I asked about expectations of us as nurses, hours, salary, contract, etc. They were relying on Washington Alaska RMP to help them, which made sense, as no one there had expertise in establishing and managing the clinic.

I had prepared a written statement for the board expressing my love of the area and the mountains, my mountain climbing experience, my independence as a public health nurse, the excitement of learning new skills, my work ethic, my love of the nursing profession, my professional experience, and my belief in myself. Gretchen and I stressed that we worked together as public health nurses and felt confident we would work very well together in the clinic.

They also asked Dick about his plans for graduate school and how that would work for us as a married couple. Dick gave vague answers about being able to write his master's thesis in Darrington and would then "write a book." That seemed to satisfy any concerns they may have had.

The next week, Carolyn Minnick from Washington Alaska RMP called Gretchen and me and told us that the Darrington Clinic Board had agreed to hire us. I was thrilled. In January 1972, I gave notice to the Seattle King County Department of Public Health. I was leaving for a great professional opportunity.

Gretchen and I attended a training program to prepare us for our role in opening the Darrington Clinic. The clinic was scheduled to open on April 10, 1972. We had a little over three months to prepare. But how were we to prepare for this exciting and challenging opportunity? The Washington Alaska RMP had the funds and the resources to help us.

Gretchen and I needed advanced education in assessment skills, problem-solving, and decision-making in managing medical problems. At the time, there were no formalized education programs in which we could enroll to address these needs. It would be years before there would be a master's degree program for nurse practitioners anywhere in the United States. There was also a lot of anxiety among the five physicians in Arlington, as well as from the School of Medicine at the University of Washington and the Washington State American Medical Association. Would we see ourselves as "junior doctors"? Would we know our limitations? What *were* our limitations?

Marguerite Cobb, the chairperson of the Department of Family and Community Nursing at the University of Washington, was very involved in determining the curriculum of what was to be a nine-week educational and training program for us. We got to know her very well during this time. She was about 60 years old and a strong, opinionated, passionate advocate for the nursing profession. I learned so much from her; she was a true role model for me. She and the other members of the University of Washington nursing faculty understood the value and potential of the registered nurse. Marguerite also knew how uncomfortable most physicians were about the concept of an independent nurse practitioner clinic. We shared a strong belief that many primary care problems could already be handled appropriately by registered nurses, and that some added skills and knowledge would increase the nurses' self-confidence and ability to handle them more comprehensively. So, the written educational plans for Gretchen and me stressed recognizing one's limitations and the constant, candid evaluation of one's own competency. Of course, anyone in healthcare, whether a nurse or a physician, at any time in their career, should always be thinking along these lines.

How would Gretchen and I be able to see patients independently in Darrington under the present restrictive Washington State Nurse Practice Act? We had to have some concrete support from the physicians in Arlington. We needed at least one of them to allow us to write prescriptions under his license to start out with, at least until we could get the Washington State Nurse Practice Act changed.

There were five general practitioners in Arlington: Ben Burgoyne and Norman Zook, who were in practice together; Dale Huber and John Hahn, also in practice together; and Sam Nebel, who had his own practice. They were all "old school" doctors who performed all kinds of procedures that only physician specialists are allowed to do nowadays. They performed hysterectomies, cholecystectomies, and other surgeries, in addition to seeing patients and delivering babies.

Sam Nebel was cordial but generally ignored us. He was the loner among the Arlington physicians. He was not interested in working with us, but he wasn't against us either.

Norman Zook was a very sober, polite, and religious man. Unlike all the other physicians in Arlington, he never made appointments for patients. All his patients were seen on a first-come, first-serve basis. He was pleasant to us but quite reserved.

Ben Burgoyne was an excellent and experienced clinician. He was kind and patient, with a wonderful sense of humor. He had a fatherly, supportive manner with us. His support staff really loved him, which is always a good sign.

Dale Huber was a shrewd businessman, and it was rumored that he "owned half of Arlington." He was a very skilled and serious clinician. Being paid for his services was of the utmost importance to him, and it was said that he would confront patients in the Arlington grocery store who owed him money. It was widely known that he did not get along with his partner, John Hahn.

John Hahn was very much against nurses coming to Darrington. He was known to be a cold and difficult man to deal with. He virtually never smiled. When I had a scheduled appointment to see patients with him, he refused to even let me in the exam room. Dale Huber, his partner, allowed me to work with him instead that day.

The Arlington physicians were generally uncomfortable with us and did not know what to do with our Darrington Nurse Practitioner Clinic. At some point, John Hahn expressed interest in being the consulting physician for us. We panicked, sure that he would try to sabotage the clinic. The pharmacist in Darrington, Elden Abbott, was in complete support of our proposed Nurse Practitioner Clinic and reassured the Arlington physicians that he would make sure communication about what we were doing there was shared by all. Finally, Ben Burgoyne agreed to be our consulting physician. This was a huge relief.

During our nine-week training program, we saw patients in Arlington with Ben Burgoyne, Norman Zook, and Dale Huber. We also spent time with physicians at the Harborview Medical Center emergency room, learning how to suture wounds and give joint injections. We saw patients with physicians in the community clinics in Seattle. We were instructed in intubation procedures with Charles Bollinger, the anesthesiologist at the Cascade Valley Hospital. We spent time with Elden Abbott, the Darrington pharmacist. We worked with pediatricians at Snohomish County Well-Child Clinics. We rode with Medic 1 on the streets of Seattle, handling a multitude of emergencies. We worked with laboratory technicians, pediatricians, and ophthalmologists at the Everett Clinic. We worked with gynecologists at the Mason Clinic. We did all this in nine short weeks!

Gretchen and I understood that this nine-week training program was just the beginning. Our education and training would continue on an ongoing basis.

The plan was that the clinic would be self-supporting on a fee-for-service basis in three months' time. A grant from Washington Alaska RMP was provided to support clinic operations during this initial period. Gretchen and I were to be paid a salary of $900 per month for the first six months, and then $1000 per month after that. That was significantly more money than I was making as a public health nurse. The clinic would have a full-time receptionist, a cleaning person, and a bookkeeper.

When Gretchen and I arrived in Darrington, the 20-foot sign that used to read, "This Town Needs a Doctor" now read, "Welcome, Gretchen and Lynne."

CHAPTER 4

Life in Darrington, Washington: 1972–1977

DICK AND I got together with Gretchen to figure out our living arrangements in Darrington. Since Dick would be leaving for graduate school in Vermont at the end of August, we decided to rent a house with two bedrooms. After Dick left for Vermont, Gretchen and I would live together in the house. We were all facing something new and unknown. A shared living situation would give us more stability as we began this adventure.

We rented a two-bedroom rambler with a huge yard and an enormous vegetable garden. The house was just two blocks from the clinic. We had a beautiful view of Whitehorse Mountain from our front yard. At night, the snow- and glacier-covered mountain seemed to glow and shimmer in the moonlight. I loved seeing it right outside my window.

Whitehorse Mountain from our house in Darrington

The Darrington Clinic was scheduled to open on Monday morning, April 10, 1972. On March 24th, the Darrington Clinic Board held a town meeting to introduce us to the people of Darrington. It turned out to be quite an event. About 150 Darrington residents came to the clinic to meet us. Ben Burgoyne came to the meeting and was introduced as our "physician consultant." Others who attended this momentous occasion were Allen Remington, the administrator of the Cascade Valley Hospital in Arlington; Marguerite Cobb, professor from the University of Washington School of Nursing; and reporters from *The Everett Herald*.

Ben Burgoyne was quoted the next day in *The Everett Herald* as saying, "I will stand behind these girls all I can. All the little things and not-so-little things can be taken care of by these girls."

Although this happened over 53 years ago, it still makes me cringe a little to hear us referred to as "these girls." At the same time, I smile a little as well. It was a different time.

Nancy Bascom was hired as our full-time receptionist. She was in her mid-20s and had been born in Darrington. Her father, Elmer Wood, was a retired logger and had just built Darrington's second tavern. She personally knew nearly everyone in town. Edna Bryson was our cleaning woman. She was a bright, cheery, and hardworking woman with frazzled gray hair. She was married to Fred Bryson, an old-time logger and fur trapper. Fred was generally a man of very few words, but over the years I learned all sorts of amazing stories about life in Darrington from him. Fred knew how to survive in the mountains.

Monday morning, April 10, 1972, finally arrived, and the Darrington Clinic was open. I wore a little white dress with pastel blue flowers, nylon stockings, white shoes, and a white lab coat. In the first hour, television trucks arrived from channels 4, 5, and 7 from Seattle! By noon, the television cameras and trucks were gone. Gretchen and I were seeing a few patients when suddenly, two firemen drove up in the Darrington ambulance and ran into the clinic.

"There has been an accident in the woods! You have to come with us!" they shouted.

Gretchen stayed in the clinic while I grabbed our previously prepared emergency bag, jumped into the ambulance, and sped away. I neglected to bring a coat and was just wearing my white dress with pastel blue flowers.

The firemen had no real information except that some man was hurt in the woods. We rode for about two long hours on the freshly plowed, snow-covered logging roads. On either side of us, the snow banks towered over the ambulance. Finally, we stopped. As I jumped out of the ambulance, I sank into the snow to my knees.

The two firemen grabbed me and hoisted me to the top of the eight-foot snowbank, where I was quickly knee-deep in snow. Another logger led me about 50 yards to the site of the accident. A man was lying faceup on a blanket on top of the snow. A log had rolled over him. Later, at the Cascade Valley Hospital, I found out that he had multiple fractures of his pelvis. He was barely conscious and in shock, but could whisper a few words to me about how much pain he was in.

I knelt down in the snow. started an intravenous drip, and administered some morphine. The loggers and I stabilized him on a back board, and four men helped to lower him down over the huge snowbank to the ambulance. We rode in the ambulance with the injured logger for two more hours, until we were finally back in Darrington. Then it was 30 miles to the Cascade Valley Hospital in Arlington. What a relief to transfer the responsibility of my patient to Ben Burgoyne, who had received our call from the ambulance that we were en route!

After that experience on the day the Darrington Clinic opened, I kept a pair of sturdy leather boots, wool pants, and a heavy coat in the ambulance for the next time. And there were many "next times" in the future for me.

Those first few months were a whirlwind for us. There wasn't a single minute when we were not doing something or figuring out the best way to treat a patient. Elden Abbott, the pharmacist at the Darrington

Pharmacy, was such a help to us, confirming dosages and uses of prescription medications and even helping us with the choice of medications.

A few weeks after the clinic opened, Gretchen and I got a call at 11:00 p.m. about a 65-year-old woman who was having trouble breathing. We told her husband we would meet him at the clinic. We jumped into the car and arrived at the clinic just as they drove up. We had called the Darrington ambulance from home, and it arrived at the same time.

The woman was one of the members of the Darrington Clinic Board who had interviewed us months ago. Listening to the labored, gurgling sound she made with each breath, we knew she had acute pulmonary edema. What we didn't know was that she had also had a massive heart attack, which was causing blood and fluid to back up into her lungs, resulting in acute pulmonary edema. She was dying right in front of us, 30 miles from Arlington and the Cascade Valley Hospital. We started oxygen and loaded her into the ambulance. On the way to Arlington, she stopped breathing. Although we rendered CPR in the ambulance, we couldn't save her, and she died.

I felt very bad about this for a long time. I had to learn the painful lesson that, while we always want to make a positive difference for all our patients, there are times when no matter what we do, we cannot change the outcome.

My role as a nurse practitioner was to help my patients improve their lives without judgment. I think this frame of mind comes naturally to the best nurses. Living and working in a small town like Darrington required discretion and a nonjudgmental frame of mind. Typically, each person we treated knew most of the people living in Darrington and might be related to many of them. I learned quickly to be cautious of what I said about anything to any person. Even an innocent casual comment might be construed as negative criticism of someone else.

Dick and I, together with our friend Suzanne Spencer, climbed Whitehorse Mountain for the first time about a month after the clinic opened. There are a few different routes up Whitehorse. I prefer the route straight up the face of the huge Whitehorse Glacier. There is another route through the forest to the west, called Lone Tree Pass, that takes you straight up to a single huge Douglas fir tree, which you can see standing on the snow just at the top of the ridge. I have climbed Whitehorse several times and it is a new and exhilarating experience every time.

Summer in Darrington is a beautiful time of year. The red cedar and Douglas fir trees were shedding all their snow, and the creeks were full with rapid, glistening mountain water cascading down steep slopes. The hiking trails started to appear beneath many feet of melting snow in the forest. It was hiking and climbing time in the Cascades!

As the summer of 1972 came to a close, Dick got ready to go to Vermont. I had saved enough money to pay his tuition for the year. He revealed to me that he owed several thousand dollars in student loans from his undergraduate days at Morningside College. It took me almost three years, but I paid that loan off as well.

I was very hopeful about Dick entering the master's program at the University of Vermont. This was a great opportunity for him to move forward in his career, not to mention in our life together. I believed it was worth every sacrifice. I had saved enough for a little apartment for him in Burlington and living expenses, so he would be able to focus totally on his all-important coursework. He thought he could finish in two quarters and then write his master's thesis in Darrington. He left Seattle in September, would be home for Christmas, and then would be home for good in March.

Life was a continual whirlwind in Darrington that fall. We were busy with patients every day. On the weekends, one of us would stay in town, while the other spent time learning joint injections or suture techniques at one of the hospital emergency rooms in Everett or Seattle. We were steeped in medical journal articles. We were constantly working and trying to learn more at the same time.

In Darrington, the police were seen as friendly, important, and helpful by residents. That view was antithetical to how my Seattle patients saw the police when I was a public health nurse. In Seattle, my patients were nervous and suspicious of police and did not see them as advocates. Unconsciously, I came to feel the same way about them when I was working in Seattle. I was unaware of my feelings toward police until I moved to Darrington and experienced them in an entirely different and positive way.

Sometime during the fall of 1972, Gretchen became angry and moody. She was difficult to talk with. She would alternate between being depressed and lashing out verbally for no apparent reason. One day, while we were working at the clinic, she went home for lunch. When she did not come back, I called her, but there was no answer. I walked the two blocks back to our house to find out what was going on. When I walked in the door, she was unconscious on the living room floor. She was breathing, but I could not rouse her. Her vital signs, blood pressure, pulse, and respiratory rate were stable, but she wouldn't wake up.

I grabbed her shoulders and yelled, "Gretchen!" but got absolutely no response from her. I was frantic. I called the ambulance, loaded her into the back, and we drove to Arlington. She was completely unconscious all the way to Cascade Valley Hospital. Charles Bollinger, the anesthesiologist, evaluated her. Then, in the emergency room, she just woke up. All her blood tests came back completely normal. There was no obvious cause for her unconscious, unresponsive state.

Charles Bollinger thought Gretchen's condition was psychogenic in nature, and her place at the Darrington Clinic was precarious. He contacted Ben Burgoyne and alerted him to the fact that Gretchen was in trouble. I, too, was concerned, but when I tried to talk with her about it, she became angry and verbally combative. She was a strong, articulate woman who was no longer rational. I found it difficult and frightening to stand up to her.

Gretchen's behavior continued to become more and more erratic. I tried to reason with her, then tried being more confrontational, but nothing worked. She became delusional and thought I was the one with the problems. She was intense and aggressive. Some of our mutual friends actually believed her and thought I was the crazy one. However, my friend Suzanne Spencer knew how ill Gretchen was and how dangerous the situation was. She had also tried to confront Gretchen. Suzanne was in graduate school in Seattle and living in a house partly owned by Gretchen. In response to Suzanne, Gretchen became outraged and belligerent. They had a confrontation in the house in Seattle, and Gretchen actually threw something at Suzanne in the kitchen. She then told Suzanne to move out of the house immediately.

I believe this period of confrontation with Gretchen was when I truly grew up and became a responsible adult. The stakes were so high; the viability of the Darrington Clinic was at risk. So I pushed back.

Performing as a nurse practitioner in Darrington was something I knew I could do, even alone. I also knew I could not continue to work with Gretchen in her present state. She was mentally ill and receiving no help for her problems, which she refused to even acknowledge.

In February 1973, I told Helen Lemmon that Gretchen had serious mental health problems and that it was impossible for me to continue working with her. Fortunately, Charles Bollinger, after his experience with her in the emergency room, had notified not only Ben Burgoyne, but also Carolyn Minnick of Washington Alaska RMP. Helen Lemmon and the Clinic Board, after talking with me and consulting with Ben Burgoyne, asked Gretchen to leave. She moved out of our house, left Darrington, and went back to Seattle, where she began teaching at the University of Washington School of Nursing.

Several years later, Mary Ann Draye, the chairwoman of the nurse practitioner master's program at the time, told me that Gretchen had gotten worse after she left Darrington. It was a very sad situation. I think she eventually got some much-needed mental health therapy.

It was such a relief to me when Gretchen left. No part of the job as the nurse practitioner at the Darrington Clinic was as frightening as continuing to work with her. It didn't matter that Dick was still in Vermont. A sense of calm came over me. I had a job to do, and I knew I could do it now.

I also knew that Kasha Barnowe, the public health nurse from Snohomish County, was interested in taking Gretchen's place. It would take many months, but knowing she was coming made me feel more secure. Kasha loved the mountains, too, and had a lot of experience hiking the trails around Darrington.

One of the big challenges for the clinic now was reimbursement. The initial grants from the Washington Alaska Regional Medical Program had been spent. Some logging companies were making donations to the clinic, but we were not being paid for seeing most of the patients. Washington Labor and Industries stated that they would not reimburse us for any of our services unless Ben Burgoyne was present. But he was in Arlington and we were in Darrington. The Washington State Department of Public Assistance was paying for services, but Medicare would not. Even King County Medical-Blue Shield would not reimburse us for our work.

By fall of 1972, Darrington residents were outraged. They mobilized to try and get insurance reimbursement for the medical care we were delivering at the Darrington Clinic. Arliss Abbott, wife of Elden Abbott, our Darrington pharmacist, wrote an article published on December 6, 1972, in the *Seattle Post Intelligencer*. Another colorful long-time resident, 88-year-old Alice Eleanor Lambert, who lived alone in a cabin outside of Darrington, wrote a passionate letter to Washington State Senator Warren G. Magnuson, who wrote back telling her he was fully behind our plight.

Finally, on March 23, 1973, about a year after the opening of the Darrington Clinic, Senator Warren G. Magnuson came to Darrington to meet with Kasha Barnowe and me. Kasha was preparing to take Gretchen's place. Ben Burgoyne was also there, along with the television cameras and lots of Darrington people. Senator Magnuson pledged to the huge crowd that he would work hard to encourage the Washington State Legislature to act, and act now.

The clinic was now very busy. I was averaging between 15 and 20 patients every day, in addition to night and weekend calls. Ben Burgoyne was always available by telephone, and he got to know me well and trusted me. He would come to the clinic once a month for an afternoon, and I would present certain patients I was treating to get his expert opinion.

One of the challenging problems I faced in Darrington was helping young girls with unwanted pregnancies. January 22, 1973, signaled the passage of *Roe v. Wade*. Before *Roe v. Wade*, I counseled girls about their choices, which nearly always involved helping them inform their parents. Most of the time, I arranged meetings between the girl, her parents, and myself. Depending on the parents, this could be a primarily supportive interaction or a painful and miserable one. After January 22, 1973, it was an entirely different experience.

One day, in late January 1973, I received a telephone call from old Doc Riddle himself. He was still living in his house next to his "hospital," which was now vacant. He asked me to come to the house, as he had a "bad bursitis" in his shoulder. His house was just across the street from the clinic, so I walked there with my medical bag.

Doc Riddle was a tall, very thin, very frail white-haired man. I wasn't exactly sure how old he was, but he had practiced medicine in Darrington since 1929. When I arrived, he was kind and welcoming. He asked me if I could do a joint injection. I replied that I had been taught how, but had only done a few of them.

He smiled and said kindly, "I will walk you through the procedure."

So I gathered my equipment, lidocaine and cortisone, and filled my syringe. I was ready to go. He steadily and quietly walked me through the steps of the joint injection.

After I finished the procedure, he smiled and said, "Very skillfully done, Lynne."

I will always remember that. The next month, Doc Riddle died.

Many Darrington residents didn't like to leave town for any reason. Driving from Darrington past Oslo, which was about 12 miles from Arlington, was referred to as "going down below." Many people told me they had not been down below for a few years and were not anxious to go anytime soon. Despite the fact that Darrington was only 30 miles from Arlington, it always seemed much farther than that. To a large extent, Darrington was isolated and in its own little world.

In March 1973, Dick finished his coursework at the University of Vermont and came home. In those days, we still had significant "chemistry" that helped bridge the obvious differences between us. I had really missed him. I was worried that he did not seem motivated or confident in pursuing his goals, but I still believed in his potential. He was my husband, and I believed in our marriage. Dick told me that he started smoking marijuana in the evenings in Vermont. That really frightened me—I hated mind-altering drugs of any kind, especially after the years of exposure to my dad's alcoholism. Dick told me he wrote what he thought was a brilliant paper one evening while smoking marijuana. The next morning, he read the paper and told me it "didn't make any sense and was drivel."

Dick tried to reassure me by saying he would start writing his master's thesis right away, which was all he needed to complete his degree.

On Mother's Day weekend in 1973, Dave Clemens, from the US Forest Service in Darrington, his wife, Sue, Dick, and I took a fantastic trip in the mountains. We started at the end of the Suiattle River Road, northeast of Darrington, and hiked the 14 miles to Miner's Ridge above Image Lake. We actually packed cross-country skis and skied along Miner's Ridge and across Image Lake, which was completely covered with snow and ice. We stayed overnight in the Miner's Ridge Lookout since Dave, as a forest service employee, had the keys. I took glorious pictures of the sunset over Miner's Ridge and Glacier Peak. I still think about that trip. Perfect weather, incredibly beautiful views, the peace and quiet of nature, and just us there in that heavenly place.

Meanwhile, the Washington State Nurses Association and their lobbyist, Marguerite Ouchi, were hard at work trying to persuade the Washington State Legislature to pass the Nurse Practice Act that would legitimize "advanced and specialized levels of nursing practice." It was very exciting when they succeeded. On April 4, 1973, it was passed with overwhelming votes from both the House and the Senate and was signed into law by Governor Daniel Evans. The success and publicity of our Darrington Nurse Practitioner Clinic was thought to be the key to passing this new Nurse Practice Act.

The law, of course, was just a first step. Its actual wording was "advanced and specialized levels of nursing practice as authorized by the Washington State Board of Nursing." It was up to the Board of Nursing to define these new levels of nursing practice and which nurses could perform them. We had come far, but we still had a long way to go.

Although the new law was passed in April, it didn't go into effect until June 1973. The Board of Nursing had a lot of work to do to define what the new law meant and how to implement it. The Board of Nursing is a seven-member board, six of whom are registered nurses and one who is a nonprofessional public member. All members are appointed by the Washington State governor for five-year terms.

In 1973, there were no standards of practice anywhere in the United States for advanced and specialized levels of nursing practice. None of the other 49 states had faced anything like this. Even the American Nurses Association, the national nurses' organization, did not develop a certification examination for nurse practitioners until more than three years later, in November 1976.

Looking back at my years in Darrington, it seems that so many of the serious emergencies happened in the middle of the night. No one calls in the middle of the night for something minor. Countless times I was called, roused out of a dead sleep, and had to immediately head out to an unknown medical emergency. I was the first responder for any and all emergencies in town and out in the countryside. Multiple times, a local policeman would call and enlist my help. One time, it was a fight that had broken out, leaving one man with an open fractured skull; another time, it was a serious accident at the timber mill that tore a man's arm and part of his shoulder off. Those are just a few examples of the health emergencies I had to confront.

My friend Suzanne Spencer was getting married to Dave Uvelli that summer of 1973. Suzanne was now in medical school. The wedding took place at her parents' house in West Seattle. There, I met Berdi Safford and John Hruby, a married couple who were also attending medical school at the University of Washington. I instantly felt a connection with Berdi, who became, like Suzanne, one of my best friends. Berdi was warm, enthusiastic, and seemed to love the mountains as much as I did.

Debbie Grimm, Doc Riddle's 13-year-old great-granddaughter, had severe asthma and was one of the few in Darrington who went to Seattle for healthcare. Her care was managed by pediatric pulmonologists at Children's Hospital. When she had asthmatic attacks, I would treat her with medication delivered by an IPPB machine in our clinic and also give her parenteral medications. Then, I would telephone her doctors at Children's Hospital to determine what else I could do to help her, and when to make the 80-mile trip in the Darrington ambulance to Children's Hospital.

This was all happening in August 1973, and I was dying to get out of town to hike in the mountains. I was just passionate about it, and it was prime hiking time. But Debbie needed me, and I eventually had to ride to Seattle Children's Hospital with her in the ambulance. She arrived wheezing but otherwise stable and was admitted. I drove back to Darrington with my firemen. With Debbie under care at Children's Hospital, it was now time for me to hit the trail in the mountains.

Normally, I would always go hiking with Dick, but as time went on, he seemed to have lost much of his enthusiasm for the mountains. I wanted to go on a circular high route in the meadows and lakes around Glacier Peak. This high route was called the Rivord Lakes High Route. The beginning of the trip was on a maintained trail, but the middle and end part of it involved route-finding along a "high route." High routes are trail excursions along the high ridges of mountains and involve a variety of route-finding and technical difficulty. The entire trip was described in a now out-of-print book called *Routes and Rocks*, published by The Mountaineers of Seattle. I had been reading and salivating about this trip for more than a year. I pleaded with Dick to go with me, but he would not.

I drove to the Milk Creek trailhead at the end of the Suiattle River Road, about an hour's drive north and east from Darrington. I kept written journals on most of my hiking and backpacking trips. The value of written records is to remember what an experience was really like and what it felt like. On this trip, I wrote how much I missed Dick, "my dear hiking and climbing companion, my wonderful man." I cannot imagine ever thinking that way now, after all I have been through since with my ex-husband. But there it is in writing—a true expression of what I felt at the time.

The first 11 miles I hiked that day were so beautiful. Even now, when I am hiking, I feel an excitement, a thrill of just being in the mountains. The experience itself is electric for me. At first, the trail wound through a lush evergreen forest, then it entered deciduous woods before opening out onto glorious meadows of flowers. The trail climbed steadily across the meadows and then switchbacked up through huckleberry bushes. The day ended at my camp above the treeline at Mica Lake, on the shoulder of Glacier Peak. That's when I discovered that my pack was way too heavy. I could barely get it back on after taking it off during a rest stop. But I told myself I could still manage and make it work.

The next morning, the weather was uncertain, with swirling clouds and a drop in temperature. I had reached the point where one had to "route-find" without an actual trail to follow. I was well above the treeline and had to traverse the north-facing, snow-covered slopes to the next beautiful lake, Lime Lake. Part of the problem was the snow on the north-facing slopes softens and melts later than the snow on the south-facing slopes. I had my heavy pack on and my ice axe out as I walked on the hard snow. At the time, the way did not seem that steep to me. I would slip a bit on the hard snow but easily catch myself. In retrospect, I was inexperienced, and it was not smart to traverse the snow with a heavy pack, especially alone. I should have gone below the snow slopes, but the steep terrain may have made that impossible. I should have retraced my steps and gone back, but I did not.

I was taking pictures of the views across the valley and feeling good. I didn't sense being in any danger. Then, suddenly, I slipped on the hard snow and started sliding down the slope. I tried to stop and "arrest" using my ice axe, but it was too late. My ice axe was in my hands above me, not under me, and I had gained too much speed. At one point, I started to go down headfirst, but I was able to turn and correct myself. Then, I suddenly hit the rocks below with my boots and stopped. Very shaken, I stood up and tried to assess my wounds. I had taken off layers of skin from my forearms and elbows and badly lacerated my knees. But I was alive. My camera, which had been around my neck, was lost.

It took me a while to clean myself off and bandage all my wounds. I still have scars on my forearms and elbows from the injuries that day. All I could think was that I had to get out of there and get back home. I was able to hike below the snow slopes and finally reach Lime Lake. Just before the lake, I met the only human beings I would see on the entire Rivord Lake High Route: three young Caucasian fishermen carrying their fishing equipment. They just stared at me. I started crying. I was a complete mess, with dirt all over my torn clothes and bandages on my arms and legs. I tried to explain what happened to me. They just kept staring. Finally, I asked if Lime Lake was just ahead. They said yes, and I walked past them up the meadowed slope and down to Lime Lake.

I have talked about how much I love the mountains and lakes along the Rivord Lakes High Route. They are some of the least visited and most pristine high mountain lakes in the Cascade Mountains. But after falling down the snow slope, I just could not bring myself to enjoy them. I had to muster the strength to find the route out and get home safely.

So I pushed on, past Lime Lake, up and over the saddle at the end of it, and on to the two Milk Lakes, which are considered to be the most beautiful of all. They were gorgeous, but I continued on. I thought that if I stopped, I might not have the strength, mentally or physically, to get out.

After the Milk Lakes were the upper and lower Twin Lakes. Then I climbed northward over heather to the trees and cliffs above, and down again on a gentle ramp of snow and heather. After that, there was a long traverse to the top of the cliffs overlooking Rivord Lake. It was nearly 7:00 p.m. when I dropped down over the slopes to the outlet of Rivord Lake. I made camp for the night there.

I woke up the next day at daybreak and climbed west through scattered trees to reach a small lake at the foot of Lime Mountain. My whole body was stiff and sore. From that lake, I descended a steep open slope to the largest lake of all, Box Mountain Lake. For the first time since my fall, I caught a real trail, although barely maintained. The trail wound around the lake and then sharply descended 4,500 feet in just two miles. It was so steep that you could not actually walk down it directly, and I found myself almost falling down the slope. It was excruciatingly painful on my thigh muscles. After many hours, I finally broke out of the trees, got into my car, and drove home. I tried explaining to Dick what happened. I don't think he understood, but then how could he? He wasn't there.

I had recovered mentally and physically by Labor Day Weekend 1973, and convinced Dick to join me on a trip to Cub and Iswoot Lakes. The lakes are on the last 12 miles of the famous Ptarmigan Traverse, a route from Cascade Pass to Dome Peak in the North Cascades. The lakes were not visited often, as it was a long, steep 11 miles to Cub Lake. People in Darrington thought the Sasquatch had been seen there about four years prior.

During this time, I got pregnant with my first son, Eric. I had always wanted children—but sometime in the future. I was much more concerned with getting Dick on his way in his philosophy career. And I was the only one of us who had a job. Dick was not at all happy with the thought of having a baby, and he made that very clear to me.

After the initial shock, I moved forward with my life. My pregnancy was a healthy one, and I felt strong. That year, we celebrated New Year's Eve with an overnight cross-country skiing and backpacking trip over Bluet Pass. I was five months pregnant. We went with John and Berdi, and Dave and Sue Clemens. At Bluet Pass, we skied in 15 feet of snow. The dark green Douglas fir and red cedar were heavy with blankets of white. We pitched our tents, and the temperature dropped well below freezing. We made a big campfire, but it was still too cold for us to stay up to celebrate until midnight.

After 20 months in Darrington, I was feeling the stress that came with being on the job 24 hours a day. To avoid the ringing telephone, I would have to leave town. One of the most difficult parts of the job was never knowing when someone would need me due to an accident or sudden illness. When the telephone rang, I would have to stop whatever I was doing in order to meet the emergency. In the five years I was in Darrington, I accepted that this was part of the job. I only felt free when

I was driving out of Darrington. When I drove up and over Scagglin's Hill and was halfway to Arlington, then I could breathe and finally relax.

But there was a downside to leaving Darrington. If I was gone when someone needed me, I felt so guilty. Once, when I was visiting friends in Seattle for a weekend, a teenage boy drowned in the Sauk River. So many people in town told me they wished I had been there. It's unlikely that I would have been able to save him, but what if I could have? This was another hard part of the job.

In January 1974, Ben Burgoyne stepped down from his role at our Darrington Clinic. He had been wonderful to work with and so supportive, and we would really miss him. At the same time, I had been attending a medical education conference in Seattle on respiratory illness, and ran into Dale Huber. He and I talked, and I asked him if he would be interested in taking Ben Burgoyne's place. Ben Burgoyne was a fatherly, kindly, very religious family man. Dale Huber was a shrewd businessman, an astute clinician, and a bit of a ladies man. He had just left his wife of 30 years, had a new woman friend, and was taking sailing lessons. We were paying Ben Burgoyne $300 a month for his services. Dale Huber told me he would do it, but he wanted $350 a month. I agreed because we did not have much of a choice.

On April 10, 1974, we had a two-year anniversary celebration at the Darrington Clinic. We had made it. Kasha Barnowe was now living in Darrington and had joined me in our practice. It was wonderful to have her. Present were members of the Darrington Clinic Board, including its chairman at the time, Katie Robinson; Carolyn Minnick from Washington Alaska RMP; and Dale Huber. It was an emotional and very happy moment.

In the winter of 1974, the owners of the house Dick and I were renting wanted to sell it. We couldn't afford to buy it—I had used most of what we had to pay off Dick's undergraduate college tuition. Dick wasn't working and was still trying to finish his thesis.

Fortunately, we found a four-bedroom, two-bath, split-level house for sale. It was on an acre of land two miles out of town. The bank was sponsoring a lottery for the sale of the house. Whoever won would be able to buy the house and start making house payments without any down payment. I put our names in right away. By some miracle, we were chosen. We were able to buy the house for $18,500 and get a mortgage without any down payment!

By May 1974, it was clear Dick was making no progress on his master's thesis. He had been home from the University of Vermont for one year. His thesis advisor finally gave him a deadline to finish his thesis, or his master's degree would be in jeopardy. I was furious with Dick. How could he let this happen? I told him what I expected: he would start studying every morning at 9:00 a.m. At noon, he could take a one-hour break for lunch and start studying again at 1:00 p.m. He was to write down the times he started and stopped writing.

After a few weeks, I asked to look at his progress. He broke down in tears and told me he had just fabricated the times he wrote down. He hadn't written anything at all. I was outraged. By this time, I was eight months pregnant and working more than full-time. To me, it was now a desperate situation. I could see that our marriage was in real jeopardy. But I still couldn't imagine life not being married to him—and we were going to have a baby in one month!

I kept doing something that would continue on and off throughout my 14 years of marriage to Dick. When I saw him starting to fail, when his balloon would start sinking, I would find a way to propel his balloon up. My hope was that he would then be able to figure things out by himself. He would learn how to keep his balloon afloat himself. But he never did.

My next plan to get him to finish his master's thesis was to tell him that he must sit down in the morning and just start writing. After working all day, I would insist on seeing what he had written, and then I would type it out, which sometimes took me half the night. The next day, I would get out of bed, work all day at the clinic, come home, and start typing again late into the night.

Finally, his thesis was done. It was 100 pages long. I didn't know if it was any good or not, but it was finished. Two weeks before I went into labor, we mailed the finished product to his thesis advisor at the University of Vermont.

The people of Darrington threw us a huge baby shower, attended by more than 100 people. We received so many gifts, love, and goodwill from everyone. And the food was amazing; everyone brought their best dishes.

The paperwork on our new house was finally completed. On June 29, 1974, we moved the last of our boxes in. I was exhausted. That night, we drove to Seattle to get some rest and get away from the telephone. We stayed overnight with one of my old public health nursing friends, Cherie LaMaine, and her husband, Jeff.

At 5:00 a.m, I woke up feeling uterine contractions in earnest. I had a friend, Sharon Bradley, who was a labor and delivery nurse at Virginia

Mason in Seattle. I did not want to have our baby in Arlington, so I had planned to have him at Virginia Mason. In 1974, the legitimacy and safety of medications and spinal anesthesia in obstetrics were being questioned for the first time. Nearly all women at that time had babies with the aid of spinal anesthesia. Nothing was known for sure, but standard practice in labor and delivery care were being reconsidered and reevaluated, even by the medical profession. I wanted to avoid medication and spinal anesthesia if I possibly could. Richard Soderstrom at Virginia Mason was one of the only obstetricians in Seattle at that time who was supportive of allowing a woman to make that choice.

Dick immediately drove me to Virginia Mason. I quickly went through the first stage of labor. Finally, after eight hours, Eric Barber Vigesaa, at eight pounds nine ounces, was born. It was an experience and the thrill of a lifetime.

When Dick and I drove back to Darrington with baby Eric two days later, there was a huge new sign on the right side of the road that read "It's a Boy!" and everyone in town knew what that meant.

I received some memorable letters from my dad at this time. He was so happy about Eric's birth. Interestingly, he wished my mother had been with me. Honestly, I do not think that having my mother there would have been helpful. She never volunteered, and I never asked.

Breastfeeding our beautiful baby boy went well. It was three weeks before I felt strong enough to go back to work, so patients just came to our house when they needed help during that time. I did my best to examine them in my living room and call in the needed prescriptions. Finally, after close to a month, I felt ready to start thinking about work at the clinic.

My milk supply was very good, and I pumped and froze quite a bit of breast milk. I had no access to an electric pump, just a hand pump. We also had no diaper service. Merle Green, a friend of mine in town, gave us a ton of cloth diapers. We had a good washing machine in our new house, and it ran all the time.

I started back full-time at the Darrington Clinic five and a half weeks after my delivery. It would have been so much better to have more time at home with Eric before I had to go back to work, but Dick was home during the day with him, and I went home at lunch every day to breast-feed him. Eric did fine and so did the Darrington Clinic, but it was really hard on me.

Dick was not content with just taking care of Eric. As many learn, parenting is an all-consuming task and can be exhausting. On the weekends, he would sometimes take the car and go to Seattle to visit bookstores or see friends. During this time, when I was needed in the middle of the night by a patient, a wife of one of the firemen would come over and take care of Eric. The people of Darrington had such positive energy and were so willing to help me.

When Eric was almost three months old, a friend in Darrington told me that a teacher was needed to teach the history of philosophy to the servicemen stationed at Whidbey Island Naval Air Station. I immediately went home and gave Dick the telephone number to call.

Every day, and I mean every single day for two weeks, I asked him, "Did you call about that teaching job?" After two weeks of no action, he finally called. They sent him the paperwork, and he filled it out. A week later, I came home from work and found him sitting in a chair, looking depressed.

"I got the job," he said, morose and miserable. He was sure that servicemen were not interested in philosophy.

Dick would be teaching an evening class once a week at the Whidbey Island Naval Air Station. He went off in total misery to his first class, but late that evening, when he came home, he was elated.

"It went really well! It was fun! I was able to engage them!"

He went on to have a very successful semester class. It was a great experience for him. I thought this would finally get his career off the ground, but he never even looked for another job.

Kasha Barnowe was a wonderful addition to our clinic. She was a serious new nurse practitioner and was doing a fine job. Kasha was also emotionally solid and stable, which I needed after my experience with Gretchen. She was a great lover of the mountains and often took her nieces and nephews.

"You can hike with a baby in the mountains," she told me. She and I planned a mountain trip with Eric.

On Labor Day Weekend 1974, Kasha and Dale Abbott, our pharmacist's son, joined Dick and me for a three-day backpacking trip with nine-week-old Eric. We hiked the entire Lost Creek Ridge Trail surrounding Glacier Peak—from the White Chuck River to Kennedy Hot Springs, up to Lake Bryne, then Camp Lake, then along the gorgeous meadowed ridges to Hardtack Lake and Round Lake, and finally down to the North Fork of the Sauk River, a total of about 15 miles. Lost Creek Ridge Trail is an amazing trip of green meadows, alpine lakes, and views of snowy peaks all around. I still think about that trip with tremendous fondness.

Eric was a beautiful, loving, and healthy baby. He was an easy baby, too. He was a great nurser, slept well, and presented the perfect picture of normalcy and well-being. I couldn't imagine life without him. I had much to be grateful for.

In late September, Dale Abbott suggested to me that we climb Lookout Mountain, which is not far from Darrington. It began with about a mile of trail partway up the mountain, after which there was no trail to the summit.

But Dale told me, "Lynne, it will just be another mile up through the trees, then a mile of meadows, and then we will be there at the top!"

We could do it in one day, but what about Eric? Elizabeth, Dick's mother, had moved to Seattle, and she came to Darrington to take care of Eric while we made the climb. I had plenty of breast milk frozen for the day.

So Dick, Dale, his father, Elden, and I hiked up Lookout Mountain on a warm and sunny Saturday in late September. We started up the trail to its end, and then climbed through the woods to the ridge above us. At this point, we planned to hike along the top of the ridge to the meadows. We tied a red ribbon to a tree on the ridge to let us know exactly where we needed to head down on our way back. This was an important step, as we were hiking without the guide of an actual trail.

Up, up, up we went. Finally, we saw the lush green meadows just beginning to turn yellow. Ripe blueberries were everywhere on low-lying bushes. We could see the summit above a rock slide. At long last, we reached the summit. It was so beautiful, and I felt such exhilaration. I remember saying to myself, "I am still here in the mountains! Having a baby did not keep me away!" It was a triumphant feeling.

But then we started down the mountain. We wove our way through the trees along the ridge. But where was the red ribbon we had attached to the tree? I thought we should have reached it by now. We kept on moving down the ridge. At some point, we decided to just get off the ridge and head down. That was a mistake.

The way down was extremely steep. We encountered huge Douglas firs and red cedar trees that had fallen, and we had to climb up and over them. I wasn't tall enough, so Dick had to hoist me up and push me over those massive tree trunks. At times, the fallen trees were so huge that none of us could get over them. We had to walk hundreds of feet around them on a very steep incline. It was getting darker. We had flashlights but no overnight gear. And what about Eric? Dick's mother was deaf and couldn't use the phone. Would there be enough breast milk for him?

I regretted so much the stupidity of this ridiculous ascent of Lookout Mountain. What was I thinking? What kind of mother was I? I felt like screaming, but I had to control myself and think of one thing at a time. My legs and arms were scraped and bloody. I focused on one step at a time.

It was just past 9:00 p.m. when the four of us broke out onto the trail leading back to the trailhead and our car. When we got back to our car, who was there waiting for us in the dark but the Darrington chief of police, Penny Bryson, and the whole ambulance crew. They had heard from Elden Abbott's wife, Arliss, that Lynne Vigesaa, the Darrington Clinic nurse practitioner, and her husband, Dick; along with Elden Abbott, the town's pharmacist, and his son, Dale, had not come back from the mountains. They formed a search party and had set out to find us.

And so we drove home. Eric was asleep, and Dick's mother was not particularly concerned that we were so late in coming home. I promised myself that I would never let this happen again. And I never did.

Back in the Midwest, my dad had received another job transfer. My parents and Jacquey, now a teenager, had moved to Carlisle, Massachusetts, just outside of Boston. My brother was in and out of the house during his years at college, and my sister Carol had stayed behind in Chicago to attend Roosevelt University.

In 1974, my mother had decided enough was enough and filed for divorce from my dad. He was furious; she was determined. She asked for and received half of all their assets. She could have gotten a lot more and probably some maintenance for life, but she felt "independent" and did not want to act like a dependent ex-wife.

Their divorce made sense to me. I had confidence that my dad would do okay in the long run, and I understood my mother not wanting to live with all that alcoholic violence and uncertainty any longer.

My other siblings worried that my dad would fall apart without my mother. That didn't happen. It seemed to me that his drinking lessened a bit after their divorce. He traveled a lot for his job, and he loved his dogs: Frau, his German Shepherd, and Jenny, his poodle. He also took every opportunity to visit me in Darrington when he was doing business on the West Coast. He loved coming to Darrington. I knew his opinion about Dick had not changed one bit, but he never crossed the line with any bad behavior or even the slightest negative comment.

While I was working at the clinic and Dick was taking care of Eric, my dad would spend the day at the Red Top Tavern, which he referred to as the Red Top Café.

"I'll be at the café," he would tell me when he stopped by the clinic to say hi to me in the morning. He loved talking with the loggers and the old Darrington men. He bragged about me whenever my name was mentioned. The men told me later he often said, "She's my daughter!" I never worried about him. He was having a great time.

Once, when my dad was at the Red Top, one of the loggers began having chest pain. When the ambulance arrived to take him to the clinic, Dad jumped into the ambulance and escorted the firemen as they loaded the man on the stretcher. Dad just loved it.

My dad loved to fish. There was a young man in Darrington, Boone Vincent, who was known as a great fisherman and knew all the places to go. I would hire Boone to take Dad down to the Skagit River to fish for salmon and steelhead. Boone would also take Dad north to Baker Lake to fish for Kokanee and rainbow trout. It was a beautiful area, and on the weekends Eric and I would go with them.

One August, when Eric was 13 months old, Carol and Jacquey visited us in Darrington. Jacquey had just finished her freshman year at Hampshire College in Amherst, Massachusetts. August was the best month to hike in the mountains. The weather was usually excellent, and the melted snow allowed us to get on the higher elevation trails. I had been waiting all year and was just dying to be in the mountains again. We had some memorable experiences hiking during their visit.

In the summer of 1976, Jacquey visited us again, this time with Steve Sutcher, a wonderful man she would eventually marry. Dad was also with us, and we all drove up to Ross Lake, the headwaters of the Skagit River. We rented a boat and had a wonderful time. These are great memories.

------◆·◆------

Meanwhile, in Olympia, the seven members of the Washington State Board of Nursing were struggling with the meaning of "advanced and specialized levels of nursing practice." The Washington State Legislature had authorized these new levels of nursing practice in the spring of 1973. Now, it was up to the Board of Nursing to define what that actually meant.

The Board of Nursing is an administrative agency of the state government, responsible for controlling the practice of nursing in the State of Washington. The members of the board are appointed by the governor to serve as public servants. They are not controlled by representatives or lobbyists of any profession. As public servants, their primary concern is the welfare and protection of the public. The Washington State Legislature delegates power to the Board of Nursing to make and execute laws regulating the practice of registered nursing.

The board already had some strong, insightful, and experienced nursing leaders on it. Some were already pioneers in the practice and education of registered nurses. But none of them had any personal experience with nurse practitioners or the expanded role of registered nurses. There was a recognition that new expertise was needed on the board—someone who had actual experience in the expanded role. All present members were in the midst of their five-year terms. Dan Evans, the governor of

Washington State, had to wait until a vacancy opened on the board before he could appoint a new member.

That vacancy was coming up in 1975. It was around the end of 1974 when I got a telephone call from a member of Governor Dan Evans's staff, asking if I would consent to become a member of the Washington State Board of Nursing for a five-year term starting in June 1975. At first, I thought, *How can I do this, working full-time in Darrington and still care for Eric?* But I said yes. The opportunity of contributing was too great to consider saying no.

That five-year term was truly a once-in-a-lifetime experience. We met monthly at the State Capitol in Olympia, and sometimes even more often in different places across Washington State. One of the most memorable parts of that experience was working with the strong, forward-thinking nursing leaders already on the board. These nursing leaders in Washington State were not nurse practitioners, but they were pioneers in their own right.

One of them was Ruth Barney Fine, RN, MN. She was the Director of Nurses at University Hospital in Seattle, and later an associate professor at the School of Nursing at the University of Washington. She was tough, smart, and knew the value of excellent nursing care, and she understood what it took to bring that excellence to the patient.

Thelma Cleveland, RN, PhD, was a true visionary who had founded the Intercollegiate College of Nursing (now Washington State University College of Nursing). She brought baccalaureate nursing education to the eastern part of Washington State for the first time.

And then there was Betty Harrington, RN. After many years working and teaching at the Sacred Heart Hospital School of Nursing in
Spokane, Washington, it became clear to her that quality nursing education belonged in colleges and universities, and not primarily in hospitals.
She was instrumental, with skill and sensitivity, in closing Sacred Heart
Hospital School of Nursing and transferring the students to community
colleges.

During those five years on the board, these nursing leaders and I learned
a lot from each other's experiences. It was new territory for all of us.
In 1975, applications started to arrive from registered nurses wanting
the legal title of "Nurse Practitioner." Everything was complicated by
the lack of any standardized program of study and poor documentation
of any education. It was impossible to develop a unified and consistent
application of educational and practice criteria. There was a complete
lack of any qualifying examination. There wouldn't be a nurse practitioner master's degree offered by the University of Washington until
1978, with graduates only finishing at the end of 1979. And the Doctor
in Nursing Practice degree (DNP) was not offered at the University of
Washington until 2007. At one point, we stopped accepting applications
and went back to the drawing board.

Those of us on the Board of Nursing waited not-so-patiently for the
American Nurses Association to develop criteria and a national examination for the expanded role of the nurse, and for the University of
Washington to offer a master's program for the nurse practitioner. It
became clear that the biggest challenge was to figure out how to safely
authorize prescriptive authority for nurse practitioners.

In continuing to tackle the challenge, the Board of Nursing appointed
a task force composed of registered nurses, physicians, and pharmacists

to make recommendations regarding the prescribing of drugs by future registered nurse practitioners. Emerging from those meetings were a majority and a minority report. The majority report was vague and non-committal, consisting of a bunch of questions:

- Should an MD have to cosign a prescription written by a nurse practitioner?
- Should the nurse practitioner have to be employed by a physician?
- Should a pharmacist be part of the team?
- Should the nurse practitioner work off a formulary?
- What drugs should be on the formulary?

The minority report, from John S. Holcenberg, MD, associate professor at the departments of medicine and pharmacy at the University of Washington, was scathing:

> Nurses are poorly trained in the basic and clinical sciences needed to understand drug action in the patient and his or her diseases. In remote areas, the pharmacist also has not been trained in the clinical problems associated with drug therapy. If prescribing by nurse practitioners must be started, it should be done only with direct MD backup.

We felt we were back to square one. Then, in October 1976, the Board of Nursing conducted a meeting with members of all three governmental boards: the Washington State Board of Nursing, the Washington State Board of Medical Examiners, and the Washington State Board of Pharmacy. This group decided that a committee should be established to develop a "formulary of non-allowable drugs: for which prescriptive authority should not be granted to the nurse practitioner." As the only nurse practitioner among the members of all three boards, I was quite frustrated by the whole process. But there was no other state in the country that had faced these kinds of questions, and we had no other example to guide us.

These meetings were not comfortable or enjoyable. There was so much tension. During the actual meetings, members were barely cordial and polite, but during the breaks and after the meetings, the interactions were unnerving and upsetting.

After one of the meetings, a member of the Board of Medical Examiners, Robert Willkens, MD, leaned over the table, looked directly at me with a menacing face, and said angrily, "There is really no place for nurses seeing any patients independently. And I don't believe you belong in primary care, either. If you have an ENT problem, you should see an ENT specialist!"

I didn't know how to respond, so I just stood up and walked away.

As this struggle continued, two important events occurred. First, in November 1976, the American Nurses Association finally developed and administered the first certification examination for Adult and Family Nurse Practitioners. I sat for this examination with a few other nurses and passed it. The Board of Nursing started carefully granting nurse practitioner status to specific "pioneer" nurses who met certain educational criteria and passed the American Nurses Association certification examination. I was one of those nurses.

The second and critically important event occurred on January 13, 1977. Senate Bill 2090 was passed as an amendment to the Washington State Drug Act that allowed registered nurses to prescribe legend (prescription) drugs if authorized by the Board of Nursing. This bill did not mention anything about physicians, pharmacists, or other boards. The authorization for registered nurses to prescribe drugs was only to come from the Board of Nursing. Washington became the first state to legislatively allow registered nurses independent prescriptive authority to prescribe drugs. And that authorization was to come from nurses themselves, not physicians or pharmacists.

Any formularies we were working on, positive or negative, were abandoned. Nurse practitioners would now be able to prescribe medications within their scope of practice, as did every other professional with prescription authority. Those of us on the Board of Nursing would work on developing educational and practical criteria for nurse practitioners to be able to apply for prescriptive authority.

The Washington State Medical Association went ballistic. In 1978, the House of Delegates of the WSMA recommended that their physician organization sue the Washington State Board of Nursing based on the failure of the State Board of Nursing to implement and secure "joint recognition" of additional acts by the medical and nursing profession. Meanwhile, board members were receiving threatening letters from attorneys hired by WSMA. There were also statements written by WSMA:

> It is not in society's best interest that nurses be allowed to perform "medical acts" independent of direct physician supervision. The educational preparation of nurse practitioners did not have any standardization and did not provide the knowledge and skills that were needed.

The Washington State Medical Association's written response added that there would be more doctors graduating from medical schools and, as they had physician assistants now, there would be decreased societal needs for nurses.

We went back to our drawing board. We examined the role of prescribing medications in primary care healthcare. We all knew it was a very important component. In fact, in many instances, it was essential for the completion of the assessment, diagnosis, and treatment cycle for the provision of complete care to clients in primary care settings. Nurse practitioners had to have their own authority to prescribe medications in order to function.

The physicians on the Board of Medical Examiners wanted to have control over what we as registered nurses did with the prescribing of medications. They already had total control over physician assistants. But we were not their assistants. We were registered nurses with our own profession and scope of practice. We would have control over our own educational and practice requirements, as well as licensure.

By August 1979, we had the rules and regulations regarding nurse practitioner prescriptive authorization written. It included detailed, specific educational and practice requirements to be eligible to apply for prescriptive authority. Also, by this time, the University of Washington had a master's degree program in place for registered nurses who wanted to become nurse practitioners. The legal term for nurse practitioner eventually became ARNP: Advanced Registered Nurse Practitioner. And the American Nurses Association had its certification examination well developed for nurse practitioners. We would be able to use both the master's degree and the ANA certification process as criteria for ARNP licensure.

A date was set in September 1979 for an open meeting of the Washington State Board of Nursing to announce the implementation of independent prescriptive authority for nurse practitioners. A few weeks before the meeting, headlines in *The Seattle Times* and *The Seattle Post Intelligencer* read, "The Washington State Professional Physicians Association (WSMA) is preparing to sue the Washington State Board of Nursing for allowing nurses to independently prescribe drugs."

The backlash from the public against WSMA was clear and swift. They did not like the idea of doctors suing nurses.

At the meeting in September 1979 in Olympia, the entire auditorium was filled with hundreds of people from all over the state, including reporters from Seattle. My pulse was racing, and my face felt warm. It was a scary and exciting moment. Before we started the meeting, there was a hush in the audience. Suddenly, a spokesman for the Washington State Medical Association stood with a microphone and made an announcement in front of the cameras and the press: the WSMA had decided to give us their full support. There was a rush of loud cheering and clapping from the big crowd. We had won. The Washington State Medical Association had capitulated. It was widely thought that it was because of the public outcry against doctors suing nurses.

I was in the last year of my five-year appointment to the Washington State Board of Nursing. I was proud of the work we had done. In May 1980, I was the first nurse practitioner (ARNP) to receive independent prescriptive authority in the State of Washington. At first, it did not include most "scheduled" drugs—the small number of potentially abusable drugs, such as demerol and morphine. But after two years, all legend drugs, both scheduled and non-scheduled, were included in independent nurse practitioner prescriptive authority. It was a great achievement, and the first independent prescriptive authority for nurse practitioners in all 50 states.

Back in Darrington, once my five-year appointment was up, it was as busy as ever. The phone rang all the time. We saw patients five days a week, and we were also busy on weekends with true emergencies. For chronic or non-emergent problems, we tried to "train" people to call us on Friday rather than wait until the weekend.

One weekend morning, I got a call from a young mother concerned about her child, who had been sick for many days. I gave my "very nice" speech that I would be happy to meet her and her child at the clinic this time, but next time, please just call on Friday, and I would fit her in.

After we hung up, I drove to the clinic and opened the doors to let some fresh air in. I waited for over an hour. No one came. Finally, I called the mother and said that I was at the clinic waiting for her. She began shouting at me in a rage. How dare I not see her child at any time of the day or night! She would not come to the clinic! I tried to quietly explain my reasons, but then I just started crying and couldn't stop. I was just so tired.

I had left the clinic doors wide open, as it was summer. While I was sitting there, crying and trying to explain myself to this woman, a tall elderly man with long white hair and a scraggly beard walked into the clinic and stared down at me.

He looked at me, paused, and then said, "Lady, if you are going to deal with the public, you are going to have to get a tougher skin than this!"

That man was Toby Freeze. He was somewhere in his 80s at that time, and had owned the Darrington Water Works for many years. He was thought to be the first White child born in Darrington. He was a very ornery, tough guy. He gave me the best advice that day, and I've never forgotten it. He said he had noticed the clinic open on a Saturday morning, wondered what was going on, and just decided to drop in. I was so glad he did.

I got a phone call from the firemen one afternoon that they were on their way to pick me up. There was a motorcycle accident ten miles toward Rockport. They arrived, and I jumped into the truck. As we approached the accident scene, I could see two motorcycles lying side by side on the road, and another motorcycle lying about 100 yards away. There were two very distressed young men in black motorcycle gear by the side of the road. I knew one of them. He was Kenny Bryson, one of the sons of Edna Bryson, our clinic housekeeper. He told me there were three of them riding very fast, each on their own motorcycle. There was a turn in the road, and as they rounded it, one of the motorcycles did not make it, and was propelled down the road, landing a long way in front of them. They couldn't find their third friend. Kenny was ashen.

It was August, and there was road dust coating the trees and foliage on the sides of the road. The dust was always there in August, where a little rain and many cars had spread it on the surrounding foliage. It made all the green bushes and trees a dull, uniform gray from the ground to many feet above my head. The firemen and I looked everywhere. Where was the missing man? Finally, as I combed the sides of the road, I could just make out the image of a man, hanging upside down in a tree just barely off the road. He was covered by the same coat of gray dust as the trees around him. The motorcycle accident had flung him up into the tree. He was dead. It was a horrible sight. I never got used to these sights. My job then became to comfort his two surviving friends and meet with his family.

At the end of January 1976, Dave and Sue Clemens, along with Dick, little 18-month-old Eric, and I, drove to the Olympic National Park on the Pacific Ocean and hiked the three miles into Cape Alava. The rugged coast is mostly roadless and isolated and offers some of the wildest, untouched beaches remaining in the continental United States. January is a particularly "wild" month, with winter storms on the coast. But the Olympic Coast also has majestic sea stacks; secluded coves; deserted strands of smooth, sandy beaches; contorted, salt-sprayed maritime forests; and tidal pools bursting with sea urchins, sea stars, limpets, barnacles, and a myriad of other sea creatures.

We pitched our four-person tent on the beach, explored the tide pools, had a delicious dinner, and then went to sleep. All was quiet when we went to bed, but in the middle of the night, a huge wind came up and blew harder and harder. Then the heavy rain started. We thought it might actually blow our tent down—the sides were straining, and the top was lifting. In all the wild places I had ever pitched a tent, I had never had this concern before, but this wind was different. So, in the middle of the night, we took the entire tent down and moved it deeper into the trees. All four adults worked earnestly in unison to move it, and Eric, amazingly, took it all in stride.

In the morning, the rain and wind had subsided, and the sun was out. With Eric in my backpack, we combed the beach where the high tide had reached. We found four oriental glass fishing floats that had come all the way across the Pacific Ocean. Such a thrill! Dave and Sue took two of them, and I still have the other two on our window sill at home.

Day-to-day life in Darrington underwent a huge change after Eric was born. I was working my usual long hours, but now there was a toddler in our house making messes that needed to be cleaned up. Dick was home all day, and I would return home after working more than ten hours to a house in complete shambles. John and Berdi once made an unexpected visit, and Berdi told me that the house was a complete disaster. Eric was playing by himself, and Dick was reading a book in a corner of the living room. He told Berdi that he had "more important things to do than clean up Eric's messes."

In June 1976, when Eric was two years old, he and I flew to Boston to see my dad. It was a wonderful trip. We visited Hampshire College, where Jacquey was studying. We drove to Syracuse and visited my best friend, Pat Smyth, at Columbia University. It was the first time I had seen her in eight years. Dad, Eric, and I toured the Finger Lakes and then went to Niagara Falls. We also went to the Thousand Islands, between the borders of Canada and the United States, along the St. Lawrence River. Such history and beauty!

Dad took us to Canton, New York, where he grew up. We toured St. Lawrence University, where both he and his father had graduated. We drove to Lake Ozonia, where we vacationed as a family in the 1950s and where my dad spent time as a boy. I dove into that beautiful, clear, cold water—it hadn't changed since I was an 11-year-old girl, and was still a thrilling experience.

In September 1976, I had a few vacation days and longed to get into the mountains again. Dick was complaining of a painful knee and said he couldn't go. I decided to go on a three-day backpacking trip by myself, but this time there would be no "route-finding"—it would be a real, established trail all the way. Dick dropped me off at the trailhead at Curry Gap and I started there. I followed the Bald Eagle Trail, scrambled to the top of Johnson Mountain (6,700 ft), swam in the Upper Blue Lake, and went to Dishpan Gap and Pilot Ridge. I wrote in my diary:

> The way was so beautiful, with Glacier Peak
> and open meadows for two miles, then
> descended through trees to Indian Pass
> (5200 ft). Up again and hiked along the
> meadows. I am now camped about three
> miles from White Pass, with a beautiful
> view of Johnson Mountain, the Pilot Ridge,
> Sloan Peak, Bedal Peak, Three Fingers,
> Liberty, Big Bear, Bullen, and the North
> Fork of the Sauk River. I am sitting here
> gazing at this incredibly beautiful site.
> The sun has just set behind Pilot Ridge.
> I have been dreaming about this all year long.

As I descended, the fog lifted, and I hiked back to the trailhead, where Dick and Eric met me.

Dick was not happy that I had been gone for three days. He looked at me sternly and told me, as if it were my fault for leaving, "Eric has started stuttering."

Eric had such advanced verbal skills at age two that it wasn't uncommon for the appearance of some transient stuttering. His stuttering soon disappeared and never returned.

At the beginning of 1977, I knew that I had to get my master's degree. I was already a licensed nurse practitioner. I had pioneered the role, and because of that, the Nurse Practice Act had changed to make what a nurse practitioner does legal. I had already experienced how "practice precedes law." But going forward, nurses would have to earn a master's degree to become nurse practitioners. The University of Washington had just enrolled their first class of registered nurses in the first master's degree program for nurse practitioners in the country. I knew that if I did not get a master's degree, I would regret it later in life.

But how was I to get a master's degree when I lived and worked in Darrington and had a two-year-old? To make matters more complicated, there were prerequisites necessary for entry into the program. I had to have one class in statistics and one quarter of anatomy and physiology at the University of Washington.

The class in statistics was simple—I could do a correspondence course offered by the University of Washington. Long before any online classes were available, we had the good old United States Postal Service. I registered for a correspondence course on statistics in the winter quarter of 1977.

The hard part was the anatomy and physiology class; there was no correspondence class. Instead, it was an evening class from 6:00 p.m. to 8:00 p.m., two days a week, for the entire 12-week winter quarter. There was no way I could attend all of those classes while living and working in Darrington, 80 miles away. I didn't know anyone who was taking the class, so I had to take a chance. I bought a cassette tape recorder, a package of cassettes, and a bunch of padded, self-addressed stamped envelopes, and drove to Seattle to attend the first class.

The class was held in one of the big auditoriums at the UW Health Science Complex. I walked in, saw a young woman in the front row, and sat right next to her. I didn't know her, but she looked both friendly and serious at the same time. I started taping the class while also taking notes. After class, I told her of my predicament, and she offered to help me. I gave her the tape recorder, tapes, and self-addressed stamped envelopes. She agreed to tape the lectures and mail the envelopes with the tapes on her way home from class. It seems almost crazy that my plan would work, but it did.

After Eric was in bed each night, I would play the tapes and take notes. 12 weeks later, at the end of the winter quarter, I drove back to Seattle, attended the last class, and took the final written examination. I got an "A" in that first quarter of Anatomy and Physiology. With my prerequisites completed, I applied to the University of Washington and was accepted into the master's nurse practitioner program for the 1977 fall quarter.

Besides needing to get my master's degree, after five years in Darrington, I was ready to leave—actually, I felt I *needed* to leave.

First of all, I did not want to raise Eric in Darrington. Despite the beauty of living at the foot of the Cascade Mountains and the fascinating people who lived in and around Darrington, the school system wasn't very good.

Additionally, although I enjoyed listening to the tales of the Darrington mountain men, loved hiking with Dave and Sue Clemens from the Forest Service, and enjoyed drinking a few sips of homemade moonshine made by Darrington Tarheel folks, I wanted to be around people with access to more education and a broader life experience. The 24-hour nature of the job was getting to be more and more difficult for me, too.

And then there was Dick. If there was a chance for him to ever realize his dream of becoming a college philosophy professor, we had to get out of Darrington. Dick was also more than ready to go, although any impetus for moving forward had to come from me.

I explained to the Darrington Clinic Board that I needed to get my master's degree and thus needed to leave Darrington. Everyone in town was very unhappy, and no one really understood. But Kasha would still be there, and the professors at the University of Washington School of Nursing were looking for another nurse practitioner to take my place, which eventually happened.

We decided to rent out our house in Darrington. The rent would cover the house payment and give us a little extra as well. In Seattle, we found a two-bedroom, ground-floor apartment that opened out onto a grassy little courtyard where Eric could ride his tricycle. It was a few miles north of the University of Washington.

CHAPTER 5

Back in Seattle: 1977-1979

B Y JUNE 1977, I had settled into our apartment in Seattle, ready to begin work toward my master's degree in late August. My mother and Jacquey were both in San Francisco that summer. I couldn't afford the airfare, so I decided to take Eric, who had just turned three, with me on a Greyhound bus. The trip was a total of 24 hours each way. It would be an adventure.

The bus left Seattle at about 4:00 p.m. Eric and I settled into our seats. We traveled all night long with a variety of people, mostly low-income. I had packed all sorts of snacks and fun little games for us, and Eric did wonderfully.

Our time in San Francisco with Jacquey and my mother was absolutely great and so much fun. I was proud of Eric; he was so well-behaved and smart. My mother had been divorced a few years and was excited about her new life, eager to tell us all about it. Jacquey was, and still is, the best aunt for Eric that anyone could ever wish for. She was so interested in him just for himself. She was giving and loving, as she still is today.

The 24-hour trip back to Seattle didn't have the excitement that the bus ride to San Francisco had. It felt painfully long. But the entire trip was so worth it to me.

Just before my classes started in August, Eric and I took another trip back to upstate New York with my dad. Dad paid for our airfare to Boston, or it would have been impossible for us to go. It was another wonderful, meaningful trip visiting relatives from my dad's early life that I had never met before. All these people are long gone now, and I feel so fortunate to have met them and interviewed them about their important memories.

When Eric and I returned from our visit with Dad, Dick couldn't wait for some marital romance and intimacy. I couldn't find my diaphragm, and six weeks later, I found out I was pregnant with our second son. I had just started my first quarter of graduate school.

Life in Seattle was a whole new world of excitement and challenges. I decided to get a Master of Science (MS) degree rather than a Master of Nursing (MN) degree. If I wanted to get a PhD in some other field in the future, an MS was preferable to an MN, as it was thought to be a broader degree. To get an MS, I would have to satisfy a language requirement and choose a minor degree. I decided I would earn an MS in nursing with a minor in physiology and biophysics. I took a refresher course in Spanish at the University of Washington and was relieved that I only had to pass a written examination in Spanish, as I was much better at reading and writing Spanish than speaking it.

Dick eventually found a job at the Seattle Department of Neighborhoods P-Patch Community Gardening Program. He would be working as an assistant to the head of the program. I enrolled Eric in a preschool near the University District called Rainbow Valley Child Care Center.

The master's program at that time was six quarters; four quarters were straight academic, and two quarters were clinical, seeing real patients. Because of my five years at the Darrington Clinic, I planned to challenge out of the two clinical quarters and just complete the four academic quarters, in addition to the physiology and biophysics classes I needed to complete my minor degree. I also needed to write a master's thesis. Theoretically, if I pushed myself to complete my master's thesis, I could complete all my studies in four quarters.

My experience at the University of Washington was mixed. Higher education for nurse practitioners was an evolving process. It was an excellent program, though, and I learned quite a bit. In 2007, the master's degree program was ultimately discontinued and replaced by a Doctor of Nursing Practice (DNP) degree.

The problem for me as a student at the University of Washington was that I was already licensed as a nurse practitioner by the State of Washington. My fellow students were seeking qualifications in the master's program to obtain this license. As I had pioneered the role, I was doing it backward. However, none of the professors teaching in the program were licensed yet, and that made many of them uncomfortable around me. In addition, I was on the Board of Nursing at that time and at the forefront of writing the new law. I tried to stay in the background as much as I could. I just wanted to get my master's degree and move on with my life.

Meanwhile, on the home front, Dick's salary was minimal, and we were really hurting for money. To earn more money for the family, I started working weekends as a public health nurse for the Seattle King County Department of Public Health. That extra income really helped.

Eric seemed happy at Rainbow Valley Childcare Center, but both Dick and I wanted him to be really challenged in a learning situation, not just in a day care. The University of Washington had a preschool for "gifted" children. They determined a child's eligibility after an IQ test and an extensive interview with the child and the parents. Testing a young child's IQ, especially in 1977, was difficult and not thought to be very accurate, so the test was administered in a one-on-one interview between the child and a clinical psychologist. At three years old, Eric was starting to read on his own and could do some math computations. We applied to the preschool, and Eric scored over 160 on the IQ test. He was accepted into the Child Development Preschool. It was a full-day preschool, and Dick agreed to be responsible for dropping him off and picking him up each day.

It was a stressful time. I was happy Dick was finally working, even though he wasn't trying to further his career at all. But the worst part was when his two younger sisters, Valerie and Suzie, moved to Seattle. During that fall and winter, they became obsessed with *The Rocky Horror Picture Show* and introduced Dick to it. Although critically panned on its initial release, it soon became a cult classic and was shown at midnight on Saturdays at Seattle's Neptune Theater for years. People would go again and again, often dressed like some of the characters. They would stand in line for at least an hour to get into the movie, getting stoned on marijuana in the process. During the movie, the audience, now stoned, would talk back to the screen, miming the scenes and shouting and lip-syncing the character's lines.

Every weekend for months, Dick and his sisters would go to the Neptune Theater. Dick would get home sometime after 3:00 a.m. and then sleep past noon on Sunday. I thought the whole thing was meaningless and reckless behavior. I couldn't imagine why any principled, intelligent, serious-minded adult would waste time seeing this movie multiple times. It also brought back all the fears I had about out-of-control, frightening behavior with drugs and alcohol. And now all the energy and purpose that Dick should have focused on his career was going to *The Rocky Horror Picture Show*. At the time, it seemed like a living nightmare.

Dick also was not happy about my second pregnancy. He told me he wanted to have a serious talk with me at the beginning of the third trimester of my pregnancy. His thesis advisor at the University of Vermont was sponsoring a Philosophy Collegium in Perugia, Italy, for five weeks that summer, and she had invited him to come. Dick felt this was a unique opportunity for him to finally get a job teaching philosophy. He said he knew he would be leaving soon after the baby was born, but he thought it was worth the sacrifice.

I was understandably very ambivalent, but this was the first time he had shown any initiative in finally doing something with his life and contributing to our married life together. Maybe this would finally be "it," and he would start moving forward on his own. Unfortunately, my decision to reluctantly agree to this Italian trip was a huge mistake.

On Tuesday, June 20, 1978, I began the first day of my fourth and last academic quarter. My second son was also born that same day. My labor was just barely over three hours from start to finish, so we arrived at Group Health Hospital Medical Center just in time. A short while later, Kell Barber Vigesaa, at eight pounds eleven ounces, was born. He was another beautiful baby boy. I was filled with excitement and exhilaration.

I was in the hospital for just one night. When we arrived home, we found that one of my friends, Cherie LaMaine, had made lasagna and left it for our dinner. But by the time I arrived home with Kell, Dick's sisters, Suzie and Valerie, were already sitting in our kitchen, uninvited, and eating it.

Also around this time, Dick announced that he wanted to be called "Richard" rather than Dick. To me, Richard never seemed to fit him; he will always be Dick in my eyes. I will, however, refer to him from here on in this memoir as Richard.

One week after Kell was born, Richard left for Perugia, Italy. After the events surrounding *The Rocky Horror Picture Show*, my relationship with him was strained in a way that it had never been before. But I think it was just one more in an accumulation of disappointments in our marriage. Richard was on his way to Italy, and there was nothing I could do about it now. I just had to push forward. In addition to my schoolwork and taking care of my children, I was still on the Board of Nursing. We were in the middle of several intense hearings situated outside of Seattle. It was all very overwhelming.

Richard would send me periodic letters from Italy, where he was staying in a monastery, enjoying delicious Italian food, and fraternizing with the other students in the Philosophical Collegium. He was having a wonderful time. Richard assured me that this trip would be the key to finally launching his career in teaching philosophy at some college or university. But that never happened. To my knowledge, he never made a single effort to get any job in philosophy while he was there or after he returned.

During my last academic quarter, Kell accompanied me to all my classes. He was a happy, good-natured baby, which made it a lot easier. My classmates were kind and accommodating. I would sit in the back of the classroom with Kell, taking notes with one hand and holding him with the other, nursing him when he was hungry. If I dropped a cloth or pacifier, my classmates would pick it up for me.

As the quarter drew to a close, my classmates became a lifeline for me. During the written final examinations, I nursed Kell while my classmates took the final. When the first classmate finished, they took care of Kell for me while I took the final. I will never forget their help and kindness.

I had formally petitioned to challenge out of the last two clinical quarters of the master's program. Finally, on July 20, 1978, when Kell was one month old, I received a letter from Barbara J. Horn, Ph.D., professor in the School of Nursing Department of Community Health Systems, approving the waiver of the last two quarters. In the letter, she wrote:

> The approval for this waiver was based
> on your experience of pioneering the nurse
> practitioner role in the town of Darrington
> from 1972 to 1977, your responsibilities as
> a member of the Washington State Board
> of Nursing, your excellent record in the
> formal graduate school courses, your
> publications, and your activity on a timely
> thesis.

I could finally see the end of the road.

After five weeks in Italy, Richard came home. He had started smoking cigarettes again, which terribly upset me. At one point, his sisters complained about me to him—and he took their side, right in front of me. I felt totally humiliated.

It was now September 1978. I had finished graduate school and completed my thesis. Kell was three months old, and Eric was four years old. We were living in a cramped little apartment. We needed to find something bigger, and I needed to get a job.

The medical community in Arlington, Washington, had changed considerably since 1972, when I first arrived in Darrington. Two new, young family practice physicians from the Doctor's Hospital Residency Program in Seattle had moved to Arlington and started a practice together. Gerard Hooke and Charles Chaffee, who was known as just "Chaffee," were both board-certified family practice physicians, not merely general practice physicians like the other Arlington doctors. Gerard and Chaffee reached out and wanted me to come work with them after I graduated. I was thrilled with the opportunity, which would also bring me closer to my former patients in Darrington. I agreed to start in December 1978.

Meanwhile, we had to get out of that cramped little apartment. We couldn't afford to buy a house in Seattle, but we could afford one in a town just to the northeast, called Bothell. Bothell was closer to Arlington than Seattle and would make an easier commute for me. In addition to our house in Darrington that we rented out, we also owned a parcel of forested land adjoining it. The collateral in those two properties could be used to buy a house in Bothell.

CHAPTER 6

Life in Bothell:
January 1979—March 1982

RICHARD AND I purchased a four-bedroom, split-level home in Bothell and moved in December 1978. I was hoping 1979 would be a new positive start for our family.

As soon as we bought our new house, Richard suddenly quit his job working for the P-Patch Program in Seattle. He never consulted with me. He was only making minimum wage, but it was something. He said he needed to put his full effort into finding a teaching job in philosophy. He also argued that he could not take care of our children during the day. He insisted that Eric and Kell needed to be in full-time day care or preschool so he would have the time and energy to look for a new job.

I felt so good in my new job at the Cascade Valley Clinic in Arlington, working with Gerard and Chaffee. Right away, I was busy. A good number of my old patients in Darrington would drive up to Arlington to see me. I was also seeing lots of new Arlington patients. The Cascade

Valley Hospital granted me hospital privileges, and I was making rounds there. The longer I worked at the Cascade Valley Clinic with Gerard and Chaffee, the busier I became, and the more money I was making.

I was still a member of the Washington State Board of Nursing and in the final stages of getting independent prescriptive authority for nurse practitioners into law. It was finally implemented in August 1980. A front-page article appeared in *Family Practice News*, a national newspaper for family practice physicians. It featured a picture of me examining a patient, with the heading:

"Lynne Vigesaa, family nurse practitioner, has been part of a family practice unit for two years and was recently given prescriptive authority by a state Board of Nursing."

In part, the article read:

> "She's like a third member of our family practice unit" is how Dr. Gerard Hooke describes the relationship that he and Dr. Charles T. Chaffee have with Lynne Vigesaa. "She already has hospital admitting privileges. You wouldn't know that she wasn't a doctor," Dr. Hooke told *Family Practice News*. . . ."We originally thought she would be a backup for us for the overflow of patients, but instead she has developed her own following. She functions as a practitioner in her own right and utilizes us as a backup. She calls on us, and we call on her."

The interviewer asked Gerard if my being one of the first nurse practitioners in Washington State to be given the authority to independently prescribe medications would affect his practice. His response:

"I welcome it. It was frustrating to both of
us that I previously had to countersign for
her. It seems appropriate to me. I know
what her training is, and I know that she has
the background and the judgment to accept
the responsibility."

Eric was blossoming in his new preschool. He was socializing well with the other children and excelling academically. His preschool teacher told me that he was "the most intellectually curious child I have ever met."

Kell was happy at his day care, too. I was finally making enough money for the family. We even bought a second car, a red VW Rabbit.

The problem was Richard. What was he doing with his time? Where was the job that he was supposed to get? We started arguing more and going to marriage counseling, but it never resulted in any action.

In July 1980, my mother called me and said she and a few of her new friends would be renting a house in Cape Cod, and would I like to come and stay with them for a week?

"Just me?" I asked.

"Just you."

I thought about it. My children were six and two years old and were in full-time day care. I had a job with paid vacation time. I could actually go to Cape Cod again! I had visions of those glorious, cold, saltwater waves cascading over my head in the Atlantic Ocean.

That week in Cape Cod was very memorable for me and filled with different experiences. First, there was the experience of my mother. She was now divorced from my dad and living a free, fun-filled life. She was renting a house about a mile from Ballston Beach, the beach of my childhood. I loved that beach so much. I still wear a "Ballston Beach" cap while playing golf.

After all those years of an unhappy marriage, my mother was in a new phase of her life. She rediscovered that she liked to party and have a good time. I tried to put aside my memory of how she used to be and experience her as she was now. I had dinner with my mother and her friends at the house every night. Afterward, they would play cards and drink. Around 10:00 p.m., I would go to bed. They would continue drinking, laughing, and carrying on until well after 2:00 a.m. I would suddenly wake up with the noise and then try to go back to sleep.

The next morning, I would wake up at about 8:00 a.m. Everyone in the house would still be dead asleep after their wild night before. I would eat a quick breakfast, put on my bathing suit, pack some snacks, a towel, a good book, and tiptoe out of the house to go to Ballston Beach.

As I got closer to the beach, I could hear the crash of the waves and smell the salt water. I would set my towel and possessions on the sand and head into the water. After riding many waves, I would come back out, dry off, and walk down the beach, with its high sand dunes and beach grass. Then I would return to my place on the sand and read some of my book.

Around 1:00 p.m., my mother would appear on the beach. She would bring a delicious lunch, and we would relax together on the sand. We had some good conversations.

A few days after my trip to Cape Cod, I found a sheer, light-pink night-gown hanging in the back of my closet. It wasn't mine, and when I asked Richard about it, he said that Karen Lassen, a young woman friend of my mother's from Berkeley, had stayed a few days at our house in order to attend Seattle's production of Wagner's *The Ring of the Nibelung*. This occurred while I was visiting my mother in Cape Cod. He said she must have accidentally left the nightgown. It seemed a bit strange, but at the time I did not question it.

I was ready to continue hiking in the mountains with my boys. I was strong enough to carry two-year-old Kell in a backpack, and Eric, at age six, was quite the hiker himself. I have beautiful pictures of us on Sawyer Mountain and Tonga Ridge in the Cascade Mountains.

During that summer of 1980, our long-time friends, John Hruby and Berdi Safford, suggested that the four of us do the Ptarmigan Traverse in the North Cascade Mountains. The Ptarmigan Traverse is a weeklong, off-trail high route weaving between the glaciated peaks that dominate this gorgeous part of Washington State. This is how one mountaineering site, summitpost.org, described it:

> This is not the Pacific Crest Trail and not
> for hikers. Essentially a mini-expedition,
> it requires off-trail wilderness navigation,
> extensive glacier travel, self-reliance, and
> commitment. The rewards are the views,
> the climbs of the peaks so remote that
> this traverse is their most common
> approach, and the adventure of it all.

The Ptarmigan Traverse was too exciting a mountain adventure to pass up. Edna Bryson in Darrington agreed to take care of our two boys. Both of them loved Edna, so we felt comfortable having them stay with her.

Richard and I both wrote in a diary during the Ptarmigan Traverse, and I have enjoyed reading our entries and looking at the fabulous pictures we took of this great adventure along the way. This area of the North Cascades is one of the most spectacularly beautiful I have ever seen. There are incredible hanging glaciers, green meadows dressed with multicolored wildflowers, and majestic rock peaks. The first four miles are on a trail to Cascade Pass, but then the rest of the traverse, until the very end, is a matter of route-finding across green meadows, steep snow fields, crevassed glaciers, and rock scree.

Rereading my diary of that trip, I experienced again the resentment and anger I felt toward Richard. The entire time, Richard was completely focused on himself, his route-finding, and his pace. It was a potentially hazardous trip, but he rarely cared where I was or how I was navigating by myself. It was less about the two of us sharing an adventure together; in so many ways, this trip was a microcosm of the problems in our everyday life. Richard was not there for me, like most days of our marriage.

Changes at the Arlington Practice

In February 1981, Gerard and Chaffee decided to part ways. I never knew exactly what the problem between them was, but the separation seemed amicable. They remained friends and colleagues, but established separate practices in Arlington. Each of them wanted me to join their practice. At the time, I thought Gerard was the more mature, stable physician, so I decided to work with him.

I officially joined Gerard's practice on February 19, 1981. I signed a new contract with similar compensation, which included benefits and malpractice insurance. I was seeing the same patients, and we had the same good office staff that we had when Gerard and Chaffee were together.

Gerard had dreams of building a big new house on 40 acres of land he had just bought outside of Arlington. He was focused on making his dream home come to life. First, he had to build a road through the 40 acres to reach the site where his new house would be. Then, he had to bring in water, electricity, and gas. It all cost a lot of money before he could finally begin building the house itself. Initially, the plans were just for a beautiful, big house, but got more and more extravagant. He kept borrowing increasing amounts of money. By the time he turned all those loans into a house payment, the monthly amount was more than $4,000. That was an extraordinary amount in 1981.

Now he had a cash-flow problem. Out of the blue, he told me, "I have to lower your salary, and I don't have the money to pay you, despite how many patients you are seeing."

I was stunned. He still wanted me to be a part of his practice, but I would need to work for less money. He couldn't tell me how much less.

In the end, Gerard and I were at an impasse. I realized I had to find another job, and quickly. The Seattle King County Department of Public Health and the U.S. Public Health Service Hospital (soon to be renamed Pacific Medical Center) had combined for a joint venture, and had a primary care and family planning clinic in North Seattle. They were advertising for a nurse practitioner. The chief medical officer, Frank Baron, interviewed me and offered me the job. I immediately accepted.

The one problem was the salary. I was making well in excess of $30,000 per year with Gerard. This new job only paid $22,500 per year. I told Richard he had to find some kind of job that would bring in at least $7,000 per year just to keep our current standard of living. By that time, Kell was in preschool and Eric was in second grade. Richard *had* to get a job.

I gave Gerard two weeks' notice. The staff gave me a lovely going-away party, and that was the end of my career at the Cascade Medical Center in Arlington.

CHAPTER 7

The Next Two Years:
March 1982—April 1983

AFTER I PUT pressure on Richard to find a job, he was furious. It was all my fault, he told me. If I would just stop nagging him, he would be able to move ahead. Finally, after a huge shouting fight, I made an agreement with him. I wouldn't say anything about getting a job or taking on more responsibility at home for a full six months. I would leave it all up to him. And I kept that agreement.

Richard's father and his new wife, Joyce, suddenly arrived for a visit during this time. They only announced they were coming a few days earlier. They lived in Minnesota on Social Security Disability and had limited financial resources. They arrived without any departure date. We eventually discovered they had to wait for their next disability checks to arrive in the mail before they would have enough money for the airfare home. No one knew exactly when their checks would arrive, so no one knew when they would leave.

Although Richard's dad and Joyce were very pleasant, their visit only made more work for me. Neither of them felt the need to pitch in and help with anything around the house. Depression about my marriage continued to grow.

On the other hand, my work at North Seattle Health Clinic was really fun and interesting. The clinic included nurse practitioners, a few registered nurses, and one family practice physician, Michael Lippmann, who was also the medical director of the clinic. We primarily saw low-income patients for acute illness, health promotion, and family planning. I had more experience than anyone else at the clinic. I was confident in my clinical judgment and what I could offer. Michael Lippmann had only graduated a year before from his family practice residency. He was quiet and somewhat introspective. During the weekly clinic meetings that Michael chaired, I was enthusiastically supportive of the plans he had for the clinic. I also had ideas of my own that Michael was interested in. The other nurse practitioners were inexperienced, and although the clinic was affiliated with Pacific Medical Center, it was essentially a government-run health clinic. The salaries were low for everyone. Everyone arrived exactly at 8:00 a.m., and the building was completely empty at 4:31 p.m. It was an atmosphere of doing the bare minimum, nothing extra.

From Michael Lippmann's point of view, his job changed for the better when I arrived, something he told me many months later. After a month or so, he started seeking me out to ask my clinical opinion on a variety of medical issues. We talked a lot about clinical cases and all sorts of other subjects. He was also interested in hiking, but had little experience. He talked with me about hiking and climbing—what places to go and what equipment to get.

For me, it was uplifting to have such a positive connection with a doctor at the clinic. With the exception of my two wonderful sons, my life at home was depressing. Working at the clinic with the camaraderie of Michael Lippmann was a sharp contrast. At the time, I was aware of how rewarding and fun it was to work with someone who would actually follow through on mutual plans and ideas.

It wasn't just working at the clinic that I looked forward to. Working with Michael Lippman was the real draw for me. I became aware of how his eyes just seemed to focus on me when I walked into the conference room, and I loved the way he always smiled at me. We thought about healthcare in the same way. Michael was so responsible. He had a job. He made money. I could rely on him in the clinic. He did what he said he was going to do. The contrast to Richard was striking.

For the first time in my 14-year marriage, I was seriously attracted to another man. But I knew there was no way I was going to act on that attraction. There was no future in it; I was married to Richard. I had two children. I did not approve of extramarital relationships. I could think about it, but that was as far as I would ever take it.

Meanwhile, my friends Dave and Suzanne were planning a climb of Eldorado Peak during the first week of August. Eldorado is an 8,868-foot glaciated peak with a famous, snow-covered "knife-edge ridge" at the top. I had heard stories of this mountain and thought that, with a strong climbing group, we could do it. Also joining us on the climb were my good friends Barbara Krieger and Buzz Shaw. Richard was not interested in going.

On Friday, August 6, the day before the climb, I spent the day seeing patients at the clinic. The clinic closed at 4:30 p.m., and it was close to

5:00 p.m. before I completed my charts and finished reading a journal article. I didn't think anyone else was in the clinic that late. All was quiet.

Suddenly, the door of my office opened, and there was Michael Lippman. He just stood there in the doorway for a minute and then closed the door behind him. I was frozen. After a minute, he walked up to my desk. I stood up, and he put his hands on my shoulders and said he could not remember when anyone had ever touched his life as strongly as I had these past five months. He said any feelings of "disconnection" that he had in his life completely vanished when I started working at the clinic. He went on to say it was more than just being his "ally" at work. He then put his arms around me and said, "You are the woman who I always needed but never ran into."

I am able to put quotations on his words because the next day he wrote me a letter with these words and more. And there were many other letters, all of which I have saved.

All I remember is telling him, with so much emotion in my voice, how bleak my own married life had been for so long—with a husband I couldn't rely on, whom I could not respect or even love anymore. It was like a big dam broke, and all this misery and longing flooded out of me.

Michael and I did not stay long at the clinic. I needed to get home to prepare dinner for my family, and get ready for the climb. While I drove home, I was struck by a revelation. In the last 14 years of my marriage, I had been running a race, running long and hard toward some goal for my life with Richard. But now, I looked back and the finish line was behind me, but I was still running. I needed to finally stop.

I didn't say anything to Richard that evening. I was busy with my boys and preparing for the climb the next day. Very early the next morning, I drove off to the North Cascades National Park and Eldorado Peak.

The climb was a difficult one. Just the approach up the 2,000 feet of boulders with heavy packs to our high camp in the meadows was strenuous enough. I have a picture of Suzanne Spencer, Barbara Krieger and me on Saturday night at sunset, sitting in that meadow, with stunning Johannesburg Mountain (8,200 ft) behind us. Suzanne and Barbara are still two of my closest friends. I never said anything to them at the time about what had just happened the day before, but I knew my life had changed forever. I felt deeply that it would be for the better. It really didn't matter what might happen between Michael and me. I was going to end my unhappy marriage to Richard, a marriage that had been going nowhere for years. I did not have to settle anymore. There was a possibility of something good out there for me.

The Sunday climb to the summit is one I will always remember. We all put crampons on our boots to grip the hard snow and ice on the glacier. I roped up with Dave and Suzanne. Suzanne was leading, I was in the middle, and Dave was at the end. The route up the Eldorado Glacier was straightforward, although long and steep.

At first, the snow climb seemed very doable. But as we ascended, the snowy, icy ridge became narrower and narrower. Finally, we found ourselves actually standing on the beginning of the famous knife-edge ridge. The top of the ridge was so narrow that there was barely enough room for my two boots. The surface of the snow and ice dropped precipitously, more than 1,000 feet on either side.

I went a few feet more and then yelled to Suzanne, "I don't want to go any further."

Suzanne yelled back, "Lynne, it is just a few more feet to the actual summit!"

We made it to the summit shortly afterward. We didn't stay long before carefully retracing our steps down the knife-edge ridge. Soon, we were back to our camp in the high meadows. What a thrill that climb of Eldorado Peak was!

Suzanne and I on the knife-edge ridge of Eldorado

We made our way down the 2,000 feet of big boulders, jumping from one to another with our heavy packs on our backs. Finally, we reached the top of the trail which would eventually lead to our car. We were miserable, and how every bone in our bodies ached! But even sore and tired, we were elated with the incredible experience we'd just had.

Back home, I read Eric and Kell their stories and tucked them into bed. Richard was waiting, but I said very little and just went to bed. I got up very early the next morning, and Richard got up with me, sensing something was wrong. I told him I had something important to say, and started by summarizing the past years of our marriage, and all the broken promises and unmet expectations. I ended by telling him about Michael Lippman's conversation with me two days earlier and what it had meant to me. I did not want to settle anymore for the kind of relationship and marriage that Richard and I had had for so many years. I felt calm and decisive.

At first, Richard did not fully understand what I was saying. He said something to the effect that he was glad we were "clearing the air." He acted as if it was just one more talk, like so many we'd had over the years. I explained that this time it was different—I was done. I wanted a divorce. He was totally shocked. I told him he had to move out. He called Buzz Shaw, who had recently separated from Barbara Krieger, and made arrangements to move in with him. He begged me not to actually file for divorce, and I reluctantly temporally agreed.

When Eric woke up, we explained that we loved both him and Kell more than anything, but we weren't getting along well, and Dad would be living with Buzz for a while. Eric nodded and said that he understood. But Richard didn't leave it at that.

He started crying and saying over and over again, "Don't you understand, Eric, that Daddy is leaving and not coming back?"

Eric was reduced to tears. Richard had made this all about him, and not about helping Eric through this difficult time. It made me sick. More than ever, I wanted to move on from this man.

I certainly knew that divorce is hard on children. It was one of the reasons I had stayed married to Richard for 14 years. But when Michael Lippman came into my office late that Friday afternoon, it was as if my life suddenly opened up in a monumental way, and I knew I did not have to live in this depressing, loveless marriage any longer. There was happiness somewhere out there for me. I would somehow make it work for my children.

When I received our phone bill that month, it was more than $150—a huge amount of money in those days. The bill included two lengthy long-distance calls that Richard had made to Karen Lassen, who had stayed in our house and left her nightgown behind. The calls were made just two days after I told Richard I wanted a divorce. I was furious. It would be hard to pay that bill.

What I didn't fully comprehend at the time was that you can never be "done" with a man who is the father of your children. That being said, I have never once regretted my decision to divorce Richard. My only regret was not doing it sooner.

The next few months were tumultuous. All my friends stood by me then, and still do now. Work was stressful at best. After our encounter, Michael Lippmann became afraid and somewhat regretful of having expressed himself so strongly to me, a married woman with two children. But he was also strongly attracted to me, as I was to him.

In September, I formally filed for divorce. I suggested that Richard and I meet at Costas, a small restaurant in the University District. He arrived very morose and depressed, tearful and dejected. I told him that waiting to file for divorce made no sense, as there was no question in my mind that it had to happen, and the sooner the better. Afterward, as we walked out of the restaurant, Richard started to collapse, and I had to hold him up. As we approached his car parked on the street, he fell against the side of the car, moaning and crying. His body was partially limp. I managed to get him into the passenger seat and safely belted in. I couldn't get him to articulate any understandable words. I drove his car south a few blocks to the emergency room of University Hospital.

I parked his car, got a wheelchair from the emergency room, and wrestled Richard's limp body into it. He was conscious, but refused to move by himself.

I waited in the University Hospital emergency room for several hours while Richard was fully examined and evaluated. The physicians determined that he needed an inpatient psychiatric evaluation. Unfortunately, there were no beds available in the hospital's psychiatric unit. A bed was finally found at Everett General Hospital, and he was transferred via ambulance there.

If I had ever doubted my decision to get a divorce from Richard Vigesaa, there was not a shred of doubt now. I could not respect a man who fell apart at such a critical time, rather than rise to the occasion. I knew he was safe for the present at the hospital. I continued to move forward with the divorce.

Sometime shortly after he was discharged, Richard looked tearfully at me and said, "You are really going to miss me."

The truth is, I never have missed him. I should have left long before then.

I sought the help of my longtime good friend from Mountain Lakes, George Bowden. George was the brother of my first high school boy-friend, Bob. He was now a lawyer working in private practice in Everett, Washington. I hired him for my divorce. I decided to have the divorce papers delivered to Richard while he was still at Everett General Hospital. He would have professional support in the hospital to help him process the divorce and respond to the divorce papers.

Richard was in the hospital for about a week, and then discharged to Buzz Shaw's house. He spent his time looking for a job and collecting unemployment insurance. Buzz told me later that Richard spent a lot more time making sure he got unemployment insurance than he did look-ing for a job.

I discovered that the court expected me to pay Richard alimony for one year because he wasn't working when I was married to him. I wasn't sure I had the money to support my boys, myself, and Richard too. I was told by the court that was my problem. We owned that piece of wooded property in Darrington, and two houses with mortgages in Darrington and Bothell. The equity in our house in Bothell equaled the equity of the wooded property and the Darrington house combined. I agreed to split the assets: each of us got one car, I got the Bothell house, and Richard got the wooded property and the Darrington house.

The court told me I had to sell the Darrington house and the wooded property within six months and give Richard the money from the sales. He had no responsibility to see the house and the property even though they were now his. The responsibility was all mine. If I didn't sell the house and property within six months, I would have to pay Richard interest on the money until I was able to sell them. Fortunately, I was just able to sell everything within the deadline.

I wanted full custody of our boys; Richard wanted joint custody. I agreed to joint custody because otherwise he would have fought it, and it would have cost a lot more money and time in court. We settled on joint custody with the stipulation that the boys would live with me. I would be the custodial parent, and that fact could not be changed unless I agreed to it. And I would never agree to not having my children live with me.

George did an excellent job as my lawyer. The divorce was finalized on January 3, 1983. I was finally free of this painful and unhappy marriage. However, many of life's challenges were just beginning for me. Somehow, I thought life would be easier now. I knew I would be a good wife to the right man, and I was now focused on trying to find him. When I look back on my life, I have very few real regrets. However, I do regret spending so much time and energy on trying to find the "right man" when my children were so young. In 1983, the professional thinking in social work and psychiatry was that if a woman wasn't married by the time she was 40 years old, her chances of ever getting married again were slim. I was 36 years old, and I didn't think I had much time left to find the right man.

At first, I was totally focused on Michael Lippmann. He was conflicted about me, though. On one hand, he was very attracted to me. I was also a major strength for him at the North Seattle Health Clinic. He relied on my energy and support. I also scared him; I was way too serious and focused on a committed relationship. I was a big package with my two sons. Michael and I went back and forth in a "semi-relationship" during the first part of 1983.

Grandma Frieda was now 90 years old, and her health was failing. Uncle Joe, her son and my mother's brother, had made the decision to move her into a nursing home. In February 1983, I decided to take my two boys, now ages eight and four, and fly out to Northwood to see her. I wanted to make it fun for the boys, so I brought cross-country skis for all three of us. There weren't many hills in Iowa, but there was lots of snow for our cross-country skiing fun.

Eric, Kell, and I flew into Minneapolis-Saint Paul Airport. I had asked my Uncle Joe to pick us up, not realizing it was two hours from Northwood. Uncle Joe was not happy that my mother had divorced my dad. He was "down on women" at that time in his life. He also wasn't happy about my divorce. When he met us at the airport, his first words to me were angry ones, telling me that the only reason he agreed to pick me up was because I had my two little boys with me.

Despite the way Uncle Joe treated me, I was glad we had made the trip. Uncle Joe's wife, Aunt Mary Ellen, was friendly and welcoming. My boys got to know Grandma Frieda a little, and I got to spend precious time with her. She was physically weak but mentally still present. I had seen her eight years earlier when she came to Seattle to visit me after Eric was born. Her physical deterioration since then was sobering and sad, but her kind and loving personality was still present.

Eric and Kell loved cross-country skiing. We flew over the snow-covered cornfields in Iowa. Some cornstalks were still peeking through a foot or two of snow, but we skied over them too. All in all, it was an important visit.

The chief medical officer of the North Seattle Health Clinic was Frank Baron, the doctor who had hired me. Frank was a general internist who worked at the Seattle Public Health Hospital, which had recently been renamed Pacific Medical Center. In April 1983, Frank called me and told me there was a nurse practitioner position now available at Pacific Medical Center. The salary was significantly higher, and he wanted to know if I was interested. I was! I applied for the job and was hired immediately. The increase in my salary made a big difference, and it was the start of a 20-year career for me there.

CHAPTER 8

Pacific Medical Center:
May 1983–June 2003

WORKING AS A nurse practitioner at Pacific Medical Center (PacMed) opened unimagined doors for me in my career. For the first time, I was working with physicians who weren't primarily interested in money. In addition, they were really interested in my decision-making process and the quality of healthcare I was providing.

The advent of licensed nurse practitioners in Washington State, who could work independently without being associated with physicians, was completely new and sometimes threatening to others. At Group Health Hospital Medical Center in Seattle, nurse practitioners had to be members of the registered nurses union, and could not become members of the medical staff. The nurses union was strong but rigid with regard to rules and regulations. The physicians had little control over the nurse practitioners because they weren't part of the medical staff. In contrast, physicians had complete control of physician assistants, who were legally "the arm of the physician." Over the next year, most nurse practitioners disappeared from Group Health and were gradually replaced by physician assistants.

However, at PacMed, everyone was an equal member of staff. A few months after I arrived, I was asked to be the supervisor of all the nurse practitioners and physician assistants there.

The organization for the medical staff was named PHASE (Pacific Health Associates of Seattle). The PHASE board governed the entire medical staff. Members of the PHASE board included the chief of internal medicine, the chief of pediatrics, the emergency room physician director, chiefs of all specialty areas, and me as supervisor of nurse practitioners and physician assistants. I was the only member of the PHASE board who was not a physician.

It was quite an experience to be an equal member of the PHASE board, which met monthly. I served on the PHASE board for almost 20 years, right up until I left Pacific Medical Center in 2003. The physicians on the board didn't know what to make of me at first, but over time I was accepted as a long-time board member.

One of my responsibilities was to hire, evaluate, and manage the nurse practitioners and physician assistants at PacMed. At that time, nurse practitioners worked as primary care providers with their own panel of patients in the adult medicine clinic and also evaluated patients in the emergency room at Pacific Medical Center. In 1983, about 40 percent of hospital admissions came from the emergency room. The majority of our patients had multiple, complex health problems.

I knew excellent nurse practitioner candidates, many of whom had been my classmates. I hired several of them, all of whom would go on to have long careers at Pacific Medical Center. The physician assistants at PacMed did not feel limited to being only "the arm of the physician." Together, the nurse practitioners and physician assistants came up with the title of "physician associates" for our group, and from then on were called the "associate staff" at Pacific Medical Center.

At this time, Richard continued to live in a house rented by Buzz Shaw. A few months after our divorce, Richard met Susan Loitz, a woman 13 years younger than him and just out of law school. Still unemployed, he began living with Susan. Richard remained primarily unemployed for the next seven years. Finally, Eric, who was then in high school, suggested that Richard take a class in computers. He took an introductory computer class and was hired by Microsoft as an entry-level employee. His salary was much less than one-half of mine. After they were married, Susan Loitz's huge income as a lawyer could not be factored into child support. I still had to pay him a large sum for the six weeks in the summer when the boys stayed with him.

In the spring of 1983, my dad came to visit and stayed with me for several days. My sister Carol also came out to see Dad for an afternoon. Dad's behavior toward Carol was so terrible—really reprehensible. He was drinking beer continually and said many inappropriate things of a sexual nature to Carol. I was shocked and outraged, and told him to his face to "stop it now!" It wasn't clear to me at the time what was behind all of this.

Eric, Kell, and I did a lot of hiking and camping with friends that summer in both the Cascades and the Olympics. In the summer months, I tried to spend as much time as I could hiking in the mountains or at the ocean with my boys.

One day in September, I was at my desk at PacMed when the receptionist knocked on my door and said there was a man who wanted to see me about something important. The receptionist ushered him into my office. His manner was cavalier and impersonal. He asked me to verify my identity, and then abruptly handed me a court subpoena. He said I was being sued by the family of a former patient from the Cascade Valley Medical Center in Arlington. I was in shock. I had no idea what he was talking about.

I first called my malpractice carrier from my employment with Gerard Hooke. I was ridiculously naive about the ins and outs of malpractice insurance. I knew I had malpractice insurance coverage as part of my employment contract, but I didn't know I had the type called tail coverage. This meant that in addition to the monthly premiums, there was also a "tail" that needed to be paid when I left Gerard's medical practice. This tail coverage would cover any malpractice lawsuits that might occur after I left the company. The insurance company informed me that my tail coverage had not been paid. As a result, I had no malpractice insurance. And now I was being sued.

The insurance agent told me they had sent several notices to my office in Arlington after I had left, saying there was just a small window of time left for me to pay the tail. The window of time had long since elapsed. When I called Cascade Valley Medical Center, Gerard Hooke's office said that the multiple notices from the malpractice insurance company had been ignored by the clinic manager—Gerard Hooke's wife, Amanda Hooke. In fact, the insurance company had sent three registered letters to me at my former work address at Cascade Valley Medical Center, but no one had forwarded the letters to me.

I called the insurance company again and tried to find out my options. I really had only one: I had to pay the insurance company $1,684 within the next seven days. If I did, I would have malpractice coverage for any other malpractice claims that might come in the future. However, I would have no malpractice coverage for this present lawsuit. And there was no way to get it now.

I was frantic. I called my dad, explained the situation, and asked him for a loan. He never hesitated. I paid all the money back to him in several installments over the next year. However, I still had an active lawsuit against me. I finally found out why I was being sued. Two years earlier, I had seen a woman in her mid-50s who was a long-time smoker. At the time, the standard of care for people who smoked was to get a routine chest X-ray as part of a physical examination. She was feeling well and had no symptoms of lung disease, but she had a 20-year history of heavy smoking. I ordered a chest X-ray at Cascade Valley Hospital. The radiologist read the X-ray results as having no disease, and I had received his written report stating that fact. But now, two years later, the woman had developed a malignancy in her brain. On evaluating her, they looked again at the chest X-ray, and thought, in retrospect, that there actually was evidence of a malignant tumor. The undiagnosed lung cancer had now metastasized to her brain. The lawsuit named Cascade Valley Hospital, the physician radiologist, Gerard Hooke as my employer, and me as the one who ordered the chest X-ray.

Once again, I called upon my friend and lawyer, George Bowden. He thought I would eventually be dropped from the lawsuit, and that the radiologist and the Cascade Valley Hospital who employed him would incur most of the risk. After many months, that's exactly what happened. However, George was not happy that I had a written contract with Gerard Hooke that stipulated malpractice insurance was part of my contract, yet there was no malpractice insurance for me when I got sued. I had to pay for my own tail coverage, and I had also incurred lawyer and court expenses. George thought I should sue Gerard for breach of contract.

Over the next few months, George and I sat with a judge who would rule in my case. Gerard Hooke also was present with his lawyer. I couldn't believe Gerard could look me in the face in that courtroom and insist that he had no obligation with regard to my malpractice insurance. The judge ruled that Gerard had to pay me $1,684 for my tail coverage, as well as all my attorney expenses. I didn't ask for anything more in my lawsuit—no "pain and suffering" compensation. I wanted to be as fair as Gerard was not.

Gerard refused to pay me what the court had ordered him to pay. Once again, I called George Bowden. George asked me to find out where Gerard did his banking. That was easy. I was still friends with his staff at the clinic. I called Dorothy, his lead receptionist and bookkeeper, and she gave me the information. Then George went into action. He contacted Gerard's bank and had his account frozen. Gerard couldn't even meet his employee payroll without paying me first. The money from the lawsuit suddenly appeared in my bank account. And that was the end of that.

During this time, my dad was diagnosed with lung cancer. Although he was only 68 years old, he was in terrible shape health-wise. All that drinking and smoking for so many years had taken its toll. The prognosis was that he had less than a year to live. In fact, he actually had seven months.

Also during that fall of 1983, I received a disturbing call from my sister Carol. She was agitated and speaking very fast.

She said, "I have had 'incest amnesia,' and I was sexually assaulted by Dad when I was a little girl."

I thought to myself, *I can't believe this*, but I knew from her voice that *she* really believed it. I tried to be supportive and recommended that she get counseling.

It took me two weeks to admit to myself that Dad fit some aspects of the clinical picture of someone who would sexually molest his daughter. I remembered the sexually explicit comments he had made to Carol the previous spring. I started thinking about the past. Was there anything about Dad's behavior when I was growing up that was alarming? A memory of something came back to me.

Carol was a beautiful child, quiet, with big blue eyes. When she was about three or four years old, I remember one of my dad's friends pointing at her and saying, "Better watch out for that one, Carl!"

Dad laughed. "Yeah, I know what you mean."

I was eight years old and didn't understand what they were talking about, but I still remember how uncomfortable those words made me feel.

In December, my brother, John, flew out to Seattle from Boston with my dad. Dad had lost a lot of weight, was on oxygen 24/7, and looked terrible. But he still had a lot of fight in him. It was clear to me that he did not comprehend that this was a terminal disease. Dad began radiation treatment ordered by the oncologist. He also started seeing Frank Baron, the chief medical officer at the North Seattle Health Clinic who had told me about the nurse practitioner job at Pacific Medical Center. With the radiation treatment, Dad began experiencing nausea and vomiting.

Soon after my dad arrived at my house, my mother flew to Seattle to talk with him about changing his will. My parents had been divorced for ten years, and I was the executor of his will. At the time of their divorce, their assets were divided equally. Although my mother could have received a lot more from their divorce settlement, she had decided not to ask for any maintenance. But now, ten years later, she wanted the money when he died. I remember their meeting so clearly. My dad, my mother, my attorney, George, and I gathered around the dining room table. My mother told my dad that the money that was designated to be divided between the four of us children really belonged to her, and she wanted it. It didn't matter to her that they had been divorced for ten years. Despite the fact that he was nauseated and periodically vomiting from the radiation treatment, he was alert and following the conversation. Ultimately, Dad decided to make a change to his will and give my mother an additional $130,000. The rest of the money would be divided between the four of us children. George also took over the steps needed to get his house in Carlisle, Massachusetts, on the market.

I knew Carol had talked with my mother about being sexually abused by my dad. Would my mother confront my dad about it? But she never did. Her focus was on the money.

It was nearing Christmas 1983. John had left and then returned for the holiday with Lily, my dad's mid-sized poodle. Dad called her "Lily-White," and he was so glad to have her with him again. She was completely devoted to him, and he was equally devoted to her. Her one problem was that she frequently peed on the rug in my living room. I tried everything I could think of to solve the problem. She tended to pee on the rug in the early morning, so I began setting my alarm for 2:00 a.m. to let her out. As I staggered out to the living room, Lily would get up and stare at me.

Then, without a sound, she would squat and pee on the rug in front of me. Lily did this for the entire seven months she lived with us.

As Christmas drew near, I began thinking about which Christmas cookies to bake. "I don't think I have the energy to make bonbons this year." I said to myself out loud.

My dad overheard me. "Oh, you have to make the bonbons! I may not be here at Christmas next year!"

He said it almost as a joke, but I just froze. I knew he would likely not be here next Christmas. I immediately started making a batch of bonbons, and made them every two weeks until the end of June 1984, when Dad died.

During the seven months that Dad lived with me, his health failed as the lung cancer gradually took over his body. Hospice was involved, but it wasn't the proactive and comprehensive hospice support we've come to expect today. Basically, they just helped me hire a home health aide to stay with Dad when I was working.

Dad was quite demanding. He became angry if I left the house for a few hours on the weekend to visit friends. He was frightened—and I was physically and mentally exhausted. Even though he needed oxygen to breathe, he was still addicted to smoking. He also constantly asked Eric and Kell to get him a beer from the refrigerator. I caught him smoking in the house a number of times while on oxygen.

Every four to six weeks, Jacquey would fly in for the weekend. There was a lot of paperwork to go through—insurance forms, medical bills, all the maintenance and selling of his home in Massachusetts. Jacquey also gave me a break from Dad's demands. She was just as wonderful then as she is today.

Sometime in the spring of 1984, I got a call from George Austin, a 40-year-old divorced insurance broker with an 11-year-old daughter, who worked with a friend of mine. She, unbeknownst to me, had given him my name as a possible date. After some conversation, we agreed to meet. George Austin would come to be known to many of my women friends as "The Bad George." My attorney and good friend George Bowden is, of course, "The Good George."

Although George Austin was truly not a good man, he was temporarily helpful to me. He was strong and decisive. For the first time, I had someone who would insist that I get some nightly help, as he could see I was trying to function at work with no sleep.

Several times that spring, I asked Dad directly what had happened between him and Carol. All he would say was that a few times, after coming home from an office party smelling of cigarettes and alcohol, he had tried to get into bed with my mother. She would wake up very angry, tell him he smelled and then say, "Get into bed with Carol!" Carol had the only other bedroom that could easily accommodate a double bed. He never admitted anything specific, but his words seemed like an admission of some sort.

There are lifelong consequences of fraught relationships in our family: father and daughter, sister and sister, mother and daughter, father and son, brother and sister. How could our father treat each of us in such different ways? We all had very different experiences with him. Why was Carol the victim of sexual abuse but not Jacquey or me? Jacquey and I were able to get the very best out of our father for some unexplained reason. He could still be abusive and scary, but this was balanced by generous support, respect, and love. Dad could hold his liquor so much better in his younger days. As his oldest child, I was definitely the beneficiary of that. As the years wore on, he drank more, and the deleterious effects on his children became more extreme.

The same could be said about my mother, but for different reasons. She also treated the four of us in different ways, some better than others. She was resentful of the life she had as a mother of four. Although she willingly chose that life, once she was actually in it, she didn't like it. However, many years later, she became a responsible woman and a much better mother. She was a more patient, loving, and accepting mother to Jacquey than she ever was to John, Carol, or me.

On Father's Day 1984, I offered to make some of Dad's favorite dishes, but he didn't want anything special to eat. He didn't want to go for a drive, which was unusual. The next day, Monday, he didn't have the strength to get out of bed and into his wheelchair, even with my help. He had a very frightened, helpless look on his face. Alarms were ringing in my head. I called hospice, and they immediately canceled all the home health aides and scheduled registered nurses to come round the clock. I called my siblings and told them Dad was much worse, and that they should plan on coming very soon to see him.

On Friday, Dad was still alert and conscious, but very weak. John and Jacquey both arrived that evening.

Late Saturday morning, Carol arrived, tense and angry. Without saying a word to me, she went out to the backyard where Jacquey was at the time. I couldn't hear what was being said, but I could see Carol yelling, pointing her finger at Jacquey; Jacquey had her hands over her face and was sobbing. I was furious. I went outside and told Carol she needed to leave. She stormed out of the backyard and drove away.

On Sunday afternoon, June 25, 1984, after John and Jacquey had left and Dad and I were alone, he passed away.

The boys were spending the weekend with Richard, so after Dad died, I got my tent, stove, and backpack, and drove out to the Olympic Peninsula—to Lake Ozette and the trailhead to Cape Alava. I felt so completely lost. I started on the trail through the dense forest of western red cedar, licorice ferns, and salal. After a little over three miles, I could hear the waves crashing on the beach. Finally, beautiful Cape Alava! I pitched my tent and tried to somehow get a hold of myself. I kept remembering the good times Dad and I had in the past.

A week or two later, Carol called me. She said she wanted to spend some time with my boys. I was uncomfortable with that, given her recent behavior. I told her she could see them at my house, which made her furious. She started yelling at me, and I finally told her that if she continued, I was going to hang up. She then said menacingly, "I dare you to hang up . . . I just dare you!"

I hung up—and didn't talk with her again for nearly 38 years.

After Dad died, George Austin and I started dating seriously. Although he supplied the strength and help I needed around this time, I discovered that there was a cruel and abusive side to him. But I was desperate for some caring and stability, and he seemed to supply that—at least for a while.

George had an 11-year-old daughter, Katie. She lived with her mother in California, but traveled to Seattle frequently. George was devoted to her. I really liked Katie, too, and I established a good relationship with her. For George's birthday, I took some lovely pictures of Katie, and she gave them to him as a present. He was surprised and delighted. Katie was his soft spot.

After seeing George for several months, he and I flew to St. Augustine, Florida, to buy a metal hull for a new sailboat he was building. It was a difficult trip. He wasn't very nice to me. It was subtle most of the time, but hurtful. I kept thinking eventually he would relax and be kind. Of course, abusive men never are.

Our relationship lasted less than a year, and I have George's daughter Katie to thank for that. One day, Katie called me at work. She was crying and told me that whenever I left their house, another woman would arrive. She said she wanted me there and not "that other woman." I calmed her down and thanked her for the call.

The next day I confronted George with what Katie had told me. He was furious with me. Who did I think I was, after all? We exchanged a few harsh words, and he grabbed my arm and twisted it painfully. That, thankfully, was the end of my relationship with George Austin.

Late into the summer of 1984, I went on some wonderful backpacking hikes with Eric and Kell. We loved Eunice Lake and Tolmie Peak in Mt. Rainier National Park. We hiked and camped at Summit Lake, near the park. We also did Rachel Lake and Rampart Ridge in the Cascades. Once, we were hiking to Rachel Lake when the rain started and totally drenched us. We had to pitch our tent along the trail before we even arrived at the lake. It sounds like a difficult time, but it was really fun. I served Eric and Kell hot breakfast in their sleeping bags in the morning.

I love looking at the pictures of my boys, smiling and all bundled up in their rain gear and backpacks.

One time, on an overnight backpacking trip to a lake near Snoqualmie Pass, I actually packed a small inflatable raft. It's hard to believe I managed to stuff it in my pack with everything else, but somehow, I did. Eric, Kell, and I had such fun paddling the raft to an island in the lake. We had a wonderful time exploring the island.

Hiking and backpacking with Eric and Kell in the North Cascade Mountains

Penny Crom was one of the nurse practitioners I hired for PacMed in 1984. Although she was six years younger than me, we had a lot in common. We both loved the mountains. Penny was a more experienced hiker and mountain climber than I was. She was also an avid competitive bicyclist.

One day, Penny and I were chatting together in the clinic conference room at lunch when she suddenly asked me, "I know you have been married before. What do you think of marriage now?" I answered truthfully that, although my marriage had been a mistake, I still believed marriage could be a positive, fulfilling experience. Then she said, "Chris and I are getting married, and I really trust him." Penny Crom and Chris Mroz got married a few months later on March 9, 1985. They are great friends of mine to this day.

After their wedding, Penny and Chris stayed in a cozy cottage called Sea Sprite Cottage on the ocean at Tolvanna Park, just south of Cannon Beach, in Oregon. On Penny's recommendation, I rented Sea Sprite Cottage for spring vacation with my boys three years in a row. Eric and Kell loved riding beach cycles on the hard, wet sand along the waves; exploring the tide pools around Haystack Rock; and flying kites.

Penny was a skilled downhill skier and a member of the ski patrol at Crystal Mountain Resort. I had done very little downhill skiing, but I loved cross-country skiing. What I really wanted to learn was telemark skiing to get around in the back country in winter. Penny told me telemark skiing lessons were being offered at Snoqualmie Pass, so we signed up for a few weeks. I improved, and it was so much fun, but it was hard to keep pace with Penny.

In April 1985, I took Eric and Kell to Disneyworld in Florida for a week. We stayed right in the Magic Kingdom in a little camping trailer, secluded in the woods. The three of us never had to leave the "magic" of Disneyworld. We would wake up, walk through the woods, and catch a boat that motored us across the lake to breakfast and more of the amazing Magic Kingdom. We didn't have a care in the world that week. Over the next two years, we went to Disneyworld twice more, for a week each time. Those were wonderful times with my boys.

My sister Jacquey was very devoted to Eric and Kell, and they just loved her in return. Jacquey is really "half-kid" herself; she understands what it's like to be a child. Jacquey was the associate director at the University of California Lawrence Hall of Science, which focused on teaching science to children in new and creative ways.

Eric and Kell would visit Jacquey every summer for a week. I would send "Boy A" down on an airplane, and he would spend an idyllic week with Aunt Jacquey and Uncle Steve doing all sorts of fun activities. I would then drive down to Berkeley with "Boy B." Boy B and I would have fun going down the Oregon Coast and visiting the California redwoods. When I got to Berkeley, I would leave Boy B with Aunt Jacquey and Uncle Steve, and drive Boy A back to Seattle with me. We would alternate which boy was A and B every year.

Eric and Kell with me in Berkeley: picking up Boy A and dropping off Boy B

In 1985, Pacific Medical Center closed its hospital; it was an older building and needed renovation. Also, there were many other hospitals in Seattle. There was a need for outpatient clinics in other parts of the city and suburbs. Pacific Medical Center clinics sprang up in several suburbs around Seattle: Kirkland, Bellevue, Renton, Lynnwood, and North Seattle. Several of the nurse practitioners I was supervising went to work in these new clinics. Although the main hospital on Beacon Hill was closed, we still had pediatric and adult medicine outpatient clinics and saw plenty of patients.

I had been the first of my female friends to have children. Now nearly all of them did. My athletic women friends and I started "Mothers Climbs." We were all proud to be mothers and still active enough for mountain climbing. In the summer of 1990, Debbie Anderson, Terri Wolber, Penny Crom, and I spent two days in the North Cascades National Park climbing Black Peak, an 8,975-foot rocky, non-volcanic peak. It was a gorgeous day, with perfect blue sky and minimal wind. In the pictures we took, I saw that I was the only one wearing a rock helmet and seriously worried about falling. But we all completed this beautiful rock climb in one piece.

I was still looking for a good man, with little success. All my women friends were in long-term, stable marriages to really wonderful men. I wondered if all the unmarried men in their 30s and 40s were flawed, dishonest, or incapable of commitment. Fortunately, I escaped any pregnancy or disease. I had my heart broken several times, but only one was really devastating.

Back in August 1983, when I had been divorced from Richard less than a year, I got a call one day from Rich Spivak, the man I had been engaged to during my sophomore year at Western Reserve University. I hadn't seen or heard from him in 17 years, and it was quite a shock to hear his voice. He had his own company, The Potomac Group, in Cleveland, and he told me he was separated from his wife and had a ten-year-old son, Ben. He occasionally had business in Seattle, and during that fall we had dinner together. The spark of our previous relationship years ago was still very much there, but there was no talk of trying again.

In August 1988, long after Rich's divorce was final, he came to Seattle on business again. We had a lovely dinner and started a passionate love affair. Each of us flew back and forth between Seattle and Cleveland over the next two years. We went to an extravagant bar mitzvah in New York City and spent a week in fancy Hawaiian hotels on both Maui and Kauai. He met all my friends, and I met his friends.

Rich didn't really like Cleveland, but he loved the Pacific Northwest. Our plan was to wait until Ben graduated from high school, and then Rich would move to Seattle, and we would get married.

I was fine with this plan. I had my career, my children, all my longtime friends, and I loved the Pacific Northwest. I was comfortable waiting and seeing each other long-distance until our children were in college. I think Rich tried at the beginning; he wanted our relationship to work. But in the end it just wasn't okay for him. If he didn't have a woman with him all the time, in the same city, he couldn't sustain a happy life.

So on October 1, 1990, I received a letter from Rich telling me he had to end our relationship; he couldn't live with his life on hold. He also informed me he had been seeing another woman for the past two months.

I had never experienced the crushing feeling of having my world turn upside down like that. On October 23, 1990, I wrote Rich. Rereading the letter now, it sounds pretty dramatic, but it was exactly how I felt at the time. In part, the letter reads:

> You have always been, and are still, the
> love of my entire life. You have always been,
> and are still, one of the most significant
> and important people in my life. Over the
> past two years, you have become a huge
> focus of my everyday existence, and have
> been inextricably involved in my vision of my
> future. . . . Since receiving your letter ending
> our relationship, I have been in the most serious
> depression I have ever experienced. . . . I must
> focus all of my strength now on trying to recover
> from this, the single greatest loss of my life.
> Under the circumstances, I cannot call you,
> write you, or see you in the foreseeable
> future. I must get better again. I cannot
> live with this amount of pain.

This was the first time since college I had known real depression. Eventually, though, as the winter turned into spring, life started to look better. Penny Crom called me in May and said that Piro Kramar, an ophthalmologist at PacMed, was leading a climb of Mt. Rainier in July.

"Lynne," Penny said, "let's go—we can share a tent!"

I was so excited. Piro was an internationally-known climber, having been on an all-women's climb of Annapurna, a 26,545-foot high peak situated in north-central Nepal. Just the thought of this climb lifted my spirits.

Penny picked me up at 5:30 a.m. on July 18, 1991, and we drove to the White River Campground on the north side of Mount Rainier. We met Piro and a few others from PacMed at the campground and hiked up to Glacier Basin. From Glacier Basin, we ascended the Interglacier to Camp Schurman (elevation 9,500 feet) and Steamboat Prow. Early the next morning, we put on our crampons, roped up, and began climbing. Piro was leading, I was in the middle, and Penny was at the end of the rope. It was a truly exhilarating experience. We wove around some deep crevasses, putting one foot carefully in front of the other. The air was clear, cold, and beautiful. Reaching the summit that day in July 1991 with Penny and Piro was an amazing experience.

We descended back to Camp Sherman and spent the night there before hiking back to our car at sunrise. We were very elated and very tired. After that climb, the world looked so much more welcoming and happy to me. Worries I previously had about my life retreated to the back of my mind.

———————◆•◆———————

Work and climbing mountains were important to me, but not as important as my children. Making sure Eric and Kell received an excellent education was one of my top priorities. Eric had excelled in school ever since kindergarten. In grade school, he was in a special program that included parental participation and allowed him to learn at his own pace. He was a straight-A student, and all his teachers were very complimentary of him.

Eric took swimming lessons at our local pool, and became an excellent swimmer. He swam competitively on a local swim team, Wave Aquatics, and lettered all four years in high school. He also worked as a lifeguard at Juanita High School, and taught swimming lessons.

Kell entered kindergarten at age six in September 1984, in the same program at Northshore School District that Eric was in. He had the same teacher as Eric, Shirley Hawkes. She was a wonderful teacher who had a strong, positive emotional connection with Eric. Shirley was a good choice for Kell too, but he presented other challenges. At the start of the year, he had a difficult time resolving conflicts with his peers, but he worked hard to improve his social skills. Like Eric, he also excelled in reading.

Kell's first-grade teacher was Laurie McLean. She was new and inexperienced. There was immediate conflict between her and Kell. She wrote in her winter report:

> Kell is a bright child who is not working up to his potential. He is often uncooperative and resistant to instruction. He needs to resolve some issues that are beyond the scope of school.

The following spring, I had a school conference with Laurie McLean. She said Kell was "angry, detached, drawing inward, internally distracted, choosing to play alone, having social conflicts with other children, and having poor conflict resolution."

At the end of his first-grade year, I decided to put Kell in a traditional grade school. Interestingly, many years later, when I was working as a nurse practitioner in dermatology, Laurie McLean came into my clinic to see me as a new patient. We recognized each other, and she remembered Kell too. Laurie told me that looking back, she realized with regret that she hadn't treated Kell with the expertise and compassion he deserved.

Kell always said he hated school. I don't think it was challenging or interesting for him. Additionally, although bullying was not talked about much in those days, I now know that was a significant factor in his unhappiness. I came across something Kell wrote at the beginning of sixth grade:

> Sixth grade is going to be boring. I know
> that because second, third, fourth, and fifth grade
> were boring. Sixth grade is going to be
> like any other grade at Maywood, except
> that it will be different stuff.

At Maywood Hills Elementary, Kell made a good friend—one whose friendship lasted well into his adulthood: Eric Kingsbury. Eric is now 47 years old and a successful businessman. He lives in West Seattle, and Joe and I see him regularly for dinner. His friendship is very important to me.

Both Kell and Eric Kingsbury had similar interests. They were both members of the Columbia Boys Choir in grade school, and of a Boy Scout troop in Bothell. The troop went on several hikes, and I went along as an adult chaperone. In September 1990, Kell, Eric Kingsbury, and I did an overnight six-mile hike with their Boy Scout troop to Spider Meadows in the Central Cascade Mountains. We picked loads of mountain huckleberries, and I made huckleberry pancakes for breakfast. We had two tents—Eric and Kell in one, and me in another. I can still hear them talking and laughing in the night.

On Friday nights, Eric was often out with his friends. Kell, Eric Kingsbury, and I would go to Half Price Books, a used bookstore in Seattle. I would usually find a chair to collapse in, read, and relax, while Kell and Eric spent the time searching out interesting books. I love my memories of Half Price Books on Friday nights with the two of them.

In 1989, John, Berdi, and I decided it was time to explore the entire Bailey Traverse in Olympic National Park. The three of us, including

Penny, had done the first part of the Bailey Traverse a few years earlier. We asked Penny and her husband, Chris, to join us, along with another couple that we had met on a previous trip. But there was one complication, Penny was now five months pregnant, and her obstetrician told her he didn't want her hiking anywhere where she could not return home in one day. So that meant Penny could not join us for the whole trip. Chris and Penny decided to come just the first day with us. After that, we would go on to do the rest of the Bailey Traverse, sadly, without them.

After Chris and Penny left us, we had trouble finding the Bailey Traverse route, partially due to thick fog. We ended up in very difficult terrain. One late afternoon, we saw a huge bear slowly ambling toward us down a slope. We waved our hands and jumped up and down, trying to scare the bear away, and it finally disappeared.

Later in the trip, climbing up some rocks with a full backpack and trying to maintain my balance, I fractured my left index finger against a rock. We were off-trail, trying to find our way back. We had to climb up rocks with some exposure. I was hesitant to try. Berdi, who is taller than me, climbed up first, and I watched carefully where she placed her hands and feet. When I tried, I missed one handhold and felt myself falling backward. I told myself in a split second that there was no way I was going to let myself fall. I slammed my body back into the rocks. When I looked down, I saw my left index finger was bent at an angle. It looked to me as if it was just dislocated. I stabilized myself on the rock and started pulling at my finger to see if I could relocate the bones, but soon realized it was both broken and dislocated.

As a result, we headed back to civilization and never quite finished the traditional Bailey Traverse route. I saw an orthopedic surgeon days later, and now have two pins in my left index finger. In retrospect, it was a good thing that Penny didn't stay on that trip with us. Sometimes things work out for the best.

In September 1991, Kell entered seventh grade at Canyon Park Junior High School. I knew he was unhappy there, but I didn't realize how significant the bullying was—it was something Eric hadn't encountered during his junior high days.

Kell was very smart, but he wasn't testing as well at school as he should have. I arranged for him to be tested by Mary Oates, an educational professional at the master's level in Bellingham. She recommended that Kell receive counseling "to help him with his oppositional behaviors, as they are obviously affecting academic progress." Kell began seeing Albert Reichert, a pediatrician in Seattle who worked exclusively in psychological and behavioral pediatrics, regularly from ages 13 to 18. Dr. Reichert diagnosed Kell with mild to moderate depression and ADHD. He prescribed different medications, but nothing really worked. I kept thinking Kell would get better in time.

When I talked with Dr. Reichert many months later, he said Kell was like a quiet boy rowing a boat slowly in one direction, and I was a mother in a speedboat rushing around him. It was hard for me to know what to think about that. I was frantically trying to help Kell as quickly and efficiently as I could. Dr. Reichert's comments made me feel helpless. I didn't know any other way to be.

If I had to do it all over again, I would have moved Kell to a private school, where he would have been in smaller classes with better teachers more sensitive to his needs. I did not have much money in those days, but I would have found it. Attitudes about school were different back then. I believed you couldn't change the world to suit your child. I thought we had to help our children adjust to—and be productive and happy in—the world we had, not the one we wanted.

At home, Kell was a loving, contemplative boy and a voracious reader. A very good swimmer, he joined Wave Aquatics, like Eric. He didn't like competition, though, so after one swim meet, he said he did not want to swim competitively again. He also tried soccer and horseback riding, neither of which really held his interest.

Kell loved animals. John and Berdi gave the boys two cats, but they were really Kell's cats. One of them was a big yellow tom cat named Whiskers. Kell was so attached to Whiskers, and it was an awful day when Whiskers crawled under the hood of the car next door to enjoy the warmth and fell asleep. When the neighbor started the car, Whiskers was trapped under the hood and killed. Kell was devastated. When your child is hurting, it is so much worse than any hurt you personally might experience.

Then, Kell fixated on wanting a dog. He wanted a whippet. I searched and discovered a whippet breeder nearby, with a new litter of puppies. Kell picked out "Howie," a six-week-old male whippet. He was thrilled.

———————◆•◆———————

PacMed had opened a new clinic at Totem Lake in Kirkland, about four miles from my house. They needed another primary care provider there. Rick Ludwig, the chief medical officer of PacMed, and also my office mate, asked me if I would move from working at the main campus on Beacon Hill in Seattle, where I had been since 1983, to the new Totem Lake Clinic in Kirkland. The move would dramatically shorten my daily commute. Although I would really miss the Beacon Hill staff and my patients, I said yes.

The shorter commute was a big relief to me, and the Totem Lake Clinic staff was friendly and welcoming. There were eight full-time internal medicine physicians and a variety of part-time specialist physicians, along with a full support staff. The medical director was Jeff Brown, a young family practice physician who was married and had two small children.

After a few weeks, though, Jeff started exhibiting some strange behaviors. He began playing loud rock and roll music from his office, which could be heard clearly in the clinic hallways. I heard rumors he had been seen kissing one of the young medical assistants. Then, he started wearing aqua socks, Hawaiian shirts unbuttoned so his chest hair showed, and sunglasses when he was seeing patients. He was also hyperenergetic.

I called Rick Ludwig and told him what was happening with Jeff Brown's behavior and dress. Rick arrived at the clinic the next day and had a talk with Jeff. After Rick's visit, Jeff's behavior settled down a bit, but it still wasn't anywhere near acceptable. I knew something was still not right. Rick called to check in with me, and I told him Jeff's behavior was not much better. Rick's advice was to give Jeff some more time.

A few weeks later, Jeff appeared in my office and said he was admitting himself to a hospital for "some mental health issues." And then he was gone. He didn't tell anyone else. I called a lunch meeting with all the internal medicine physicians and specialists, and made immediate plans to take care of Jeff's patients and his administrative duties. Then I called Rick Ludwig and told him that Jeff had left the clinic. I also told him about the meeting with the physicians and staff.

"Who led the meeting?" Rick asked.

I responded, "I did."

"Okay, Lynne," Rick replied, "just keep it up, and I'll try to find a physician medical director."

For the next month, I stepped into the role of medical director of the Totem Lake Clinic. Honestly, it was really fun. I was energized. I arranged with Rick to cut my clinic hours from full-time to two-thirds (the usual ratio of clinic time to administrative time for medical directors) so I could take on the responsibilities of medical director. I had the full support of all the physicians and staff at the clinic. I think the doctors were actually relieved that they didn't have to worry about the job themselves.

One month later, Jeff Brown returned from his psychiatric medical leave. He arrived at the clinic, ready to assume his job as medical director. But now I was the acting medical director of the Totem Lake Clinic. I had moved into the medical director's large private office, which had a bigger computer system, and a table and chairs for private conversations with other staff. Jeff quickly became upset and very angry.

I called Rick Ludwig, and he arrived at the clinic the next day. A frightening meeting took place in my office. I was mostly silent. Jeff remained standing, yelling and swearing at both of us. At the end of the meeting, Rick said Jeff could continue seeing patients at the clinic, but I was to continue as the medical director. Jeff glared at me, grim and angry.

After that, it was very unsettling being around Jeff. He was angry all the time. Once, as he walked by me in the hallway, he grabbed my arm and twisted it. His grip left a small bruise. After I told him to stop, he just glared at me and continued walking down the hall.

I called Rick Ludwig. He told me he was working on a plan to move Jeff out of the clinic but for now, he said, "Just don't be in the clinic alone with him!"

I don't know why I didn't demand protection for myself. Physicians protect one another, and Rick was protecting Jeff, trying to get him out of the clinic without too much of a fuss.

When Jeff Brown finally left Totem Lake, he left suddenly. One day he was there, and the next he was gone. The following day, I went into my office. The covered bookshelves above my desk, which I always left open, were closed. When I opened the lower bookshelf, there was a cup full of urine with a dipstick in it. Jeff Brown had been in my office and left a parting message for me.

It was a relief for everyone when Jeff Brown left. I was also excited about the opportunity of being a medical director. Now, I was at the PHASE Board meetings not only as the supervisor of all the nurse practitioners and physician assistants at PacMed, but also as the medical director of the PacMed Totem Lake Clinic.

Later in 1991, Rick Ludwig left his job as chief medical officer of Pacific Medical Center, and another internist, Meredith Mathews, took his place. Shortly after this, Meredith paid me a visit at Totem Lake. He asked me, "Lynne, why are you being paid so little? You have had no pay increase to the level of medical director."

I was stunned. I was so thrilled to be the medical director that I had never thought to ask for an increase in salary. Rick Ludwig never offered a salary commensurate with my new job, and I foolishly never asked.

But now, overnight, my salary at Pacific Medical Center nearly doubled. Eric wanted to apply to several very expensive private colleges and universities. Suddenly, paying for Eric's college education was much more doable. I was flying high.

Meredith Mathews was very supportive of me. He told me he wanted me to go to a week-long national conference for medical directors in Palm Springs, California, that September. The Ritz Carlton Hotel, where it was being held, was so exclusive that, at the time, one could not be seen wearing shorts in the lobby. I found that out the hard way when I tried to go running before dinner, appearing in the lobby in my running outfit. There were lots of stares from the staff before I found out the rules.

I learned so much at that medical directors conference, and I tried to soak up all the new ideas and information. There were about 200 medical directors from all over the United States. Everyone had name tags, reading "So-and-so, MD." I had the only name tag at the conference with the initials "ARNP." I was able to attend three other medical directors conferences in the 11 years I was medical director at the PacMed Totem Lake Clinic.

That fall, Eric was a senior in high school. He had told me that, at the end of the summer, he wanted to apply for early admissions to Cornell University. This meant he would only apply to Cornell University and nowhere else. His application needed to be postmarked by September 30. If he was admitted, he would hear from Cornell at the end of December. He had an essay to write, and a voluminous application form of many pages with questions needing lengthy answers. After much nagging from me, he finally completed the application late in the afternoon of September 30, and he and I drove to the post office to mail it.

The rest of that fall was a hard one for Eric. He was such a deep thinker. He seemed morose and unhappy. One day, he said he did not feel well and didn't want to go to school. That was unusual because he was rarely sick. I went to work and left him at home.

Later that day, Eric called me at the clinic. He asked me, "What kind of injury would you have if you jumped off one of the bridges over the freeway?"

I replied that you would be seriously injured and would probably die. Just after I hung up, I became puzzled, and then alarmed. I called Chuck Cowan, the pediatrician on-call that day. Chuck told me to immediately cancel my patients for the day, go home, and insist that Eric get some counseling immediately. If he refused, I would take away the television, the car, and even food in the house until he agreed to seek counseling.

When I got home, Eric was angry and defiant. He said I couldn't tell him what to do. I tried to reason with him, using every persuasive tactic that I knew, but nothing worked. Finally, I called his girlfriend, Holly. She immediately came over. Holly was wonderful. They both sat on the front porch and spent a long time talking together. At the end of the day, Eric reluctantly agreed to see Dan O'Connell, PhD, a clinical psychologist at PacMed.

In the last week of December 1991, Eric received a letter in the mail from Cornell University. He had been accepted for early admissions.

After climbing Mt. Rainier with Penny and Piro Kramer at the end of July, in September, Piro invited all of us from the climb to her house on Vashon Island for a celebratory luncheon. I was waiting in line for the ferry when I saw Penny just ahead of me, talking to a man. She smiled and waved me over.

"Lynne, this is Max Junejo, a climbing friend of Piro's; he'll be joining us for lunch."

Max lived near the ferry dock in West Seattle, and had just walked down from his house. He was a bronze-skinned man with blackish-gray hair, a wiry athletic build, and a beautiful smile.

After lunch at Piro's house, I offered Max a ride back to the ferry dock. On the way, he told me he came from Pakistan. He was a civil engineer working for the City of Seattle, and had previously worked as an aeronautical engineer at Boeing. Max was an avid, experienced mountain climber who, unfortunately, had severe coronary artery disease and was being treated by Bob Putsch, an internist who worked with Penny and me at PacMed. I knew that because Penny had told me earlier. Max was a long-time member of the Seattle Mountaineers and had led all the most difficult and challenging routes on Mt. Rainier.

As we talked, there was an instant connection between us. Max loved the mountains as much as I did.

That winter, Max left with some of his mountaineering friends to climb some mountains in New Zealand. He sent me a postcard saying he'd see me when he returned to Seattle.

Before the three-day Memorial Day weekend in 1992, Max asked me if I wanted to hike up and camp at Lake Ann on the meadowed slopes of Mount Shuksan. I had taken my boys up there a few times in the summer, but now the way up would be largely covered in snow.

That weekend, the weather was beautiful, sunny, and gorgeous. We hit snow fairly early. When we finally reached the lake, it was completely covered in snow, as were all the meadows surrounding it. I pitched my tent nearby. Mount Shuksan, with its gleaming, hanging glaciers stood high above us. There wasn't a living soul around. It was a glorious evening.

After dinner, Max, quite embarrassed, informed me that he had forgotten to pack his sleeping bag. I thought, *You have got to be kidding!* Max ended up sleeping in my tent with his parka on and his feet in the depths of his now-empty backpack.

The next day was pristine, with sun shining on the snow and ice of the glacier. On the way back, Max took my hand and held it as we approached our car.

I tried to understand where I might fit into Max's life. I knew he had a wife, Irene, and they had two adult children. He had just retired from the City of Seattle as a civil engineer. He said that, although he was very loyal to Irene and would never leave her, they did not have an intimate marriage. They were more like "housemates." He had the freedom of coming and going without having to explain to anyone in the family where he was going or what he was doing. Later, when I met his children, his 32-year-old daughter, Yasmeen, told me she never remembered her parents ever sharing the same bedroom.

In June 1992, Irene and John Meulmans, two of Washington's most well-known mountaineers, invited Max and me to climb Tomyhoi Peak (7,451 feet) in the North Cascades of Washington State. It was a thrilling climb, and I learned some rock climbing techniques from Irene on the way up.

That night, I pitched my tent in the beautiful meadows of Yellow Aster Butte. Max shared my tent. John and Irene had to leave after the Tomyhoi Peak climb, but Max and I had a few more days.

Max looked at me with a radiant smile and said, "Lynne, let's climb Mt. Shuksan together!"

Max talked to me about his life on that trip. He was 60 years old, and I was 45. He was born in India to a Muslim family, the oldest of eight children. His father worked in an administrative position for the Hindu prince of that region of India. Max was very close to his mother, who was only 15 years older than he was. He was 16 years old when his family had to flee India to Pakistan in 1947. A few months after they arrived in Pakistan, his mother died. Max eventually earned baccalaureate degrees in aeronautical engineering and civil engineering from Indiana University and Purdue University respectively. In 1962, he moved to Seattle to work for Boeing as an aeronautical engineer.

After this climb, Max and I hiked again to Lake Ann, roped up, and began climbing to the summit of Mt. Shuksan (9,127 feet). Max had climbed Mt. Shuksan a number of times before from different routes. He led the way, showing me safe ways of walking on ice and moving from place to place with an ice axe and crampons. I had learned a lot of techniques in my mountain climbing class at the University of Washington, but Max took me to a whole other level. We climbed up a series of gullies, rock chimneys, ramps, and ledges, crossing the White Salmon Glacier and then the Sulphide Glacier. It was a thrill to climb the Fisher Chimneys, a large, three-sided rock pyramid standing more than 1,000 feet above four encircling glaciers. We free-climbed it together, Max sometimes hauling me up over a tall ledge with a rope and his strong arms. We then descended back to Lake Ann and camped.

I sensed we were falling in love. Max assured me he had a special arrangement with Irene, and that for many years they'd had no romantic or marital relationship. He wanted me to get to know Irene, as well as his adult children, Aziz and Yasmeen. I wasn't sure what I was getting myself into.

Meanwhile, out of the blue, I received a letter from my old boyfriend, Rich Spivak, right around the time of Eric's high school graduation. He wanted to see me again when he came to Seattle on business. He neglected to tell me that he'd married the woman he was seeing when he ended our relationship in October 1990. He wrote:

> You are in my thoughts every day.
> I know I am still deeply in love with
> you. You are woven so tightly into the
> fabric of my life that almost every-
> thing, in some way, is connected to you.
> Most of the time I think about you
> I smile—either inside or both inside
> and outside. I miss looking into
> your eyes. I miss the smell of your
> hair, your touch, your voice. I miss
> your incredible, loving passion. I
> have never before, or since, experienced
> such love. How we could
> get lost in each other, two becoming
> one, hours of nothing but you.
> I truly miss you.

I was completely shocked to get this letter. Fortunately, I had moved on. I called an old college friend who confirmed that yes, Rich really had married that woman.

I wrote back to Rich that there was no way I would get together with him under the circumstances. I was grateful that I had moved on from all the hurt and misery. I had my own life.

Later that summer, Max took me to his house in West Seattle and introduced me to his son, Aziz; his daughter, Yasmeen; and his wife, Irene. All were warm and welcoming. Aziz and his wife and two children lived with Max and Irene. Yasmeen was divorced and living on her own. Max told them all how much I loved the mountains and that he and I had plans for exploring them together now that he was retired.

I couldn't get enough of the mountains with Max. We did several memorable climbs with my friends, Dave, Suzanne, John, Berdi, Penny, and Chris. All felt comfortable with Max and really liked him. He was so much fun.

Berdi Safford and I climbing one of many mountains
during our long friendship

In September 1992, Max and I drove down to Yosemite National Park in California and climbed Half Dome, a famous rock formation named for its distinct shape. One side is a sheer face, while the other three sides are smooth and round, making it appear like a dome cut in half. There's a fixed rope at the top, which makes the climb a lot safer. After we left Yosemite, we drove to Berkeley and I introduced Max to my sister Jacquey; her husband, Steve; my three nephews; and my mother.

I began having dinner at Max's house with Irene and the family. Aziz frequently did the cooking. He would make wonderful Pakistani dishes. When Irene cooked, she made American dishes, such as her excellent pot roast. Irene was a heavy-set, white-haired Caucasian woman, eight years older than I was. She was very quiet, and I spent time trying to get to know her. Whenever Max and I were out and about somewhere, I made sure I called her to let her know where we were and when we would be back. I didn't realize how important those phone calls were until she told me later.

Still, I wasn't sure I trusted Max. He was a Muslim and a married man. How could this possibly be a monogamous relationship?

In October, Max was gone for ten days, climbing in the North Cascades with friends. When he came back, I met him for dinner. I decided I would be in control of this relationship, so I approached the subject by saying that I knew we didn't have a monogamous relationship. Unbeknownst to me, Max thought I meant that he was not the only man in my life.

Max responded, "Well then, I will just have to get in line with the other men."

That statement cleared things up to some degree. We then had a serious talk.

He told me that he and Irene had not had an intimate sexual relationship for many, many years. They had nothing in common except the children and grandchildren. Despite that fact, he felt he owed her a great deal. After they came to Seattle, Max sponsored most of his brothers to come to the United States and become citizens, which he couldn't have done without Irene's help. There was no way he would ever divorce her. He said that in Islam it was possible to have a second wife. It wouldn't be a legal marriage, but a religious marriage, which was much more important to him. I listened, not sure what to think.

On New Year's Day 1993, Max told me that he wanted us to be married sometime that year. He promised he would talk to Irene about it soon. I wasn't sure about any of it, but I knew I was in love with Max.

On January 12, 1993, I received another letter from Rich Spivak. He apologized for not being honest about being married, but he wanted more than anything to see me again for a weekend interlude, even though he was still married to Wendy. This time I called him and firmly said no again. That was the last time I had any contact with him.

Max was an avid squash player, and I'd often meet him for dinner after his games. One evening that January, I was waiting in the dining room of the College Club where Max played squash for him to finish. He was a little late, which was unusual. Finally, one of his friends came into the dining room and asked if I would come into the men's locker room. There was Max, leaning against the lockers and breathing into an oxygen mask. He told me he couldn't catch his breath. He did not look in acute distress, but he was perspiring profusely. I took his pulse; it was over 160 beats per minute. I immediately called 911.

The paramedics arrived quickly and determined that he was in ventricular tachycardia. They used a defibrillator to convert his heart rate to a normal sinus rhythm, then rushed him to the hospital. In a total state of shock, I called Irene, drove to her house to pick her up, and went to the hospital. When we arrived, the doctors said he would be held for several more days for evaluation.

The next day, Irene and I went to the hospital again. Irene was standing at the head of the bed, and I was standing at the foot. Yasmeen was in the cafeteria. Max looked at Irene and said that he had survived because I had recognized the danger and called 911. He added that I had become very important to him. He told Irene that he would like to marry me, and he asked if that would be okay with her. Irene, without skipping a beat, said yes.

Max looked at me, beaming, and said, "Irene said yes."

Irene gave me a small smile and a nod. That was how we made the decision to marry.

I ran down to the cafeteria to talk with Yasmeen. I was worried about her response. I said, "Yasmeen, I have something important to tell you."

She just smiled at me and said, "Is it the good news?"

I answered that I hoped she would think it was good news, and that her father and I were going to get married, and her mother had agreed.

With an even bigger smile, Yasmeen immediately replied, "I am so glad that Dad chose you!"

Later, when Max told Aziz the news, he said, "Well, finally, Dad."

Max had inherited coronary artery disease. Each of his five brothers also had it and eventually had to be treated as well. Both Max and I knew that another cardiac event might occur again in the future, even if we were careful. Max asked me later that week if I was sure I wanted to get married, knowing the fragility of his heart. There was no question in my mind. My answer was absolutely yes.

Irene wanted to make my wedding gown herself. She was a wonderful seamstress. In February 1993, Max, Irene, and I drove to a fabric shop in Vancouver, British Columbia to buy the material for my wedding dress. Irene picked out beautiful white satin material with beads, sequins, and embroidery. She even helped me pick out my wedding ring.

Kell and his best friend, Eric Kingsbury, were happy to learn of our upcoming wedding. Both of them had been to Max's house several times, and Max had taken Kell downhill skiing with us. Eric Kingsbury and Kell both really liked Max.

My son Eric was in the second semester of his freshman year at Cornell. He had a new girlfriend, Kye Soon Hong. Her parents now lived in Korea, although her family had spent much of Kye's life in the United States. She was a sophomore at Cornell. I told Eric I was getting married to Max, and that I would like him to come to the wedding. He was shocked.

"What! You are getting married to a man who is already married? What am I going to tell Kye?"

I said he did not have to tell Kye anything. I also told him he didn't have to come to our wedding if he didn't want to.

"Of course I have to come! I am your son!" he said, and abruptly ended the call. The next day, he called. He and Kye would both come to the wedding.

Now, we had to plan our wedding. Max wanted to be married during the holy month of Ramadan, which would take place in March that year. We set the wedding date for Sunday, March 21, at Max and Irene's house. Reality began to set in. Some of my friends were confused, even a bit angry. This upset me, but Max told me I couldn't expect most people to approve of marrying someone who was already married. By nature, I'm a big people pleaser, and this news of our upcoming marriage did not please the people I wanted it to.

We also had pushback from some of Max's relatives. Max was the head of his big family now in the United States, primarily thanks to him bringing them here one by one. Max called a family meeting that included his siblings, their children and grandchildren, nieces and nephews and cousins, and a lot of Muslim friends. Neither Irene nor I were invited. Seema went with Max, and she told me later about what happened.

At the meeting, Max announced that he was marrying me, and that Irene, Aziz, and Yasmeen were all in favor of the marriage.

"Who here is in favor of and will support my new marriage?" he asked. A few hands went up, but most did not. Max continued in a loud voice, "Who here will not support my new marriage?"

Most of those in attendance stood up. Max looked around, took Seema's hand, and walked out. That was the end of the meeting.

Some of my friends came to the wedding: John and Berdi, Bev and Larry Ricker, and Barbara. Bill did not come because I was marrying a man who was already married. Suzanne and Dave wanted to come, but were unfortunately out of town. Jacquey, her husband, Steve; her two children; and my mother came. Eric and Kell were there, along with Eric's new girlfriend, Kye. Of course, Irene, Aziz, Seema, and Yasmeen were there as well. We were married by Salim, a Muslim cleric who was engaged to Yasmeen. The ceremony was short and sweet. Irene gave me a big hug afterward. Aziz made a wonderfully delicious spread of Pakistani food for everyone.

After all our guests left, Irene presented Max and me with a picnic dinner of roast chicken, biryani, and roti. Max had made a reservation at a nearby hotel, and off we went.

On our way, he squeezed my hand and said a little breathlessly, "Babe, we did it!"

Max and I just after our wedding on March 21, 2003

Everyone at the clinic seemed very happy about my new marriage. Max was such a gregarious, outgoing, kind, and energetic man—everyone seemed to connect with him. But right away, we were confronted with conflicts I didn't anticipate. Soon after our wedding, we went to the College Club for dinner, and when the waiter came with the bill, I paid my portion with my own credit card, as I usually did. Max was so angry, really beside himself. There were a lot of tears on my part as I tried to figure out the problem. Max thought that by paying my own bill in front of all those men who knew him and knew that I was his wife was a sign that I did not take our marriage seriously. He wanted to pay the bill himself.

We came from such different worlds, and despite the love between us, I did not recognize beforehand the potential conflicts. I was constantly making mistakes when dealing with Muslim men. One time, I was at Max's house conversing with a young, well-educated Muslim man. I was sitting close to him on the couch because there was nowhere else to sit.

I accidentally touched his hand, and later, Max told me that was not acceptable in that setting.

Another time, I was introduced to a Muslim man at a social event, and I spontaneously held out my hand to shake his. He just looked at me stoically, with his hands behind his back, and said with disdain, "I will not touch your hand." I felt mortified.

At Muslim social events, there was an imaginary line down the middle of the room, with men on one side and women on the other. People would be milling around and mixing, but neither the women nor the men would cross that imaginary line. It was very confusing. I was always worried I would do something wrong.

Occasionally, Max hosted social events involving Muslim guests. The men would all sit together on the floor in a circle, while the women would sit in another circle nearby. I tried to sit on the edge of the women's circle, nearer the men, because their conversation was always more interesting. I never participated in the men's conversation—that would have been unthinkable—but at least I got to hear what they were talking about.

As time went by, Max and I learned to manage these challenges much better. We were both, in our own ways, working hard to see each other's point of view and make adjustments.

Most of the time, Max and I socialized with either his non-Muslim friends or my friends. I could say he was more comfortable in non-Muslim situations, but he was actually comfortable in both parts of his life. The Muslim part of his life just was more complicated when I was there.

———◆•◆———

Kell was seeing Dr. Reichert regularly and was still suffering from bullying at Canyon Park Junior High. He never talked much about it, and it's only in retrospect that I've realized what a terrible problem it was. In those days, teachers would suggest parents ask their child each day, "On a scale from one to ten, how was your day?"

Every day, Kell would say, "Mom, it was a 5.5."

One day, Kell came up with a solution to the mental torture he was enduring at school: he would change his residence from mine in Bothell to his father's in Seattle. Then, he would be able to go to a Seattle public school and not have to be in the Northshore School District. I knew he preferred living with me rather than with his father and his father's wife, Susan Loitz, who wasn't always nice to Kell. But it was better than the suffering he was experiencing at Canyon Park Junior High.

So, beginning in September 1992, Kell lived weekdays with his father and weekends with me. He was definitely happier. He tested into all the advanced classes at Nathan Hale High School in Seattle. He also took a drama class and was in a play.

Kell loved theatre, and he and I went to many productions at the Bathhouse Theatre on Green Lake together. We saw several Shakespearean plays there. He especially liked *A Midsummer Night's Dream*. He also enjoyed opera. We went to *Madame Butterfly*, *Porgy and Bess*, and *Rigoletto* during his high school years. Kell was always so much fun to be with.

Max and his good friend Eddie Bolton had worked with the Mongolian Olympic Committee, hosting a team from Mongolia during the Goodwill Games in Seattle in 1990. As thanks for their help, Max and Eddie were invited to come to Mongolia for a sightseeing trip in 1994. We would leave June 20 and return July 17. Eddie and his wife, Hille, would join us, as well as two other male friends of Eddie's. Max and I decided to combine the trip to Mongolia with a trip to Beijing. I was excited beyond words.

Both Eric and Kell had birthdays in June: Kell was now 16, and Eric now 20. We celebrated the boys' birthdays early at a Japanese restaurant in Seattle. This was the first time I would miss my sons' actual birthdays. That part was hard.

The Beijing airport was a madhouse. No one spoke English, but Eddie and Hille were also escorting a nine-year-old Chinese American boy named David from Seattle who would be spending the summer with his aunt and uncle in Beijing. David was bright, charming, and spoke excellent English and Chinese. Once out of the airport, we joined the crowd of people looking for friends and relatives. David spotted his uncle, who spoke no English; we followed his gestures and dragged our three heavy bags onto a bus, where we were sandwiched in among the Asian passengers.

After a long walk with our luggage, which we placed on carts pulled by bicycles, we reached the hotel, only to find that there had been a mistake with our reservations. We were redirected to Xidan Hotel, half a mile away. When we finally arrived and checked in, Max and I were completely exhausted. We collapsed in our hotel room and slept for 15 hours.

David's aunt arranged for a Chinese woman, who spoke some English, to take us to the Forbidden City and the Summer Palace. I loved the Forbidden City and could have spent hours there. The Summer Palace was so magnificent, and it was thrilling for me to learn more about Chinese history! We also went out to a fine Chinese restaurant and had a delicious Beijing duck dinner.

We took a bus to visit the Ming Tombs, which were disappointing because of how commercialized they were. However, the tombs themselves were visually impressive. We also took a bus about 50 miles from Beijing to the Great Wall of China. The wall, stretching and curving mile after mile along the tops of the mountains, was magnificent. Max and I could have spent days walking along that wall and experiencing the beautiful country surrounding it.

Then it was back to the Beijing airport for our trip to Mongolia. Our flight on China Air was delayed about eight hours, but we finally took off. The landing in Mongolia was unusually rough, with the pilot braking with such force that even Max looked worried. The weather was cool and breezy, quite a welcome change from the heat of Beijing. The mountains were beautiful and remote.

We were picked up at the airport by Mr. Tsend-Ochir and Mr. Terbish, the men Max and Eddy knew from the 1990 Goodwill Games in Seattle. We drove at night through the streets of the capital, Ulaanbaatar, to the apartment of our Mongolian hosts, Mr. Tsend-Ochir and his wife. There were no streetlights, and the streets were dark, dirty, and full of huge potholes. It reminded me of the very poor neighborhoods of Chicago, Cleveland, and New York I had experienced. There was a strong odor of urine in the stairwells, but our hosts' apartment was warm, spacious, and comfortable.

Mr. and Mrs. Tsend-Ochir wined and dined us; they offered us vodka, beer, whiskey, and a great variety of meats, vegetables, and salads. Max and I slept in a pull-out bed in their living room. We were exhausted and slept quite well.

Sometime during that first day in Mongolia, Max became upset by something I said to Eddy in jest. I don't remember what it was, but we worked it out over the next 24 hours, as we would do periodically throughout our trip and our married life. It was a challenge for us when my Western upbringing and independence conflicted with Max's Muslim roots and his way of trying to control what was happening around him.

One of the highlights of our visit to Ulaanbaatar was a special private concert of Mongolian folk dancing and singing, with unique Mongolian musical instruments such as the *morinkhuur* (horse-head fiddle), the *torshuur*, and the *shudraga*. We also heard the traditional Mongolian "throat singing," which was just amazing.

When it was time to leave Ulaanbaatar, we made our way to the Gobi Desert. There was one main road through the Mongolian steppe country—really just a dirt path, or in so many places no road at all. We had a minibus with our own bus driver. The way was amazingly rough, and we averaged about 15 miles per hour. Ten hours and 160 miles later, we arrived at a small, isolated settlement of gers (similar to yurts), about halfway to the Gobi Desert.

The trip through the desert was quite an adventure. One day, we visited a family of five who lived in a ger in the Gobi Desert. The family, all in traditional Mongolian dress, had 14 camels and 170 sheep and goats. I got to ride a Mongolian one-hump camel (with the wife holding the reins for me). But the biggest and most meaningful experience for me was seeing how their lives were compared to mine. How isolated I had become in America! I had never seen or experienced anything like this before.

The Gobi Desert is desolate and beautiful. South Gobi is overrun with lizards and crawling insects. This is the place where dinosaur bones were discovered, and people still find dinosaur eggs. Other things also got my attention: dramatic, reddish-brown rock formations and the deep blue sky with its magnificent expanse of clouds.

We then traveled to Terelj, about 70 kilometers from Ulaanbaatar, to the Khentii Mountains. The scenery was magnificent, with rivers, mountains, and trees untouched by logging. We stayed in a rundown hotel built by the Russians in the early 1960s. There was no hot water, electricity was marginal, and the wallpaper was peeling. However, despite all that, Max and I were very comfortable. We had a little suite to ourselves, with a sitting room, bedroom, and bathroom. The walls were thick, and we had privacy.

The food we ate while in Mongolia was varied. In the expensive hotels and at our Mongolian friends' apartment, we enjoyed a variety of meats, vegetables, salads, and rice. We had traditional Mongolian *buuz*—delicious steamed dumplings filled with meat. For breakfast, we had a wonderful pancake-like fried item, called *gampir*, with jam. However, when we traveled in the steppe country and the Gobi Desert, the food was much different—mainly bland, greasy, cooked mutton, much of which I could not eat. I lost weight when we were out on the Gobi Desert.

After our trip was over, I found a letter written to Eddie from Mr. Tsend-Ochir. It was written before our trip started. Mr. Tsend-Ochir wrote:

> "Economy of our country is still very
> bad, however now if somebody has
> money, he is able to buy food and
> other goods, which are very expensive
> for local people, not inexpensive for
> foreigners because of dollar exchange
> rate. Now, dollar bank rate is $1.00=
> 390 tugrik."

After reading that letter, I felt bad. Those of us who have never had to worry about food have a hard time really comprehending what that is like. I am now 79 years old. I was in my late 40's then. There was a lot about other people's lives that I did not understand.

At the end of our Mongolian adventure, Max and I attended NAADAM, a traditional Mongolian festival lasting three days that has been celebrated for centuries. It was in a huge outdoor stadium completely packed with thousands of people, most of them dressed in traditional Mongolian fashion. The whole week was magnificent, with beautiful blue skies and colorful flags flying everywhere. The first events featured men wrestling in traditional Mongolian costumes. The style of wrestling was very different than in the West. They would stop and rest occasionally during the match. Some of the matches lasted over an hour. No one was upset or hurt. There were no "technical fouls" or poor sportsmanship. Such fun to watch!

At the festival, we had traditional NAADAM foods: snake, beef, mutton, wheat noodles, and cabbage with steamed buns. The food was prepared for us by our Mongolian hostess, Mrs. Tsend-Ochir. She was so proud.

We saw horse racing, with pre-adolescent boys riding bareback on galloping horses. There were horses everywhere, with beautiful green hills and the city of Ulaanbaatar below us.

The next day, we observed an archery contest with both men and women dressed in traditional Mongolian attire. We saw all three parts of the NAADAM: wrestling, horse racing, and archery.

On our last day in Mongolia, we all went back to the wonderful former Russian resort and had a six-course dinner. Each of us had five glasses at our place setting: one for vodka, red wine, white wine, beer, and water or "punch." The food included cucumbers, tomatoes, cold meats, excellent soup, four different salads (cucumber, radish, cabbage, and potato), delicious pork cutlets, steak, rice, potatoes, and cake for dessert.

In my vacation diary I wrote that Max and I had spent four weeks together in China and Mongolia, day and night. There were some arguments, but it was "98 percent wonderful, and never boring." Max and I decided to consider this our belated honeymoon.

———◆•◆———

The winter of 1995 was an active one for Max and me. I had done some downhill skiing, but not much. John and Berdi were expert downhill skiers, and I learned the basics from them. On the weekends when Kell was with his father, Max and I would be on the slopes. We loved going to Mt. Bachelor in Oregon. At the end of the day, we would start up again at the top, and, with the sun setting on the mountains, ski along the ridge, and then down. It was spectacular.

That spring, Max wanted to hike up to Camp Muir on Mt. Rainier. It was his tradition to make the trip to Camp Muir when the winter weather cleared and the sun was shining again. I couldn't go with him, as I had a full schedule of patients that day. Piro Kramar told Max she would go in my place, but at the last moment something came up and she couldn't. Max insisted on going alone. He said he had done this trip many, many times by himself without any problem. Although the weather looked more or less clear, I was anxious about it. I told him to call me the minute he returned to his car, and I insisted that he plan to be off the mountain by 5:00 p.m. He agreed.

That afternoon, the weather began to deteriorate. Clouds rolled in, and the temperature was dropping. Five o'clock came and went, and there was no phone call from Max. I knew immediately that something was terribly wrong.

Half an hour later, I called the ranger station at Mount Rainier and told them Max had been on his way to Camp Muir and hadn't returned. They sent someone to see if his car was still in the parking lot. Another hour went by before someone called me back. Max's car, covered in snow, was still in the parking lot. It was snowing heavily, and no one knew where he was.

Completely panicked, I called John and Berdi at their home in Ferndale, Washington. Both of them had the flu and were really sick. I called Dave and Suzanne, and, in tears, told them of the situation. Dave kindly offered to take the next day off of work so the two of us could drive to Paradise early in the morning. I called Piro to tell her what had happened. She tried to reassure me. She said Max was "an old fox" and had been known to escape danger before.

I didn't sleep at all that night. Dave picked me up at 5:00 a.m. As we entered Mt. Rainier National Park, it was still snowing heavily. We found that the road to Paradise was closed at Longmire. Dave and I waited at the visitor's lodge there. I held a hardbound copy of The Quran in my hands for strength and good luck. After a few hours, we were told the road to Paradise had been plowed and was now open. Dave and I drove up the snowy road. When we got to the parking lot, we saw several Mt. Rainier rangers. They walked over to us and said that it had snowed heavily all night long, but there had been a small break in the weather that morning. During that time, two rangers had put on snowshoes and gone looking for Max. They were up there somewhere now.

We stood in the parking lot at Paradise for a long time. I felt completely numb. Suddenly, high in the distance, we saw a few figures snowshoeing toward us. It was the two rangers with Max in between them! When they finally reached the parking lot, I ran up and hugged Max. I felt alive again.

————————◆•◆————————

Meanwhile, I was loving my job as medical director of the Totem Lake Clinic. Not only did I have my staff of primary care internists, but I also had a variety of sub-specialists: a dermatologist, a psychologist, an ophthalmologist, a pediatrician, and a gastroenterologist who would come periodically to see patients referred by the primary care internists and me. I also had an excellent clinic manager, Sharon Kipersztok, with whom I worked closely, and who also directed the rest of the support staff. All in all, I was responsible, directly or indirectly, for about 70 people. And, most important to me, I had my own panel of patients that I saw every day.

The internists in my clinic, as well as the specialists who rotated through, were productive and fun to be with. Invariably, the women had more issues than the men. The women physicians were always trying to balance the responsibilities of home and children as well as their job at the clinic, and inevitably crises would arise. I had been doing this myself all my life, so I understood, and was usually able to work out any challenges with them.

There were some hard decisions too. One internist was just not able to perform up to my expectations. He made mistakes in judgment, and there were patient complaints. I worked with the chief medical officer to try to help him address these problems, but he never seemed to take things seriously. Finally, I had to let him go. It was hard to do, but not as bad as I thought, because I knew in the end my clinic would be better without him.

Most of the specialists at PacMed were great to work with. Tom Preston, chief of cardiology, treated me with respect and was a great resource of information about heart disease. On the other hand, Mike Schuffler, chief of gastroenterology, told me he questioned whether I could really do this job. He wasn't actually rude, just very aloof and mildly condescending. When I had to deal with him, there was a look on his face of mild disdain. I thought it would improve over the years, but it never did.

I enjoyed the monthly meetings of all the medical directors at Pacific Medical Center. Everyone was helpful and welcoming. I became friends with Betsy Plotkin, an internist who was the medical director of the North Clinic in Seattle. Betsy was an excellent internist, a good listener, and someone with whom I could communicate very well.

I was the only non-physician at Evergreen Hospital with hospital privileges. Patients admitted to Evergreen were generally quite sick, and consequently a medical or surgical specialist was nearly always involved. I primarily acted as an information source for the family and the patient while communicating and coordinating care with the specialists.

I was still living at our house in Bothell. Eric was at Cornell, and Kell was living weekdays with his father in Seattle. Kell came home every weekend to see me and his friend, Eric Kingsbury. He was still quite attached to our Bothell home, but I was now married to a man living in West Seattle and driving back and forth between our houses every few days. Honestly, I had never fit in very well in suburban Bothell; I was more of a Seattle woman. When I bought the house in Bothell, I couldn't afford a house in Seattle.

One time, when I was driving back from Max's house, I saw a little house in West Seattle with a "For Sale" sign on it. I thought to myself, *Maybe I should buy that house.* I called Jim Jacobson, the West Seattle real estate agent on the sign, and asked about it. It had already been sold, so I thought that was the end of that. But Jim Jacobson, better known in West Seattle as "Jimmy Jakes," told me he had other houses for me to look at. I called Max and told him about my idea of moving to West Seattle.

For the next few days, Max and I rode in the back of Jimmy Jake's big Cadillac and saw every house in my price range. I fell in love with one house in the North Admiral District of West Seattle, but Max thought we should keep looking. After looking at all the possibilities, I knew that little house in the North Admiral District was for me. With Jimmy Jakes's help, I sold the Bothell House and bought the house in West Seattle.

These real estate transactions take time. The summer of 1995 was very busy for me. Eric was home from college for the summer. Kye had already graduated and was working in Seattle. They were living together in an apartment just a few blocks from my new house. Kye was such a wonderful addition to my family.

Max and I also had an exciting vacation planned. In August and September, we were going to Bangkok first, then Pakistan, up to Concordia and the basecamp of K2, and then to Koh Samui, an island off the east coast of Thailand. John and Berdi were planning to join us for the Pakistan, Concordia and basecamp of K2 part of the trip. Just before leaving on our vacation, Kell and I moved into my new house in West Seattle.

On July 21, 1995, we arrived early at Sea-Tac Airport for our 7:00 a.m. flight to Los Angeles, then on to Seoul, South Korea, and finally to Bangkok. Eric and Kell were there to see us off with all the Junejos. Irene, tears streaming down her face and holding tightly to my arm, whispered softly in my ear, "Just come back!"

Our first day in Bangkok included dinner at an exclusive Thai restaurant, where we had shrimp, crab, and many Thai dishes, all expertly seasoned. We also had Thai beer. We visited a Buddhist temple after lunch, which I loved. We saw the Royal Palace only from a distance, because the queen's mother had just died and the palace was closed.

The very best part of our day in Bangkok was a long boat ride though the canals of the city. The boat was helmed by a woman who did all the rowing. We could really appreciate the culture, viewing the houseboats and wooden houses colorfully decorated and supported on posts along the canals. We saw several beautiful mosques along the canal as well.

We flew from Bangkok to Karachi, Pakistan, on July 23. When we arrived in Karachi, Max became tense and preoccupied. He told me later that he had forgotten how difficult a country Pakistan was. It was stiflingly hot, with no air conditioning in the airport. People were everywhere on the floors of the airport, all of them on their prayer rugs, kneeling and praying. Women's faces were completely covered, and the men looked tense and solemn, almost angry. I wrote in my journal that it seemed like a hostile environment. We hadn't even left the airport, and it was already scary for me and tense for Max.

Things became worse when the man who checked our passports at the immigration counter was nasty to Max. He never made eye contact with me. He did a double-take when Max said I was his wife. He glared at Max, and we had to fill out many additional forms. He told Max that we had to check in with an immigration office every week while we were in Pakistan. Max explained that it was impossible because we were headed for the Karakorum mountains. The man replied that it didn't matter and we would still have to check in every week. Max just left it at that, but throughout the rest of our trip, he worried that we might have trouble leaving Pakistan.

Max had an old friend in Karachi, Shalmir Khan. Shalmir lived in a large apartment in the city with his wife, son, daughter-in-law, and two grandchildren. The family met us just outside the airport. When Max saw Shalmir, his face lit up with his wide "Max" smile. All his tension lifted, and he looked happy and relaxed. The whole family was very gracious and kind to us, and we had a wonderful dinner and evening with them.

Shalmir and his wife threw a big party for us. Their young Pakistani friends arrived in their finest attire and had so many questions for us about life in the United States. Afterward, we went out to dinner in Karachi for a chicken tikka barbecue.

The streets were packed with small cars, trucks, donkey carts, and bicycles on our way to and from the restaurant. When we stopped for traffic or at a traffic light, we were surrounded by men, women, and even teenage children banging on the car windows and asking for food or money, which made me very uneasy.

I wanted to explore the streets of Karachi, but Max insisted that it wasn't safe, especially for me. Instead, we went to a fancy restaurant on the Arabian Sea coast with some of Max's old colleagues. It was so beautiful, and I wanted to walk on the beach, but Max said it was unsafe.

We stayed at the Faron Hotel in Karachi, about half a block from the Khan family home and place of business. At the hotel, Max fell back into a nervous, tense state, now experiencing again how challenging life in Pakistan was. The next morning we left Karachi to drive 100 miles to Hyderabad, the Pakistani village Max and his family had escaped to from India in 1947. Max's cousin Aziz picked us up, and off we went in his old car. About halfway there, we stopped for tea in an old building on the side of the road. There was terrible poverty all around us. Old wooden frames standing near the road became shelter for people wrapped up in frayed, threadbare blankets. Chickens ran wildly everywhere. I didn't see any women, and the men stared at me. I stayed close to Max, walking behind him and averting my gaze. This was not a friendly place.

We drove on, but after 30 minutes the car started making some strange noises and then broke down. All three of us tried to get it started again, to no avail. Suddenly, we saw a big, brightly-decorated Pakistani bus, which Max quickly waved down. We hopped on the bus, and away we went to Hyderabad.

Finally, we arrived in Hyderabad. Aziz managed the only gas station in town. We were invited to Aziz's house for a Sindi curry dinner. There were about 15 family members there, everyone dressed in their finest Pakistani attire. We all sat on the floor of the main room in the house. The women were all so kind and warm to me. No one spoke English, but the engaging personalities of these young women came through strongly to me. We enjoyed an authentic Sindi curry prepared by one of them. Max said no other curry in the world could compare with it, and he was right—it was incredibly delicious.

Late that afternoon, Aziz drove us back to our Karachi hotel. The next day, we met John and Berdi at the Karachi airport, and the four of us flew off to Islamabad. The airplane ride was very disconcerting—the reading lights and air flow did not work, the air was stifling, and the service was nonexistent. There was also a lot of turbulence.

When we arrived at the Islamabad airport, we were met by Kaiser Khan, who owned a travel business there and with whom Max had been in contact. He drove us to Hotel Akbar in Rawalpindi, about nine miles from Islamabad. The next day, we went to the famous Faisal Mosque in Islamabad, the fifth-largest mosque in the world and the largest in South Asia. Berdi and I were dressed appropriately, all covered up except for our faces and hands. The Faisal Mosque was expansive and ornate; it was quite an experience seeing it all. That night, we had dinner with Kaiser Khan and had a fascinating discussion about American and Pakistani cultures.

The next day, we wandered the streets of Rawalpindi with its teeming, busy market. Max was in full male Pakistani dress, wearing a light-blue shalwar kameez. He walked very proudly ahead of us. There was a traditional Rajah Bazaar going on, and it was a thrill to see it all. The narrow streets were packed with ox and donkey carts carrying all sorts of items. Throngs of people lined the streets, selling large melons, apricots in barrels, myriads of vegetables, nuts, rice, chapatis, rotis, and big slabs of fresh goat and lamb meat. Men and women weighed items on old scales and named their price. The women wore scarves on their heads, and some had their faces fully covered. I could tell Max was having fun and felt more relaxed. He was proud of his Pakistani culture exhibiting itself all around us.

The next morning at 6:00 a.m., our driver picked us up and we began traveling north and east to Skardu by way of the Karakorum Highway, a distance of 380 miles. We would spend two long days getting there.

The Karakorum Highway is 810 miles long, and connects Pakistan with China. It is one of the highest paved roads in the world and traces one of the many paths of the ancient Silk Road. Due to its high elevation and the difficult conditions under which it was constructed, it's often referred to as the Eighth Wonder of the World.

It was very hot, somewhere between 110 and 115 degrees Fahrenheit. There was no air conditioning in the minivan. However, the scenery was absolutely astounding. The area was beautiful and isolated, with steep canyons filled with clusters of stone-and-mud houses perched along the sides. We saw long, thin suspension footbridges high above the raging Indus River. There were precipitous foot trails up and down the faces of the steep terrain, thick forests dotting the hills, and glaciated peaks above.

Suddenly, we hit a big traffic jam, with at least 30 vehicles, all highly decorated in Pakistani fashion, stopped in front of us. We discovered there had been a big rock slide over the road, and men were busy removing the rocks, one by one. It took two hours for the road to be cleared.

We reached our driver's village late that afternoon. We met his family, and Berdi and I were allowed to enter his house and were offered a special drink by the women of the family. Max and the men were not allowed inside the house and the women were never allowed outside of the house. In the morning, we were back in the minivan and off to Skardu. We stopped for tea and lunch along the way and took lots of pictures. The scenery became more and more dramatic. We could now see the western end of the Himalayas! We had a magnificent view of Nanga Parbat, the ninth-highest peak in the world.

When we arrived at the village of Skardu, we stayed at the Sehr Hotel, one of the nicest hotels in the village. The staff at the hotel were gracious, proud, and kind. The next day, we were up at 5:00 a.m. and had a delicious breakfast of chapattis, parathas, eggs, mango jam, chutney, and tea. Then, we all got into jeeps and headed off to Askole. After stopping for lunch, we were off again. The scenery was fabulous. There were huge snow-covered peaks with glaciers all around us.

In the valleys were small villages. The people we saw were so industrious. There were women with their heads covered, working in small wheat fields gathering up every possible wheat stalk. The houses were built with hand-made mud bricks and stones. Everything was clean and tidy, with nothing out of place. Women carried their children on their backs.

On the way, we stopped for some delicious Pakistani tea. The trees around us were heavy with apricots. Finally, our jeep could go no farther, as the road either was too rough or washed out in places. We walked along the river, surrounded by huge, glaciated peaks with green trees around us in all directions.

When we stopped for the night, our Pakistani porters put up our tents. I wasn't used to this kind of service in the mountains! Our porters also made a delicious chicken curry dinner for us. They had carried live chickens with them which they butchered for dinner.

Max and I had a wonderful night's sleep. He held me close with such tenderness. In the morning, we were transported again by jeep, the dirt road becoming steeper and steeper. It was, without a doubt, the most harrowing ride I had ever experienced. A few times, the back wheels of the jeep were actually over the edge of the cliff. Somehow, though, we made it without the jeep careening off the cliff. Little did I know an even more terrifying jeep ride was awaiting us.

Then, we had to start walking. We came to a steep rock slide area, with small rocks and debris continually coming down the slope the entire time we were trying to cross it. The porter had us quickly run one by one across to the other side, dodging the rocks as they rolled toward us. It was terrifying. As we walked, I suddenly developed some right chest pain, which was uncomfortable and disconcerting.

We finally stopped when we came upon a much larger vehicle waiting for us. It was like a huge truck, with a large truck bed in the back. We all climbed on. I counted 16 people and lots of packs heaped in the truck bed. I was holding Max's leg tightly and sitting on Berdi's lap, ducking my head way down. The jeep seemed so top heavy that it was scary before we even started.

As we ascended the steep cliffs on sickeningly narrow gravel roads, I saw the cliffs above us, and the whole jeep leaning over with nothing below us. I was terrified as the driver tried to navigate the many hairpin turns. Sometimes the jeep's back wheels would be in the air out over the cliff. I wasn't sure we would make it and lost all track of time, but found out later the drive had been two hours long. On our way back, Berdi heard about another jeep that went over the edge, killing several people.

As the day progressed, I developed a headache and my chest pain worsened. My skin was hot and dry. I had an impromptu conference with John and Berdi. We were far from any medical facility, with no ability to get a chest X-ray. Berdi put her ear to my chest and heard the characteristic "rales" of pneumonia. Fortunately, we were carrying lots of prescription drugs with us. I started on doxycycline and cephradine, as well as some Diamox, in case I had some element of high-altitude pulmonary edema. It was hard going, but we finally arrived at the village of Askole, the last of civilization before we started on foot to Concordia and hopefully the basecamp of K2.

We camped just outside Askole. Despite the fact that I felt ill, I had no choice but to just keep going. My fever finally broke, but I was continually short of breath and the chest pain was still there as we hiked through meadowed plains.

After a hearty breakfast prepared by our cook, we were off again quite early the next day. My chest pain was finally gone, and I could take a deep breath without it hurting.

The next day, we went on a nine-hour hike through a valley. It was steep and desolate, and yet thrilling and expansive at the same time. I wrote in my journal:

> The scale of this country is so immense
> that it cannot be described or imagined.
> I am in awe. One can only experience
> it, and, by doing that, can just barely
> begin to understand its scope and
> beauty.

I tried to strike up a conversation with two of the porters who were carrying all our gear. I was just using a few words and gestures, as they did not speak English and I did not speak Urdu. Later, Max took me aside and told me sternly that I was not to talk to the porters, that as a woman I was putting myself in danger. It was becoming clear to me that my personality did not fit into Pakistani culture.

After dinner, we stood outside. The night was so beautiful, with a huge full moon. It was very cold, and Max and I huddled close, zipped together in our sleeping bags.

The next day, we left our camp at 8:00 a.m. and arrived at Concordia at 12:30 p.m. Concordia (15,360 feet; 4,691 meters) has been described by Galen Rowell as the "throne room of the mountain gods." Four peaks over 8,000 meters (26,247 feet) sit within a radius of only 21 kilometers/13 miles from Concordia.

I wrote in my journal on Friday, August 11, 1995:

> We hiked on the Baltoro Glacier to Concordia
> today. Left our camp at 8:00 am and arrived
> at 12:30 pm. Incredible, magnificent views!
> This is like a pilgrimage for Max and me. We
> started in Rawalpindi on 7/31/95, and in
> 12 days we are finally here. By minibus, by jeep,
> and by foot. I am sitting here in our dining tent,
> away from the blistering sun, with the sides
> up, viewing the incredible peaks all around us.
> K2! Finally! Mountain of mountains! I have
> read so much about it. We can see the Abruzzi
> Ridge and all the climbing camps; we can
> see the places where they were. The weather
> is flawless! Max and I are camped on a ridge
> with the mighty K2 gleaming at us. Also
> rising up in front of us are Broad Peak (another
> 8,000-meter peak), Chugalisa, Gaherbrum IV,
> etc., etc. Incredible . . . they all rise right from
> the floor of the glacier where we are now:
> Concordia.

Max and I at Concordia on the Baltoro Glacier in Pakistan;
K2 in the distance

We took pictures with our porters. They looked so hearty with their tanned faces, several of them with scruffy beards. Some looked stern, while others had a slight smile. They were all ages—young and old.

The way down the Baltoro Glacier back to Askole and Skardu was a nightmare for me. Fortunately, that nightmare has faded in my mind over the past 29 years. I was completely traumatized, primarily because of the way Max was treating me—telling me I was smiling too much or laughing too much, and generally being very disapproving of me. My son Eric had been right after all—Pakistan is no place for a Western woman.

We left John and Berdi at the airport in Karachi. Ali, our guide, accompanied us there. Berdi and I both noticed that Ali would only talk to John. He wouldn't even acknowledge us. After seeing John and Berdi off, Max and I traveled to the ancient city of Lahore, where we visited Majid, the only one of his six brothers still living in Pakistan.

Getting both of us out of Pakistan was somewhat of an acrobatic act for Max. Before we left, Max went to the immigration office in Lahore and met with some officials there. I didn't go; Max said it would be much better if the people at the office didn't see me. He gave them a significant amount of money (Max never told me exactly how much), and they stamped our passports as ready to leave Pakistan. Max told me if you want to get anything important done in Pakistan, you have to be ready to offer a bribe.

Later, I realized that Max was not physically well while we were in Pakistan. He had serious end-stage heart disease, which I had refused to really acknowledge. It was way too scary for me to contemplate. In retrospect, he was physically failing on that trip. I think he must have been just miserable coming back down the Baltoro Glacier. His physical deterioration scared him, and his way of dealing with it was by being short-tempered and angry with me, his American wife, who did not really "get" the rules of life in Pakistan.

We flew out of Thailand to Los Angeles. As we entered the big airport, there was a giant photograph of Bill Clinton, then president of the United States, covering a large part of the entire wall. I looked at that picture and felt tears welling in my eyes.

I whispered to myself, "Bill, I am back!"

———◆•◆———

It was now September 1995. Kell had just finished his sophomore year at Nathan Hale. Eric had just finished his junior year at Cornell, and was getting ready to start his senior year in Kyoto, Japan, as part of his double major in Economics and Asian Studies.

That fall, Kell periodically complained of chest pain, but by the time I had him evaluated at PacMed, it was gone and the X-ray was normal. One day, he mentioned it again, and I ordered a chest X-ray that very day instead of waiting several days to get an appointment. Finally, we had a diagnosis: spontaneous pneumothorax. The cause of most cases of spontaneous pneumothorax is unknown. It's more common in thin, adolescent males like Kell. Because it had happened several times, Kell underwent surgery to have the problem corrected. He never again had another spontaneous pneumothorax, but he had trouble emotionally and mentally recovering from the surgery. Looking back, it seemed that after the surgery, he never returned to his happier, more contented self.

I got it in my head that I wanted to remodel my house. I loved the location, but it was an older house that didn't take advantage of the potential views across Puget Sound to Downtown Seattle and the Cascade Mountains. My real estate agent gave me a recommendation for an architect. Max was not at all excited about me spending more of my money, but I really wanted to do this. Since leaving my childhood home, I had never lived in any place where I felt totally comfortable and that actually reflected me and my taste. I wanted to live in a house that really felt like mine.

That fall, I was invited to give a lecture on "The Expanded Role of the Nurse" to the Louisiana State Physicians Association in New Orleans.

Max flew there with me. I have such good memories of that trip—Max and I taking a ferry boat on the Mississippi River; listening to jazz in the French Quarter; eating jambalaya, gumbo, crawfish étouffée, and the best, most delicious Bananas Foster I've ever had.

Max was still playing a lot of squash in those days. It was such fun meeting him at the college club afterward for dinner. At dinner would be senior men, mostly physicians and lawyers, who all came alive with conversation when Max and I came to the table. Life was good.

Later that fall, some old acquaintances of Max's invited us to dinner. During the meal, the couple asked about our recent trip to Pakistan. I responded that it was both very exciting but also very difficult for me. As I write this years later, I can see how traumatized I was by my experience in Pakistan, and also how difficult it was for Max. But at the time, all I could think of was how hard it was for me.

After the dinner, I drove Max home. On the way there, he said he was angry with me because he thought I had presented Pakistan in an unflattering light. He kept saying that this was his country and his culture, and I needed to be respectful of it. I responded by getting really angry. I was furious that I couldn't express my thoughts when I was directly and honestly asked by someone for my opinion. I also felt that Max did not understand how hard it had been for me in Pakistan. I think it was the angriest I had ever been at him. When I dropped him off at his house, he walked away without a word.

When I got home, I went right to bed. My phone woke me suddenly at 2:00 a.m. It was Max.

"I'm having some chest pain."

I told him I would call 911 and be right there. I drove as fast as I could to his house.

I arrived just before the paramedics. Max was quickly evaluated, put on a cart, and loaded into the ambulance. I squeezed Max's hand and kissed him. I said a few reassuring words to Irene, who was crying, then I followed the ambulance to the hospital in my car.

Looking back, this was the beginning of the end. Max was hospitalized, and a few days later, he had cardiac bypass surgery. When he finally came home, Irene would take care of him during the day. When I got off work in the late afternoon, I would pick him up, bring him to my house, and take care of him through the evening and night. In the morning, after I left for work, Irene would pick him up and bring him back to her house. This arrangement worked well for us.

I thought Max was gradually getting better—at least I wanted to believe so. I went to all his cardiology appointments with him. Per the instructions from the cardiologist, Max wore a heart rate monitor while we were out walking along the shore of Puget Sound. We started slow. I would watch the monitor, trying to keep his heart rate stable according to his cardiologist's instructions, but it kept increasing and never stabilized. Finally, we had to stop walking; Max looked pale and exhausted. Any exercise became increasingly difficult and then impossible.

Finally, his cardiologist put him on the heart transplant list. I just refused to see that Max's life was ending. I couldn't imagine my life without him. He was the only man I'd known who had ever genuinely loved me. Max and I both had so much love and determination. How could all that goodness and happiness disappear? I couldn't face the thought of his death.

Max was not enthusiastic about the possibility of a heart transplant. He told me, touching his chest, "Babe, this is the heart that God gave me. I do not think I want anyone else's heart."

Meanwhile, I was proceeding with the remodel of my new house. Kevin Weare, the architect, suggested opening up the first floor and expanding the second floor with porches on both sides of the house. The plans exposed the beautiful easterly views of Downtown Seattle and the Cascade Mountains. I loved them.

Kevin called Joe Beck, a general contractor in West Seattle he thought had the necessary talent and experience, and who he believed would do a fine job. I remember the first time I met Joe. He was there at the house with Kevin before I arrived. He had just crawled into a cobweb-filled space between the first and second floors and discovered excess space between them from a previous, poorly-done remodel. That discovery would lead to more opportunities for my remodel. Joe was a slender, very tall, muscular man in his mid-40s, with thinning black hair and a black mustache. All three of us were excited about the potential of my house remodel.

Max was at the house with me during most of my conversations with Joe regarding the remodel. One time, the three of us were sitting at the table going over some of the plans, and Max was quite involved in the discussion. I left the table for a few minutes, and years later, Joe told me that Max had said, "I might not be here for the end of the project, but I know you will take good care of Lynne with her new house."

Max and I had never talked about the possibility that he might die any-time soon.

March 21, 1996, arrived—our third wedding anniversary. Max wrote me
a beautiful letter on that day:

> Lynne baby,
>
> Here we are, married for three years.
>
> I have not said enough times how much
> I love you. But I do love you very much.
> These last three-plus years have
> been the best years of my life. It is just
> like heaven. You have brought
> me so much joy and pleasure. You
> make me so happy. We have done so
> much in such a short time. Worldwide
> travels, exciting trips here and abroad.
> Just being with you is a joy and
> pleasure.
>
> I know how much you love me, give
> so much, and ask and expect so little.
> Sweetheart, I have tried to make you
> happy. I am sorry you got cheated with
> this lousy heart of mine. But this heart
> loves you very much. I am sure we will
> make the best of it. I am going to do
> my best with the help of Almighty God,
> in whom I believe and trust.
>
> I love you so very much,
> Max

Max and I liked to go to Pegasus Pizza, a restaurant on the waterfront
in West Seattle. We had so many memorable times there. In June 1996,

Dave, Suzanne, Max, and I went there for dinner. We took pictures outside of the restaurant. Years later, when I look at those pictures, it is so obvious how sick Max was. His face was thin, and his color was poor. I just didn't see it at the time. The pictures of Max a month after his cardiac surgery showed him looking well, like his old self. But now, six months later, he looked gaunt and pale. In retrospect, his health was slowly and steadily deteriorating over those six months.

Saturday, June 29, 1966, Max and I were at his house with the family. I was going to spend the weekend. Later that evening, Max told me he was having chest pain again and did not feel well. His vital signs were stable, but I called 911 anyway. The ambulance came and took him to the hospital, with me following in my car.

The entire night, Max and I were in the emergency room of Providence Hospital Medical Center. His cardiologist arrived, and at first it was difficult to determine exactly the cause of Max's chest pain. Maybe it was gastrointestinal and not cardiac in origin. Feeling anxious and distressed, I finally called my friend Suzanne around 6:00 a.m., told her what was happening with Max, and asked her to come to the hospital.

Just as she arrived, Max's cardiologist said to us, "Max, we think this pain you are having is cardiac in origin, and we are going to give you some medication to help."

Max turned to me, grabbed my hand, and said anxiously, "Babe, this is bad."

The nurses started a new infusion. Suddenly, Max's body went limp, and he dropped my hand. One of the nurses leaped onto his bed, straddled him, and started chest compressions. Suzanne held my arm as they wheeled Max into the operating room, with the nurse still astride him pumping on his chest.

Aziz finally arrived at the hospital. Max had tubes coming from every place possible and was on a ventilator. Later the next day, we had a conference with the doctors. Many of Max's relatives were there, as well as Kell and Eric.

I knew the truth of what the doctors were saying. Max had no functional heart left. The machines and ventilator alone were keeping his body alive. We all agreed it was time to stop the mechanical devices and give Max's body some peace. Aziz and I held hands as they turned off all the machines. The noisy room suddenly became very quiet.

Shock and despair came over me. When I went home, I remember just sitting on our bed, trying to contemplate the future. Everything looked so black. I couldn't see how it would ever get better.

Aziz called me the day after Max died. He had gone to the hospital and was somehow able to locate Max's body, which he then took back to the house. He asked me how to remove all the tubes and catheters from Max's body. Islamic, or "Sharia," law says that funeral arrangements must begin immediately after death; any embalmment is prohibited. The body is washed three times by close family members of the same sex. Aziz told me he would do it. Then the hands are laid right over left on the chest. The body is then shrouded with large white sheets.

After a long, sleepless night, I went to Max's house. I walked into the living room, and there was Max on the floor, wrapped in white sheets, with only his face showing. He looked so peaceful and so much like my

Max, it was as if he were sleeping. I knelt down beside his body and just cried and cried.

Even though I did not want it to, life went on. You think it won't, but it does. The Seattle Mosque had a big memorial ceremony for Max. The building was packed with people. Suzanne and Dave volunteered their house for a memorial service for all our friends.

Now, years later, I wish I had been able to pick up my life and move on. But I just couldn't. I saw nothing but blackness ahead of me. The one thing I did have was a personal drive to go forward. A few years later, Kell said to me, "Mom, you are just as sensitive and vulnerable as I am, but I don't have your drive."

I had reservations for Max and me to do the Seattle-to-Portland bicycle ride in June 1996. I rode it anyway and carried both my number and Max's on my bicycle. I wanted to feel like he was riding with me. Many people stopped me during the ride and asked me why I had two numbers on my bicycle. I told them all about Max.

Max was buried in a Muslim cemetery in Snohomish County. I wanted to be buried there too. Irene and I bought two plots right beside where he was buried. Several times I rode my bicycle to the cemetery. It always felt so good to ride. Did I think Max was there? Not really, but I was just looking for some relief from all the misery.

I just couldn't visualize my life without Max. I had long talks with Aziz, who was also devastated and mourning the loss of his father. Irene and I had dinners together, commiserating with each other.

I kept on searching for something to make the terrible pain go away. I read everything I could think of, but nothing seemed to express how I was feeling; it was as though I was swirling down into a bottomless hole. Finally, I picked up a book by C. S. Lewis entitled *A Grief Observed*. He wrote it just after the death of his beloved wife, Joy Davidman. I devoured that book—it expressed exactly how I felt. I ordered about ten copies and gave them to all my friends. They probably thought I was crazy, but C. S. Lewis expressed exactly the pain and suffering that was mine in that moment.

The strange thing is that, years later, I picked up the book again. It's a wonderfully written and important book, but I couldn't emotionally connect with it as I had after Max's death. I think one cannot stay in that state of profound grief, or one will not survive.

That September, I focused on my job. Eric had graduated from Cornell and was working at his first job. Kye, having graduated the year before, also had a job in Seattle. They were still living together in the apartment just a few blocks from my house. Kell was 18 years old and starting his senior year at Nathan Hale High School. He had high SAT scores and excellent grades, but suddenly didn't want to go back. He also didn't want to continue therapy with Dr. Reichert, or anyone else. Since he was 18, I didn't have the legal authority to make him go to school against his will. He started living full-time with me.

Kell said he just wanted to go somewhere other than Seattle. John and Berdi told me about a school they knew of in Redlands, California, where he could finish high school. Benchmark was a residential school for at-risk young adults ages 18 to 25. There were professionals there, including psychologists and a psychiatrist. The goal would be for him to finish high school while getting the necessary mental health help.

When I talked with Kell about the program, he said he really wanted to go there. At the time, it seemed like a reasonable thing to do. But in retrospect, it was a bad decision.

In February 1997, Kell started the program at Benchmark. He was there through the first part of 1998. It was a terrible experience for him and remained so in his mind for years. I should have brought him home for good—or better yet, never sent him there in the first place.

Benchmark took a "tough love" approach, which was exactly what Kell didn't need, although I didn't realize it at the time. After Kell left Benchmark and came home to Seattle, a new, excellent psychiatrist, Chet Robachinski, saw him weekly between 1997 and 2002. Chet is the one who told me that the approach at Benchmark was completely wrong and harmful for Kell.

———————◆·◆———————

It was now the summer of 1997. Max had been dead a full year. Kell was struggling at Benchmark. I was miserable. My friends tried to help me. They were all moving on with their own lives, and I knew I needed to as well. John, Berdi, their daughter, Sarah, and I went to Europe for two weeks. We went to Venice, then on a long backpacking trip in the Austrian Alps, and finally to the Czech Republic. It was beautiful— huge glaciers, pristine mountain lakes, Austrian mountain chalets, and walking on the historic Charles Bridge in Prague. But I remember just fighting feelings of despair in spite of all the beauty around me.

In August, John, Berdi, Dave, and Suzanne were planning a trip to Europe and wanted me to come with them. Financially, it was out of the question, since I had only just returned from the Czech Republic.

Berdi's mother heard about my situation and offered me some money for the trip to Europe with my friends. It was more than generous of her. On the trip, we met John's Czech parents in Prague, visited Florence and Venice, and took a trip down the Cinque Terre on the Italian coast. It was such a wonderful time, with great food and sights, but I fought a sense of isolation the whole time. My friends were laughing and happy. I felt only emptiness.

When I got back from Europe, I learned that Kell wasn't "following the rules" at Benchmark, and they had moved him to a motel in Redlands. He was up all night and sleeping during the day. I know it might seem like he was involved with drugs, but he wasn't. He was mentally ill, and I should have brought him home. I flew down to Redlands and stayed with him, trying to keep him awake during the day so he could sleep at night. It was terribly depressing, and I felt so helpless.

Kell finally went back to Benchmark. There, he saw a psychologist and a psychiatrist who prescribed psychotropic drugs for him. In April 1998, he expressed interest in a class on computers that was available in Redlands. The tuition was nine thousand dollars. I paid it, hoping this would be something he could focus on. I am not sure if he ever finished it, but he did complete his high school diploma in June. Eric, Kye, and I flew down to Redlands and finally brought Kell home.

I was still working long hours as medical director and nurse practitioner at PacMed Totem Lake. My clinic was busy and successful, as I was able to hire some very good physicians and other staff, who remained there for many years. There was another PacMed clinic on Seattle's Eastside: Pacific Medical Center Bellevue. It was half the size of Totem Lake, and Chuck Cowan, an experienced pediatrician, was the medical director. Chuck and I had worked together for several years, and I knew him well.

Meredith Mathews, the chief medical officer at PacMed, wanted there to be an Eastside Regional Medical Director who would be responsible for operations at both clinics. In 1997, Meredith met with me and asked me to accept this role. I was surprised and taken aback by the offer. It was an exceptional opportunity for anyone, and it was really unheard of to have a nurse practitioner in that position. Over the next few years, until I left PacMed in 2003, I was the PacMed Eastside Regional Medical Director in addition to the Totem Lake Clinic Medical Director. I continued to see my own patients as well.

During 1997 and 1998, Joe Beck was hard at work on my house remodel. It included replacing the roof, plumbing, electrical, HVAC, windows, siding, and adding another bathroom and two porches. I had to move out of the house for many months during the remodel, first to a studio apartment, then to a bigger apartment in West Seattle after Kell returned from Benchmark.

Those were terrible, lonely, depressing times for me. I couldn't seem to move on from the loss of Max. He had given me so much love, and now he was gone.

Finally, by mid-1998, the remodel was done. I loved my new house. It really was a reflection of me, my personality, and my tastes. Joe had done an outstanding job.

To celebrate, Joe took me out to dinner at Anthony's, a seafood restaurant in Seattle. Joe tells people now that we talked for two hours before we ordered any food. Although I always teased him later that we came from different parts of the same world, we had a strong personal connection. We were both struggling with sons who had serious mental health problems—Kell with depression, and Joe's son, Matt, with bipolar disease. There was always a strong, palpable warmth between us.

Joe had a Hard Rock shot glass collection. During the remodel, and for several years afterward, when I traveled to other countries, I would buy Hard Rock shot glasses for him from all different places. It was a delight for me to pick out the shot glasses and then surprise him with them.

Kell got a job driving and delivering medical records from clinic to clinic, and at that point I thought he needed to find an apartment for himself. He was 20 years old, and I thought having him establish a living situation away from home was the right thing to do. It might not have made any difference in the long term, but I still feel sick about my decision. I should have kept him home with me. On the other hand, Kell made a very good friend at that apartment building, Eric Todd, about whom I'll write more later.

I picked Kell up at his apartment every Friday and brought him home with me, then drove him back every Sunday evening. He really enjoyed being home during those weekends. Kell worked hard at his job and had very good reviews from his employer. He held that job successfully for five years.

Even after Max had been gone for nearly two years, I was still miserable and depressed. I used to tell my patients, when they experienced the death of a loved one, that it would take about a year, and then life would start to get better. But life for me was one depressing day after another. At dinners with friends, I remember feeling so lost and disconnected from everyone.

———◆•◆———

One day, my friend Bev Ricker's husband, Larry, called me. He was a member of a long-distance bicycling club called the Seattle International Randonneurs. He told me they needed more women to join the club, and he thought I could do it.

Randonneuring is long-distance, unsupported endurance cycling. It's noncompetitive in nature, and self-sufficiency is paramount. You usually begin by riding 200 kilometers (124 miles) on a predetermined route. You don't compete with other riders, but there is a time limit for completing the ride. After the 200-kilometer rides, one graduates to 300-kilometer (186-mile) rides, then 400-kilometer (249-mile) rides, and finally 600-kilometer (373-mile) rides. All this needs to be done in preparation for the most famous randonneur ride of all: Paris-Brest-Paris, also known as PBP.

Paris-Brest-Paris is a long-distance cycling event of about 1,200 kilometers (750 miles), starting from Paris to Brest on the west coast of France, and then back again to Paris. It was first done in 1891 as a professional-cyclist-only ride. In 1931, amateur cyclists were accepted into the race, but kept separated from the professional cyclists. The amateur ride is now organized by the French bicycling club, Audax Club Parisien, in which cyclists ride individually. The goal is to complete the 750-mile ride within 90 hours. Paris-Brest-Paris is held once every four years. There is hardly a level place in the entire ride; the route goes up and down between French countryside villages, winding around medieval castles and through forests and farms. The route has remained pretty much unchanged all these years.

To qualify for Paris-Brest-Paris, one must first complete a series of randonneuring events, as described above, called brevets, within the same calendar year as the PBP race.

After my telephone call from Larry, I got excited about the Randonneurs and long-distance bicycling. I saw it as a way to move on with my life after Max and rise above my depression. I had ridden from Seattle to Portland in two days many times before, but other than that, I did not have much experience bicycling. I didn't even have my own bicycle. I always rode Eric's ten-speed from high school.

It was spring 1998, and the next Paris-Brest-Paris race was to be held in September 1999. I decided to prepare myself for it. I joined the Seattle International Randonneers and signed up for the first 200-kilometer ride.

A few days before the ride, a man called me, introduced himself as Ron Lee, and said he was also signed up for this first ride. He had heard that I was a new rider and wanted to know if I wanted a ride to the starting line. After some initial conversation, I agreed, and he picked me up at my house at 3:00 a.m. We had breakfast at a Wendy's and arrived at the start of the brevet well before 7:00 a.m. At breakfast, I found out he was married, although he had been separated from his wife for ten years, and he had two daughters in their late teens. A Chinese American man, Ron was born in Seattle, graduated from the University of Washington, and was now a computer analyst working at Boeing.

Each brevet had a specific route that needed to be followed, and there were checkpoints along the way where one must present to get their control card signed. I still have my control card from that first brevet on April 4, 1998, and from all the other brevets I've completed since then. That first 200-kilometer brevet had to be completed in under 13 hours and 30 minutes. My time was 11 hours and 28 minutes.

The ride was exhausting. We stopped only to eat, drink, and go to the bathroom as quickly as possible. I pushed myself as hard as I could to complete it. That was the first of many brevets I completed over the next several years. My goal was to complete the 300-, 400-, and 600-kilometer rides, which would qualify me for Paris-Brest-Paris in the summer of 1999.

Ron had that same goal, and we rode together throughout the next year. By July 1998, I had completed the qualifying brevets. I say I completed them, but I barely managed it within the time limit. None of them were easy, to say the least.

I rode the brevets primarily with men. Ron always stuck with me, but I still tried to ride as fast as I could to keep up with the other men around me. There were a few women on the shorter brevets, but by the time I got to the 400- and 600-kilometer brevets, there were only men and me. I would get nauseated a lot on the rides and would occasionally vomit. I didn't understand why; I thought I was training enough. I just tried to pace myself more.

In May 1999, I completed a very challenging 600-kilometer brevet, which encircled the entire Olympic Peninsula, from Bremerton to Sequim, Neah Bay, La Push, Port Angeles, Quilcene, Port Townsend, and ended at the ferry terminal on Bainbridge Island. I completed it in 39 hours and 20 minutes, just under the cut-off time of 40 hours.

I thought I was ready for Paris-Brest-Paris that August of 1999. I was wrong. It was a humbling experience. Some of it is a blur now, but I do have pictures and my diary as a record. There were 14 people from our club who qualified for the event: 13 men and me.

Ron and I started off from Paris on a Monday at 4:00 p.m. We needed to be back in Paris within 90 hours, which would be the upcoming Friday at noon. After riding about 220 miles, I was nauseated and miserable. I told Ron that I had to rest and didn't think I could make it. We decided that he would continue the ride to Brest and then on the way back, he would pick me up at Loudeac, where we had hotel reservations. If I couldn't complete PBP, at least Ron could.

I arrived at the hotel and waited for Ron. After two days, he never came. I could not imagine what had happened. I thought the worst: he was dead or in a hospital. With the help of the hotel switchboard, I called some local hospitals looking for an injured Chinese American man. I told the hotel owner I wouldn't leave without knowing where Ron was.

The owner helped me out by calling one of the American organizers of the race, who then tried to find out where Ron was. Ron was also not prepared for the rigors of Paris-Brest-Paris. He had arrived in Brest, but realized that he could not finish the race back to Paris. For some reason, he had forgotten that I was waiting for him in Loudeac. He took a train back to Paris and thought he was to wait for me there.

Somehow, one of the organizers of the race found Ron in a Parisian bar with other PBP riders. Ron finally realized that I was still in Loudeac waiting for him. The owner of the hotel helped me get a train back to Paris, and Ron met me there. Both Ron and I were exhausted and sleep-deprived, which seemed to explain all the confusion.

Ron and I rested in Paris after our failed attempt at Paris-Brest-Paris. He had arranged for his oldest daughter, Tara, to join us, and we picked her up at the airport. We had a great time visiting the sights in Paris and Versailles. Tara fell in love with the Notre-Dame Cathedral, and we followed her all the way up the narrow stone steps to the top.

As Ron and I pursued our goal of completing Paris-Brest-Paris, we started a romantic relationship. He was now formalizing a divorce from his wife, and I got to know both his daughters, Tara and Nikki, very well. They are lovely women, now in their mid-40s and married. To this day, they still call and check in with me.

When Ron's divorce became final, he moved in with me. Kell was initially not happy about this. He felt that my house was a sanctuary for him on the weekends, and he did not want that interrupted. But Kell quickly became more comfortable with Ron being there. Ron was very kind and supportive of him. Every Friday night, Ron would bring home "cast-conditioned" beer from a local restaurant here in West Seattle, and he and Kell would enjoy a few mugs.

When I failed at Paris-Brest-Paris, I kept thinking that if only I hadn't stopped, or if I had eaten or drunk more, I could have finished. It was faulty thinking on my part at the time. Despite that, I started training for the next Paris-Brest-Paris in 2003. Ron felt the same way as I did and continued to train with me.

I called Joe Beck and asked him to do some more remodeling. I had him build a bicycle training room on the ground floor and add another porch, so we could move the bicycles from the house to the car more easily.

That winter, I received a call from my son Eric. He said that Kye had been on the phone that day with her mother in South Korea, telling her that she and Eric wanted to get married. The conversation went very badly, and Kye was upset.

"Mom, could you come over?" he asked.

I dropped everything and went over to their apartment.

There were no easy answers to this problem. Eric was not Korean, and he wasn't a doctor or lawyer. The very next week, Kye's mother flew to Seattle to try to talk Kye out of marrying Eric. I didn't see her on that trip. She only saw Kye and no one else. She stayed for about a week. Kye finally told her mother that if she did not marry Eric, she wouldn't marry anyone. That was the final blow for her mother, and she reluctantly agreed not to stand in the way of their marriage. Eric and Kye started planning their wedding.

Eric and Kye were married in September 2000 at the Four Seasons Hotel in Seattle. There were about 80 people there, and it was a beautiful wedding. Although the wedding went very well, it was quite stressful for me for two reasons: one, I had to deal with my ex-husband, Richard; and two, I had to deal with my sister Carol, whom I hadn't seen in 16 years. Jacquey and Steve were there, along with their three sons, Saul, Leib, and Jesse. They all tried to make Carol feel included, which I completely understood. I just tried to get through the stress of the wedding while doing the best I could as the mother of the groom.

———————◆•◆———————

At least once a month, I would go to the Bellevue Clinic to meet with Chuck Cowan, the Bellevue Clinic medical director. Usually, our meetings went very well. Sometime that fall, I had a meeting with Chuck late in the day. The clinic was empty except for the two of us.

I walked into his office and immediately saw that Chuck was very angry. I tried to find out what he was upset about. He was just fuming. He stood up and asked me to come into one of the examination rooms with him. After we entered the room, Chuck closed the door, and I sat on the edge of one of the examination tables, ready to listen to what he had to say. Chuck started yelling.

He went over to the light switch on the wall, and shouted, "Do you see this light switch? This is a pediatrician's exam room, and when the switches are mounted this low on the wall, the kids just keep turning them on and off, and it's driving me crazy!"

Suddenly, he grabbed a pencil and threw it at me. I quickly ducked and it hit the back wall. Then, using both hands, he pushed me halfway off the examination table. I barely caught myself and nearly landed on the floor.

When I think back on this, I wonder why I didn't challenge him in some way. Why didn't I tell him off? Instead, I started crying and quickly walked out of the exam room, out of the building, and back into my car.

Of course, I reported this terrible event to the chief medical officer. It wasn't that people did not believe me. They knew Chuck and his temper. They could see him doing this. And Chuck never denied it. He had been at PacMed for as long as I had, and he was a well-respected pediatrician. His wife, Ronny Levitt, also a pediatrician at PacMed, told me later that "Chuck just lost it."

Later, people would come up to me, including other male physicians, and say, "It wasn't your fault, Lynne." I'm not sure why everyone said that. I never thought it was my fault. Maybe it was just what one says to abused women. But there was no anger on anyone's part, just sadness. Everyone liked Chuck, and I did, too, until this happened. After about a month, Chuck left PacMed and started working as a pediatrician at Children's Hospital Medical Center in Seattle.

Months later, Chuck wrote me a letter of apology. I never answered it. I was sick of having to deal with abusive men: my dad, George Austin, Jeff Brown, and now Chuck Cowan. It wasn't okay, and I wasn't going to write anything to any of them to make them feel better. I was done with abusive men.

———◆·◆———

In August 2000, Ron and I decided to try a different bicycle adventure. Together with two other friends, we took a train from Seattle to Eastern Montana. We had our bicycles with us and were fully loaded, with large saddle bags on both sides stuffed with sleeping bags, tents, food, first aid, and all other necessary supplies. Once we arrived, we rode west through Montana, up and over Glacier National Park, and back to Seattle. This was not a lightweight randonneuring ride, and we had no timetable. We just took our time. The scenery was magnificent, especially riding over Logan Pass in Glacier National Park. We even saw a big moose with a huge rack, standing in a pool of water having a drink.

I thought this ride would be a good training experience for Paris-Brest-Paris 2003. It was good for overall endurance, but not the kind of bicycle-riding that would prepare me for another 750-mile ride with a time limit. I knew I could finish a 325-mile ride, but could I really finish a 750-mile brevet in the time limit given?

First, I asked around the bicycling community. What were the resources for help in the Seattle area? My problems were more than "just eat and drink more" or "just ride faster down the hills to make up the time." I had to find another solution.

In July, I went to the Washington Institute of Sports Medicine and Health. I had heard about Dr. Steven Bramwell from the Seattle sports community. His evaluation found that I was in "excellent fitness and maximum functional capacity for my age." In order to ride faster, I would need to "push up my anaerobic threshold as a percentage of my max Vo2 to 85 percent, and increase my maximum Vo2 by doing longer rides at an anaerobic threshold."

In other words, I was getting nauseated on bicycle rides because I was riding too fast and pushing myself over and into an anaerobic threshold. I needed to train by doing shorter sprints to increase my anaerobic threshold, so I could ride faster and still maintain an aerobic state at a lower heart rate. By staying in an aerobic state, I'd be able to avoid nausea and vomiting.

Through Dr. Bramwell, I contacted John Hughes, a bicycle-racing trainer in Boulder, Colorado. He had trained the winner of the famous RAAM (Race Across America) the year before. RAAM is the longest annual endurance ride in the world, starting on the West Coast of the United States and ending on the East Coast. It's a 3,000-mile race, nonstop, with no stages. The fastest riders need slightly over seven days to complete the course.

John devised a bicycle training program that he emailed to me from Boulder every week. Now I rode with a heart rate monitor. He gave me weekly assignments for riding, using my heart rate and distance for guides.

I learned so much from John Hughes about improving neuromuscular efficiency in my pedaling technique, increasing my ability to burn fat during long events, and improving the endurance of my cycling muscles. I put miles and miles on my trainer late every evening and early every morning.

In December 2001, Eric, Kye, and I planned a trip to Seoul, South Korea, to visit Kye's parents. That trip was wonderful. I had never been to South Korea before. Being "the mother of the son" goes a long way in Korean culture, and I was treated like royalty.

———◆•◆———

One day, back at home, Kell was sitting on the couch looking very distraught. Through that winter and spring, I could see he was becoming more and more unhappy. At Christmastime, I asked him what books he would like for presents. He gave me a list of 12 books to choose from, and I bought them all. He was a voracious reader, but I noticed over the subsequent months that he wasn't reading his new books. Also, he no longer seemed to enjoy many of his favorite foods.

Kell was very close to his psychiatrist, Chet Robachinski, and saw him every week. Chet prescribed many different medications, but nothing was really working. Kell heard about Electroconvulsive Therapy (ECT) and wanted to try it. Chet wasn't in favor of this treatment, but Kell was insistent.

I tried to talk him out of it, but he said, "Mom, I have been miserable and depressed for five years now, and I can't live like this any longer."

Kell got a medical release from work and moved back into my house. He underwent several ECT treatments, but they never worked, instead causing Kell to lose some of his short-term memory.

One Saturday that spring, Ron and I went on a long bicycle training ride. On the way home, we passed a construction site with some unsecured orange plastic material surrounding it. A gust of wind came up, and part of the orange plastic flew up and got caught in my front wheel. My bicycle flipped and flung me to the ground. I sustained a head injury, had a traumatic seizure, and fractured my left clavicle and pelvis. I eventually ended up at Harborview Medical Center for about four days, but fortunately, I didn't need surgery.

When I was released from the hospital, I couldn't walk and was confined to a wheelchair and a hospital bed on the top floor of our house. Aziz and Seema cooked dinner and brought it over every night.

In June, I was finally ready to return to work.

Kell asked me, "Are you sure, Mom, that you won't need me anymore?"

I was so eager for him to get on with his life that I reassured him I was fine. Several days later, I got a call from him. He was in the emergency room after attempting suicide by cutting his wrist while at work. An admission to the psychiatric unit of the hospital was highly recommended, but Kell refused. I insisted that he come home with me, which he did.

Chet Robachinski thought the episode was more of a cry for help than a serious attempt to kill himself. Chet told me that in the past, Kell had said repeatedly that the only reason he did not kill himself was because of me.

Kell decided he wanted to go to Europe by himself. Chet and I both talked with him and told him that as soon as he got better, he could go. Kell accepted this with some resignation.

I called Jacquey and arranged for Kell to fly down to Berkeley for the weekend to see her, Steve, Saul, Leib, and Jesse. Kell was really looking forward to this visit. When my boys went down to Berkeley, they always stayed overnight with my mother in a loft in her small house, less than two blocks from Jacquey. They could go to and from each house easily.

I have pictures of Kell and my three nephews from that weekend. Kell looks solemn and serious with his three smiling cousins clustered around him. He turned 24 that weekend. While he was flying home, I called my mother and asked her how the visit went. She sounded exasperated and irritated.

"Oh, he is so high maintenance!" she said. She went on to complain about his lack of engagement.

"But Mother, he tried to kill himself last week!" I protested.

"You can always use that suicide card!" she said.

Her words left me reeling. I quickly hung up. It was an uncaring, ignorant, and selfish conversation on my mother's part, and it was the last time I would allow myself to be hurt by any interaction with her ever again.

That Sunday, when I picked Kell up at the airport, he told me he wanted to go back to his apartment. I said no, I didn't think he was ready yet. The next day, he found out he had lost his job due to the suicide attempt. After five years, he was now unemployed.

That evening, Kell had an appointment with Chet. I drove him there and sat in the waiting room as usual. Halfway through the appointment, Chet called me into his office.

He started by saying, "Kell wants to go back to his apartment. He is 24 years old, and you can't keep him with you."

I protested that he had lost his job and didn't have any new structure in his life yet. Kell looked stoney-faced at me.

"I want to go back to my apartment," he said slowly, with emphasis. "I want to go tonight."

I reluctantly agreed to drive him back to his apartment that night.

I hated to leave him there alone, but he was insistent. I hugged him and told him that I loved him. Then I drove home.

The next morning, the phone rang. It was Kell! I was thrilled.

"Kell, how great to hear from you!" I exclaimed. "How is everything? I want to get a new television hookup for your apartment so that you can record your favorite shows."

He said very solemnly, "That's fine, Mom. Have a good day."

About 5:00 p.m., Eric Kingsbury, Kell's best friend, called me. He said he had a date with Kell for dinner that night, and Kell wasn't answering his phone. Eric was alarmed. I then tried to call Kell myself; there was no answer. Terror crept over me.

I immediately called Chet Robachinski. Chet was somewhat irritated with me.

"Lynne, Kell is 24 years old, and you can't keep track of him like this."

I protested that he had made a suicide attempt, and I was worried.

Chet finally said, "If you can't reach him by 9:00 p.m. tonight, then you can go over to his apartment."

At 9:00 pm, I made another call to Kell. No answer.

Ron and I got ready to leave for Kell's apartment. Eric and Kye were over at my house that evening for dinner and they agreed to follow us in their car. All I could do was review the CPR steps in my mind over and over again. The ride to Kell's apartment filled me with such dread. I was terrified.

We arrived at the apartment and banged on Kell's door. There was no answer. I called 911. Ron ran down the stairs to open the door of the apartment building so the police would be able to enter.

I felt completely paralyzed. Some of it is now just a blur. I remember Kye and me holding onto each other and crying in the hallway as we waited.

The police came. Then the EMTs. There was nothing anyone could do. Kell was dead. When they finally broke the door down, they found him lying on his bed with the television on.

I recently looked at Kell's death certificate. I had never really looked at it carefully before. His death was estimated at 4:10 p.m. There is no way I could have saved him. Eric Kingsbury's call to me was around 5:00 p.m. Even if I had driven up to his apartment then, it would have been too late. The fatal drugs in his system were effexor, oxycodone, and loraze-pam: all drugs that had been prescribed to him over the past year. He had been saving them up.

Late that night, after Ron and I got home, Chet Robachinski called me to ask about Kell. I hadn't thought to call him.

I started crying, "Kell is gone, Chet", I told him.

Chet started crying and said, "Oh, Lynne, I am just devastated!"

I knew that he really cared for Kell; he was a skilled psychiatrist and had done what he thought was best.

We had a big memorial service for Kell at Dave and Suzanne's house, attended by more than 130 people. I was paralyzed and held Ron's hand the whole time. Jacquey, Eric, Eric Kingsbury, Kell's father, and several of my friends spoke at the service. I did not speak; I couldn't. I felt near hysteria.

Chet and I had a long talk a few days later. I told him I had received a card from a good friend, Jan Suyehira, a family practice physician. She had written wise and meaningful words to me in that card, which I shared with Chet:

> I am so sorry to hear of the death of
> your son, Kell. Despite the pain and
> suffering that you are experiencing
> now, know that it is but a fraction of
> the pain and suffering that Kell was
> experiencing before he died. Kell had
> a terminal illness, unresponsive to all
> treatment and therapy. Mike and I
> have you in our thoughts.

Jan's words stunned me. They made sense. Kell really did have a terminal illness. I think Chet and I saw things a little differently after that. We had both done our best. Kell had done his best. He was not suffering any longer.

After Kell died, I knew there was no question but to go on. I had another son and a daughter-in-law. And since 2009, I have a wonderful grandson, Soren. Eric wrote to me later, "Mom, we have more memories to make together." I know that is what Kell meant when he said to me on the telephone the day he died, "Have a good day, Mom."

I mentioned that Kell made a good friend at his apartment, Eric Todd. After Kell died, Eric wrote me a letter. In part, he wrote:

> Kell and I spoke freely of our relationships with family and friends. He occasionally had harsh words for his father, but never did he express any negative thoughts about you. He spoke of you frequently and in glowing terms. He knew you loved him and wanted him to get better. He told me, more than once, that you were the reason he was still alive. He wanted to get better, and he did not want you to be sad if he left the Planet Earth. Kell loved you, and you are the reason he stayed so long. Thank you for keeping him here a little longer.

Kell and Kye at Kye's graduation from the School of Social Work at the
University of Washington, just a few days before Kell's death

I continued working at PacMed. I was 56 years old and had been there
for 20 years. I loved my job, but I was tired. The hours could be long,
and I was still rounding at Evergreen Hospital Medical Center, which
added to my workday. I had a large patient load because I had been with
PacMed so long. And then there were my administrative responsibilities,
both as medical director at Totem Lake and Eastside.

Frank Baron had been my dad's internist and had taken very good care
of him when he was dying of lung cancer. After working at PacMed as a
general internist, Frank decided he wanted to become a dermatologist.
He completed a fellowship in dermatology and was working at Minor
and James, a private practice group. Frank planned to start his own dermatology clinic on Mercer Island, located between Seattle and Bellevue.
A year earlier, Frank had asked me to leave PacMed and join him as a

nurse practitioner in dermatology, and also to manage his support staff. But because Kell was very sick at the time, I declined his offer.

After Kell died, Frank approached me again and asked me to join him. He would teach me any dermatology I didn't already know, teach me how to do surgical procedures, and I would see patients and manage his staff. He offered to match what PacMed was paying me. I felt that I needed a change, so I said yes.

I told Frank I wanted to give plenty of notice to PacMed. I owed them at least that much. Ron and I were going to France in August 2003 to ride in Paris-Brest-Paris, so I could start in September 2003. He agreed.

Meanwhile, Ron and I were seriously training. We rode the 200-mile Seattle-to-Portland ride in one day (rather than the usual two days) a few times, and I invested in a really good new bicycle. Despite these efforts, I started having problems with perineal pain after riding 300 kilometers. On one ride, I developed so much pain that I couldn't continue. I had to go to the emergency room, where the doctor said I had an abscess from pressure on the bicycle seat. I had an incision and drainage, along with steroid injections, into the abscess. I was instructed to take sitz baths, and I had to stay off my bicycle for three weeks. It was maddening. How was I to prepare for Paris-Brest-Paris with these problems?

John Hughes said I should go to the Center for Sports Medicine in Boulder, Colorado, and see Andrew Pruitt, an expert in 3-D Cycling Gait Analysis. So we put my bicycle on an airplane, and Ron and I flew to Boulder, Colorado. I had a full 3-D cycling gait analysis done on my new bicycle. The results were surprising: my bicycle did not fit me, and no adjustments on it could make it fit me. My body build was too small for the bike. Even with adjustments, I had to reach too far forward to hold the handlebars, which left me with pressure on my perineum in the wrong places. After riding several hundred kilometers, my perineum just couldn't take it anymore and an abscess would form. In those days, they didn't make a racing bike to fit my small frame. If I wanted to finish Paris-Brest-Paris, I would need to buy a custom bicycle.

Ron and I flew back to Seattle with my now "old" bicycle. After much research, I bought a custom-made, Serotta titanium racing bicycle with a leather Brooks saddle, and it made such a difference. I never had a perineal abscess, or even a sore spot, again. I was getting more and more ready for Paris-Brest-Paris 2003.

Although I had been working with John Hughes for more than a year, I had never actually met him. All our communication had been online. In March 2003, there was a PAC Tour desert camp in southern Arizona, and John Hughes would be there. Ron and I signed up to go. I was really eager to meet him in-person.

Right away, I liked John Hughes so much. He was encouraging, relaxed, and kind. I told him how nervous I was that I wouldn't be fast enough to finish.

He told me, "Ride at a comfortable, conversational pace all day, keep eating and drinking, and you will be fine!"

I did 200 kilometers there in the desert, rode in my heart rate zone, and finished well within the time limit, without any nausea or vomiting. I was thrilled.

Back in Seattle, Ron and I completed the rest of the qualifying brevets, much of them in the rain. I finished on time, but not with a lot of time to spare. I asked John if Ron and I could attend his Leadville 100K Tour, a two-week ride in the Colorado Rockies, as a final preparation for Paris-Brest-Paris. After some thought, he agreed.

Meanwhile, I made plans to leave PacMed to work with Frank Baron. Betsy Plotkin was the medical director of the PacMed North Clinic, and she had become a good friend. When she found out I was leaving, she immediately came to see me. She told me that, when she was a general internist and Frank was a dermatologist, they both worked at Minor and James. She saw many of his support staff as patients. Betsy said that Frank's support staff "just hated him." To a person, they all said that Frank was a very bad individual to work for. They said he was mean, short-tempered, and unpredictable, among other negative attributes. That had not been my experience with Frank, but I had never worked for him before. While I trusted Betsy and knew she was telling me the truth, I couldn't back out now. *It will be different for me,* I thought. *He won't treat me the way Betsy says he treated all the others.*

I left PacMed in June 2003 after working there for 20 years. It had been a great professional experience with unimagined opportunities for me, a nurse practitioner.

CHAPTER 9

---·•·---

Paris-Brest-Paris,
Island Dermatology, and Beyond:
June 2003 to the Finish

AFTER LEAVING PACMED in June 2003, I had two months before Paris-Brest-Paris. Ron and I headed to Colorado for John Hughes's Leadville 100K. It was very challenging, and John actually customized the entire tour for me, knowing I wasn't as fast as the other riders, who were nearly all young men. I was the only woman on the tour. Rather than having me grind out long, slow miles at the back of the pack, he would drive me further along the route and have me ride up all the mountain passes to the very tops. It still was monumentally hard.

The last day of the Leadville Tour was an amazing challenge. We had to ascend 6,600 feet from Idaho Springs to the top of Mt. Evans (14,150 feet). There was no time limit; we just had to get to the top. Ron pedaled past me and gradually disappeared from view. I just kept a steady pace, with my eyes focused ahead of me, up and around every switchback, higher and higher up the mountain. Between labored breaths, I would look out to the beautiful Colorado Rockies around me, with all their glory and majesty. The last few switchbacks were painful. My quads hurt, and I developed a pounding headache. I was the last one of the entire group to finish at the top, but I did it.

It turned out that Dave and Suzanne were going to be in Europe at the same time as our PBP race. They agreed to follow the race in their rented car and support us with food and water at the controls, which might save us valuable time. Their support could very well make the difference between Ron and I finishing on time or not.

The 2003 Paris-Brest-Paris started on August 18. The race was a total distance of 761 miles. There were 4,069 bicyclists at the start of the race, and 3,457 would eventually finish on time. I was determined to do everything I possibly could to finish this time around.

Ron and I with Dave and Suzanne just before the start of Paris-Brest-Paris 2003

At 4:00 pm, off we went in a huge mass of other bicyclists, soon to be spread out across many miles, all cycling toward Brest on the Atlantic coast of France. It soon grew dark, and we turned on our headlights. The Parisian suburbs were behind us, and we entered the French farmland, supposedly the flattest part of the route. That being said, the Paris-Brest-Paris route is famous for not having a single "flat" place along the entire route. The route would climb up to a village or castle, then plunge down hard before rising again.

I was one of the slowest riders, so I had little time for actual sleep. A hotel wasn't even in the picture. When we could no longer stay awake enough to ride, we took power naps, lying on the grass beside the road.

Paris-Brest-Paris is now more than 100 years old. Over all those years, the route has remained largely the same, passing through the same small, rural French villages. The people in the villages along the route eagerly anticipated the race every four years. Children, parents, grandparents, and even great-grandparents stayed up late with flashlights, cheering us on with "Andale! Andale!" as the cyclists passed by.

Ron and I rode all day and all night. We finally saw the parallel bridges that signaled the approach to Brest. We crossed a body of water on the old bridge that now serves mainly pedestrians and cyclists. The views of the Atlantic Ocean were incredibly beautiful, with sparkling blue water and rocky shores. The sun was shining, and there was a cool breeze as we rode into Brest. It was a stiff climb to the control station, where we had our control cards signed, drank some water, and, after a very short rest and some food, started on the 375 miles back to Paris.

On that last morning, when we were nearing Paris, Dave and Suzanne met us on the road, cheering us on again. They had met us at some of the controls and helped us get food and water quickly so we could continue on without wasting time. Dave held up a very amusing sign with two arrows: one pointing the way to Brest, and the other pointing the way to Paris. I believe their support was instrumental to our eventual successful Paris-Brest-Paris.

Finally, Ron and I arrived at the finish. The cut-off time for the race was 90 hours. We finished in 88 hours and some minutes.

John Hughes met us at the finish. I ran up to him, gave him the biggest hug I could, and exclaimed, "I did it!"

He gave me a great big hug back and told me I was the "biggest challenge" he had ever had in training someone for a long-distance ride.

"Why?" I asked.

He said he always trained younger men and was never presented with a 57-year-old woman who vomited after 400 kilometers.

All I could say was, "Thank you, John, for not giving up on me."

John wrote an article about us in a bicycling magazine. In part, it reads:

> Over two years, Lynne and Ron
> developed the habit of succeeding.
> When I saw them in France before
> PBP, they were completely focused
> on the event; no sightseeing for them.
> I knew they had the conditioning and
> determination to ride to Brest and
> back. They would not drop out. And
> I hoped they had the speed to complete

it before the 90-hour cut-off.

Lynne's hug and Ron's handshake at
the finish were particularly rewarding
for me. They had overcome so much
over two years, and persevered for
88 hours. Each finisher of PBP has
grown in character, problem-solving
skills, and resiliency during training, and
put those traits to use during the event.
Each has learned that she or he can
overcome great obstacles, that in life
she or he will be able to say, time and
again, "I did it."

In September 2003, I started working at Island Dermatology. Frank Baron was an excellent internist and a very smart dermatologist. I learned a great deal from him over the next five and a half years. But it was also a tumultuous work experience. As Betsy Plotkin had warned me, Frank had a very short temper and exhibited an ugly mean streak when stressed. He was, on occasion, verbally abusive, even to me. Underneath his charm and skill as a clinician, he had an angry, abusive nature.

As soon as I arrived, Frank took me aside and told me he had just fired the other dermatologist working for him because he had been perusing pornographic websites in the clinic by himself in the evenings and was having an affair with one of the medical assistants. He was a married man with two children. I was left having to pick up the pieces with the staff.

During this time, Ron and I decided to get married. In hindsight, that was a mistake. Ron wanted to get married to make a statement to the Seattle Chinese community that this was a serious relationship, and it validated his need for his divorce from his wife. I wanted to get married because living with a man while unmarried was still uncomfortable for me, even years after the women's movement.

I would have preferred a small wedding, but Ron wanted a big one. He paid for the entire wedding himself by taking a loan from his retirement fund. The wedding took place on March 14, 2004, at Semiahmoo Resort near Birch Bay in northwestern Washington State.

Ron's daughters, Tara and Nikki, were very excited about the wedding. Eric was resigned to the fact of another marriage for me, but he and Kye were still very supportive. My good friend, George Bowden, now a Snohomish County judge, married us.

I mourned that Kell was no longer with us. I placed a chair in the front row of our wedding with a big bouquet of flowers on it. It would have been Kell's chair. It made me feel better to see the chair with the bright, beautiful bouquet of flowers on it, but there was still a huge pit in my stomach. It had been nearly two years since he had died, yet it still felt raw and painful.

My friend Suzanne wisely told me that one does not really get over the death of a child. I understand that now. One cannot live with the devastation, pain, emptiness, deep sorrow, and overwhelming loss. You just take the debilitating, devastating loss and compartmentalize it somewhere inside you because you cannot face it every day and you have to go on. There are others in your life whom you love and who need you to be there.

In November 2004, I got a call from my mother. Her younger sister, my Aunt Maggie, was suddenly admitted to a hospital in Santa Monica, California. This Aunt Maggie had written me a card containing thoughtless words about Kell after his death. She had never even met Kell, and was known to be on the wacky, unpredictable side. Now she had suddenly collapsed and was in the ICU. My mother had flown to California to be with her, but she didn't know what to do. She had trouble putting coherent sentences together as she tried to tell me what had happened. I gave her some advice about what questions she should ask the doctors. My mother's typical take-charge attitude seemed to have left her at that moment. I asked her if she wanted me to come down to California to help her.

"Would you?"

Of course.

Ron and I flew down to Santa Monica the next day. By the time we arrived, Aunt Maggie had died. Aunt Maggie was long-divorced, but still had one 45-year-old son, Steve. He had been living with her on and off in her tiny, cluttered ground-floor studio apartment in Santa Monica. When he wasn't staying with Aunt Maggie, he was living on the streets. After Aunt Maggie died, Steve just disappeared. He had been diagnosed with schizoaffective disorder and also had problems with cocaine addiction. All this information was very hazy, as my mother had not had much contact with Aunt Maggie.

Ron and I spent two days searching all the homeless shelters in the Los Angeles area. One by one, we wandered through these old, dirty, and dilapidated places asking if anyone knew Steve Johnston. We tried to find a picture of him at Aunt Maggie's apartment to show people, but we found only a few faded baby pictures. After two full days of looking for Steve, we gave up for the time being.

Ron and I helped my mother clean out Aunt Maggie's apartment and arrange for her cremation. My mother seemed lost; she wasn't thinking very clearly and was very morose. Aunt Maggie's apartment was cluttered, dirty, and disorganized, and there was the smell of old urine hanging in the air.

After Ron and I left to go back to Seattle, I got another call from my mother. She launched into a long, involved story about Mary Elizabeth Lauffer, my grandfather's aunt. She had lived many years ago in Pittsburgh and was heir to a sizable fortune. Before she died in 1943, she created an irrevocable trust and left money over time to members of her family. My parents used a portion of the trust money for a down payment on their first house in Western Springs, Illinois. Another portion of the trust money was to go to Aunt Maggie's children upon her death. Steve, her only son, was now to receive $11,280.19 in a lump sum.

My mother had hired Gregory Cox, a lawyer in Berkeley, to help sort all this out. Through his instructions, I was able to discover from the Social Security Administration that Steve received $810 per month from Social Security Disability, which was sent to a post office box at the Brooks Hotel in Los Angeles. I should have thought of this before Ron and I spent two days looking for him, but now that I had the address of the Brooks Hotel, I could find Steve.

Mother and I both realized that Steve would lose his monthly disability check if he accepted the money from the Mary Elizabeth Lauffer Irrevocable Trust. He deserved that Lauffer money, but he needed his monthly disability check and Medicaid health insurance. I had several conversations with Gregory Wilcox, who told me that, by law, Steve had to give written notice to his local office of the Social Security Administration immediately after he received the distribution from the irrevocable trust. No one thought that Steve was capable of doing that on his own. He would lose not only his social security disability benefits, but also his medical insurance.

Gregory Wilcox told us that this presented a significant problem, with no clear way to solve it. It was decided that the best way was to have him, as our lawyer, write a Contract for Provision of Shelter. In summary, it read that Steve would give this irrevocable trust money to me, his cousin, and I would pay his rent of $155 per week at the Brooks Hotel with it. The $11,470 would pay for Steve's rental obligations for a period of 74 weeks. He would still have his Social Security money and any money he received from odd jobs to pay for other things. Steve's inheritance would be sheltered, and he would have use of both it and full Social Security benefits.

I thought this was a fine idea. I flew down to Los Angeles, rented a car, and drove to the Brooks Hotel. It was a rundown, dirty, two-story hotel on a dismal, cluttered street. I walked in and asked to speak to the manager. After some time, the manager, whose name was Manuel, appeared at the front desk. He had no teeth and wore old cowboy boots and a shirt stained with chewing tobacco. He was not very communicative. It was my good luck to find that Steve was there, in his room, at that same time.

The manager walked me slowly down the hall, opened the door, and yelled, "Steve, you have some company for a change!"

I walked into a very small room with no windows, completely bare except for a bed right in the middle of the room, with an uncovered plastic mattress and no sheets or blankets. Steve was lying on the mattress wearing a baggy, dirty shirt, pants, and socks. His shoes were under the bed. He had longish brown hair and a stubbled beard.

I smiled at him, held my hand out, and said, "Hi Steve, I'm your cousin, Lynne."

I spent some time slowly explaining the whole situation in detail. He seemed to understand me. The upside of this plan for Steve was that he could have extra money each month because he wouldn't have to pay his hotel bills.

I showed Steve the written documents prepared by Gregory Wilcox. Steve and I signed them, as well as a letter to the Social Security Administration. I also had Steve sign forms giving me power of attorney for both medical and financial decisions. He seemed to trust me.

Steve told me he had lots of money problems and had borrowed quite a bit of money that he couldn't pay back. He and I drove to a seedy part of Los Angeles, where a string of small check-cashing places would hold your post-dated check, give you cash, and then charge a huge interest rate. Steve owed money to all of them. He also had a checking account at Bank of America where he was overdrawn by $652.56.

We went to each of these check-cashing places and Bank of America, and I paid all his bills. He was $485 overdue on his rent at the Brooks Hotel, and I paid that too. I was then able to reimburse myself from the irrevocable trust.

I asked Steve who his doctor was and where he went for healthcare. He said he rarely went anywhere except to the emergency room when he needed to. He had some serious psychotropic medications prescribed by some physicians at the Saint John's Health Center in Santa Monica— Abilify, Lamictal, Cogentin—as well as medications for gastrointestinal problems. I called the center and made an appointment for him with Dr. Gerald Sacks, an internist.

Steve already had a medical record there. After examining him, Gerald Sacks talked with the both of us. He said Steve had some serious health problems, which included hepatitis C, cirrhosis of the liver, portal hypertension, and esophageal varies. This was in addition to schizoaffective disorder and a history of cocaine abuse. Dr. Sacks refilled his medications and referred him to a psychiatrist.

I left Los Angeles, telling Steve to be sure and keep his appointment with the psychiatrist, take his medications, and stay away from alcohol and cocaine. Each week, I sent a check to the Brooks Hotel to pay for his rent; they wouldn't let me pay for a whole month at a time.

All seemed to be going well until sometime in July 2005, when Steve called me "collect" and told me he wanted all the money he inherited, "right now." I explained why that wasn't possible, but he was still insistent. I followed up with a written letter on August 1, 2005, explaining again why this process was necessary for him to continue getting his Social Security and medical benefits and still have access to his inherited money.

On August 9 at 6:15 p.m., while I was still at work, Steve called my cell phone. He told me he was now at the Greyhound Bus Station in Seattle, having taken a bus overnight from Los Angeles. He said he was there to get his money and said, "I will kick your butt if I don't get it."

I called Ron at home, and he understandably felt there was a real risk to me.

In my limited experience with Steve in California, he had seemed harmless. His tone on the telephone was a sort of monotone, despite the threatening nature of his words. Ron would hear none of this from me. I did not argue with him. We had a lot to lose to an angry, potentially dangerous man. How did I know what Steve was really capable of?

So, Ron and I drove down to the Greyhound Bus Station in Downtown Seattle. Steve was there, standing in front of the station. He was disheveled and dressed in his usual dirty, baggy clothes. I told Steve I could not continue helping him in the face of his verbal threats. If he wanted the money, I would give it to him, but only on the condition that Ron and I would drive him to the airport and pay for his flight back to Los Angeles. Once he returned to Los Angeles, he was to call me from the Brooks Hotel. I would then speak to Manuel, the hotel manager, to make sure he was safely back at his hotel and no longer a threat to me. With that reassurance, I would transfer his remaining money into his checking account. Steve agreed to this plan, and Ron and I drove him to the airport.

Once I knew Steve was safely back in Los Angeles and away from us, I transferred all the money to his checking account, which was already overdrawn by several hundred dollars.

That's the last I saw or heard from my cousin Steve. Jacquey, with whom I share an interest in genealogy, found out that Steve died in Los Angeles on March 8, 2012. He was 52 years old. I wish I could have done more for him.

———————◆•◆———————

One time, in a teasing way, I asked Ron, "Why did you marry me?"

I expected a lighthearted or funny answer in return, but he looked at me very seriously and said, "Because you could a bicycle so well on long rides."

I was taken aback. I thought to myself, *What will happen when I am unable to bicycle, or can only manage short distances?* Maybe he was teasing, but it didn't sound like it.

I know Ron tried to make our marriage work. He was a serious man and a hard worker. He was also sensitive and attentive to Kell when Kell was fighting depression. But although Ron was born in the United States, his life was very culturally Chinese. I have always been good at communicating effectively with people. It was one of my best and most important skills as a nurse practitioner. I could usually sense if one of my patients was uncomfortable or upset. When I sensed this, I would find a way of connecting with that person in order to help them. Somehow, though, I missed all of that with Ron.

As our marriage continued, Ron became resentful of things I had no idea about. For example, sometimes I would come home from work, throw myself on the couch, and exclaim, "I had such a hard day today!" Ron never said anything at the time, but much later he told me he felt very resentful of me, like I was saying that he did not have a bad day. I was completely oblivious to his feelings. I never figured out what he was thinking or feeling until it was too late.

One day, out of the blue, Ron said he wanted a divorce. I was shocked. Within days, he had moved out of my house and into a nearby apartment. He asked me if I wanted to see his new apartment, and when I did, he told me he had signed a two-year lease. I was devastated. I cried and cried.

I suggested that we get some marriage counseling, and we went twice. Afterward, Ron said it was too late. He wanted a divorce.

His daughters, Tara and Nikki, were very upset about the impending divorce and Tara tried to talk Ron out of it. I had lunch with Eric and told him that Ron wanted a divorce. He reached over the table and held my hand.

"How are you feeling?" were my son's kind words to me.

Within days of Ron telling me he wanted a divorce, I got a call from my mother saying she had been diagnosed with small cell lung cancer. I knew the prognosis. Hardly anyone survives this aggressive form of lung cancer.

A few days later, I flew down to Berkeley to see her. Jacquey was devastated, and I felt so bad for her. After the way my mother had treated Kell, along with her callous words to me about him, I had detached myself emotionally from her. I was present for her and did what I thought I should, but that was all.

I had planned to fly down to see her once a week during her illness. But before one week went by, I called her and could tell by her voice that she was failing fast. Jacquey lived a block and a half from her and was doing all she could to help. Hospice was involved. I immediately flew down again to Berkeley.

When I arrived, my sister Carol was there with Jacquey, both looking frightened and unsure. I walked into my mother's bedroom and sat down beside her. Her eyes were closed. I gently touched her arm, and she woke up. She seemed glad to see me.

I asked her, "Mother, are you in pain? Do you want more morphine? How do you feel about taking the morphine knowing that it may make you sleepier and unable to talk with us? Either way, it is completely your choice and we want to support you."

She motioned to me quickly with one hand in a horizontal move and said, "I want to be out."

I gave her a sublingual dose of morphine. She fell back to sleep, and that was the last time I talked with her. She died the next day.

———◆•◆———

While all this was happening, I continued to try to find a way to work with Frank Baron at his dermatology practice. As difficult as he could be at times, there were two good things about Frank: he was an excellent dermatologist and a very good teacher. I learned a great deal about dermatology from him, including the diagnosis and treatment of skin diseases and surgical skills. I knew a fair amount of dermatology to begin with after all my years in primary care, but Frank taught me much more.

Gina Fragione, a physician assistant, was hired by Frank just before I came to the practice. Gina and I are still good friends and keep in touch. Both of us were shocked and disturbed by Frank's emotional outbursts and periodic bouts of just plain meanness. We never knew when he would lose his temper or say some really humiliating things to us, even in front of a patient. My resentment at his treatment of me built up over all the years I worked with him, and eventually I had had enough.

I was also the manager of all the staff at the clinic. There was one medical assistant who was Frank's favorite: Yolanda. She just adored him. He treated her differently than all the other medical assistants and gave her special favors. One time, I discovered that when Frank and I were not in the clinic, she, on her own, had tried to inject the veins of another medical assistant to treat spider varicose veins. Not only did she not have the training to do this, but she didn't have the legal authority either.

I confronted Frank with her behavior, but he refused to allow me, as a manager, to do anything about it. Any other medical assistant would be fired after an incident such as this.

He just looked at me stone-faced and said, "I own Island Dermatology, and I can do anything I want to."

Gina was paid based on her productivity, but I was paid a straight salary as a nurse practitioner and manager of the clinic. When Gina went on maternity leave, I covered all her clinical time and saw all her patients. Frank informed me that I would not be reimbursed for all this extra work. How naive of me not to have made financial arrangements with him ahead of time! But I now knew who I was really dealing with. How could this Frank Baron be the same Frank Baron who took care of my dad when he was dying of lung cancer in 1984? Human beings have different sides to them.

I tried to meet with Frank. Just that day, he had hired another clinic manager. This new clinic manager met with me instead and told me that Frank would not talk with me, and all negotiations would have to come through her. I called Ron, who was waiting in his car outside just as a precaution for what might come. Ron and I emptied my office of all my dermatology textbooks, medical journals, and possessions. We got in his car and drove away.

I was now unemployed for the first time since arriving in Seattle for my first job in 1968. I began looking for another job in dermatology. During this time of turmoil at Island Dermatology, Gina decided that she couldn't take Frank's emotional abuse anymore, and she found another job. She told me that Carla Bauman, a dermatologist in Bellevue, was looking for a nurse practitioner or physician assistant to hire. I called her office and came in for an interview. Carla Bauman hired me that day. I started working with her in February 2009.

Around this time, I got a call from Eric. He and Kye were in California on a short weekend trip.

"Mom, Kye is sick," he said. "She has a headache and is vomiting."

I told Eric to take her to the emergency room, but he said Kye didn't want to go. They were leaving to come back to Seattle in the morning.

The next morning, Eric called again; Kye was still sick. I quickly arranged to have her seen in primary care at PacMed. The doctor there asked the obvious question I did not think to ask in my anxious state: "When was your last menstrual period?"

Kye was pregnant, and both Eric and Kye were happy and excited. I was absolutely thrilled. Kye's due date was November 2009. I was going to have a grandson.

I had a very difficult time accepting the fact that I was getting a divorce. I was 63 years old. What woman over 60 cannot hold a marriage together? Ron was a good man. Why couldn't I make this marriage work? I was embarrassed and humiliated. I tried to hide the fact that Ron had left, telling people Ron was away on a business trip. Fortunately, all my female friends knew the truth and were very supportive.

I was grateful for my new job, though. Carla Bauman was a very smart dermatologist. I was fortunate in that both Frank and Carla were excellent at what they did. One cannot take that for granted. If I had a patient with a perplexing skin problem, they both could be relied on to give me quality advice and backup. I didn't have to seek advice very often, but when I did, they were always there. When it came to skin diseases, they were both smart and sharp in making the correct diagnosis and treatment.

The problem with doctors owning their business practices, as opposed to working for a large organization, is that there is no HR department. There is nothing to shield you from illegalities, unfairness, and downright avarice. It's often more serious in dermatology because dermatologists have a large share of the Medicare dollar and are among the highest-paid specialists. The more money one makes, the harder one works to keep that money for themselves.

On one occasion, I was at a large, three-day dermatology conference with about 400 dermatologists. One of the conference organizers stood up and asked for a show of hands to see if everyone was voting straight Republican that year. He was dead serious.

He announced, "We in dermatology have a greater share of the Medicare dollar than nearly every other specialty. We all need to vote straight Republican."

Another problem with doctors is they think they can do anything. After all, they are doctors, aren't they? A few years ago, it was reported that the highest incidence of single-engine plane crashes in Washington State were airplanes piloted by doctors. Carla never tried to pilot an airplane, but she thought she could run her own business and manage the support staff singlehandedly. The truth was that she was a terrible manager. During the time I worked with her, I watched her make mistake after mistake. Consequently, there was a big turnover of staff. The stress was high in the office due to her inability to choose quality people to manage her staff in a fair and consistent way.

On one occasion, when it was obvious that her present manager was not functioning well, she called me late in the evening. I was on the phone for a long time trying to encourage her to make a decision and let this person go. She finally did, but it was exhausting for me. This happened more than once.

Another shock was that, suddenly, I was making literally almost double my income, even more than what I made working at PacMed as a medical director. For the first time in my career, I was being paid a straight percentage of the money I generated. The money allowed by Medicare and insurance companies to bill for dermatology office calls and procedures was much more than was allowed in primary care. Also, many more procedures are done in dermatology, and one can bill for both the office call and the procedure. It angered me to realize the way Frank had taken advantage of my naiveté and passivity and put me on a straight salary with no connection to my productivity.

After Ron left, I didn't experience the heart-wrenching loneliness I felt after Max died. I was sad, but I knew I still had more life to live and more contributions to make. In September 2009, I spent a week in Cape Cod by myself. I rented the same little traditional "Cape Cod" house in the woods of Truro, near Ballston Beach, that Ron and I had rented two years before. I have brought all four of my husbands to Cape Cod at one time or another. Cape Cod has always filled me with excitement and exhilaration. But this time was different. I loved being there, but I was lonely. I went to all my favorite places—Highland Lighthouse, Wellfleet Bay Wildlife Sanctuary Trails—took long walks on the dunes, explored Salt Pond Trails, went on a boat trip to Monomoy Island for a long nature and beach walk, canoed in the evening on peaceful freshwater ponds, and, best of all, rode the waves at my beloved Ballston Beach on the Atlantic Ocean.

Eric and Kye's baby boy, Soren In-Woo Vigesaa, was born on November 30, 2009. This boy is now 16 years old and so monumentally important to me. I have been very fortunate to have him near me during all his years growing up.

When Soren was just a month old, Eric called and asked if I could look after him once a week to give Kye a rest. Absolutely! How fortunate could I be to have this opportunity? I took care of Soren one day a week up until he started high school. It helped that my work schedule was usually four long days a week, leaving me one free day to be with him.

In December 2009, my divorce from Ron was finalized. We had been married just five years. At the time, I was so angry with him. Why didn't he fight for our marriage? What about the marriage vows he said in front of everyone at our wedding? I told him if he wanted a divorce, he would have to pay for it himself. He did. We went to a lawyer of his choice, signed the papers, and it was done.

After we left the lawyer's office, we each walked to our separate cars. I was furious. He waited for me, standing beside his car, and I think he wanted to say something nice. I would have none of it. I just walked angrily past him, got into my car, and drove home. He had told me months before that, although he "respected" me, he could never love me. I have had no real contact with him since our divorce, although I hear about how he is doing from Tara and Nikki.

———◆·◆———

Since my house remodel was finished in 1997, I had become friends with my building contractor, Joe Beck. After the project was completed, Joe and I continued to have a close and genuine connection. We sometimes went to the movies together and would occasionally have dinner at a local West Seattle restaurant.

I sensed at the time that he might have a romantic interest in me. I thought then that it would be such a mistake to have an intimate relationship with him. I was sure it would end up with some terrible, disastrous hurt for both of us. Our relationship had no future, I thought. We came from completely different worlds. Once, I had met a few of his friends at a gathering at his house, and I had little in common with them. The majority were from blue-collar families and had no education beyond high school. They were friendly and nice, but completely different from my own friends. Almost all my friends were college graduates, and some MDs and PhDs.

My parents were both college graduates. There was never any question that, of course, I would go to college and my parents would pay for it. Joe's situation was completely different. His father only completed the ninth grade. His mother never worked outside the home and never even had a driver's license. There was no money or even encouragement in Joe's family for any education beyond high school. Joe worked evenings and weekends bussing dishes at restaurants to pay for his school clothes.

It was unthinkable that I would have had a job while in high school. My job was getting straight A's, or at least trying to.

When Joe was a senior in high school, the Vietnam War was raging. He had a low draft card number, and it was assumed he would be drafted right after graduating from high school. Just after high school, he worked at Boeing for a few months and then joined the Air Force. While in the Air Force, he took classes in electronics and anything else he was offered in the way of school or education. As he told me, when educational opportunities were offered, his hand was the first to go up.

Joe Beck had become a very important friend to me. I didn't want to jeopardize that friendship for some romantic relationship that was doomed to fail. That was what I was sure of at the time.

The fence between my house and my neighbor's house to the south was falling apart. One day, I was outside in my yard, and John, my neighbor, was in his front yard too.

"This fence is really dilapidated." I said. "Do you want to go 'halfsies' on a repair?"

"Sure," he said. "Do you know who we should hire?"

I replied, "My building contractor, Joe Beck, will do a great job."

So we hired Joe to build a new fence between our houses.

Of course, Joe did a wonderful job on the fence. John and his wife, Judy, were impressed. Unbeknownst to me, John and Judy wanted to do a huge remodel on their three-story house. A few months later, they hired Joe for the job.

While Joe was working on John and Judy's remodel next door, I decided I needed to tell him about my divorce, and now was as good a time as any. I walked over to the front door, which was wide open, and knocked loudly. Joe came to the door, covered in sawdust.

He exclaimed, "Lynne! You should have just come in. The door is open."

I stayed outside on the porch. "Well, I need to tell you something. It was not my fault. I tried as hard as I could. But Ron and I are divorced."

I can't remember exactly what he said in response. It was something like, "I'm sorry to hear that." But months later, Joe told me that he thought to himself at that moment, *I'm not letting her go this time.*

In May 2010, Soren was five months old, and Kye was suffering from postpartum depression, although I didn't realize it at the time. When I think back, I wonder how I missed it. I had some postpartum depression myself with both of my children. In retrospect, I should have clearly seen it. I should have known.

Eric and Kye had been big worldwide travelers before Soren was born. Now, they planned a two-week trip to Paris and Alsace for that May. They asked me to go with them, partly to help care for Soren. I leapt at the chance.

The trip was amazing. Each day, I took care of Soren, giving Eric and Kye the chance to go for walks during the day and out to dinner at night. Kye was breastfeeding, and she pumped enough milk for me to feed Soren when they were elsewhere. I remember spending idyllic hours walking through the Louvre with Soren snuggled against me in a front pack. He was a wonderful baby: smiling, healthy, and plump.

After Paris, the four of us took a train to Alsace and stayed in the countryside there. I loved walking with Soren. He rode with me in a front carrier, and I carried diapers and bottles of Kye's breast milk with me. I had his favorite squeezy giraffe toy in my pocket, and his pacifier was dangling on a string on the carrier. Soren and I traveled through acres and acres of cornfields and walked the small streets of a nearby village. The two of us even saw a festival in the village, with men and women dressed in bright-red-and-black centuries-old costumes. The Alsatian villages had beautiful ancient buildings and large clocks high in the courtyards. Soren and I experienced it all.

Over the years, Eric, Kye, and Soren became worldwide travelers:
This is from July 2022 during a trip to Pomarane, Italy

During this time, Joe and I had dinner together a lot. It was so comfortable being with him. We were such good friends. There was just an occasional friendly kiss on the cheek between us, but that was all.

That summer, I had a situation with an angry neighbor who owned a wooded area behind my house. There were no actual markers where one property ended and another one began. I was redoing my backyard, which was on a steep slope, putting in plants to stabilize the slope. He thought I had trespassed on the edge of his property. In an act of retaliation one day when I was at work, he cut down a lilac tree just off my back deck. When I got home, parts of the lilac tree were strewn all over my backyard. I was terrified.

The next day, I called the police, and an officer came and met me on my back porch. I was frightened and tearful, telling the officer what had happened. I felt helpless and vulnerable. Suddenly, Joe was standing beside me. It was such a relief just to feel his support. He and I talked with the police officer. The officer went to the man's house, and, of course, he denied everything. Right after that, I had my property professionally surveyed with markers, so there could be no question of the location of the property line. The man never bothered me again.

That November, Eric, Kye, and Soren—now almost one year old—came to my house on Thanksgiving Day. Kye was clearly stressed, and she was somehow upset and angry with me. I wasn't sure why, and my feelings were hurt. I foolishly tried to defend myself rather than wisely trying to see things from her point of view. She was trying to navigate the most difficult job of balancing her life with the overwhelming responsibility of being a new mother. I did not handle the situation well at all. I should have known better.

I finally mentioned something to Eric. He said Kye thought I had been critical of her as a parent. I was shocked. I had always seen Kye as a wonderful, loving, dedicated mother.

It took a few years to make up for my mistake, but now Kye is like the daughter I never had. I can talk with her about anything, and she listens and understands. She and I have brunch together monthly. I always look forward to spending time with her.

Kye and I at the Paramount Theatre

It crossed my mind that Joe might be interested in me as more than just a friend, but I saw us as just friends, and I was determined to keep it that way. I was still certain we were completely unsuited for any serious relationship. So, over the next few years, Joe and I maintained our friendship. We went out to dinner a few times during the year, and I would call and ask him for advice on my house. I would "pay" him with steak dinners. I never wanted to take advantage of him. He would sometimes call me about some health issue. Our telephone calls were warm and friendly, and they eventually became more frequent.

Morgan Freeman had been my excellent hairstylist ever since I worked at PacMed. Being prematurely gray and having to "look good" in a dermatology office, I had started having her color my hair every two weeks. In November 2010, she opened her own salon in West Seattle. I was her first client there, and Joe came to pick me up because we planned to have dinner together afterward.

Two weeks later, I was back at Morgan's salon again.

"So, do you like this guy Joe?" she asked.

I told her that Joe was my building contractor and a good friend.

"Well, Lynne," Morgan said. " You sure don't act like he is 'just a friend.' There's a whole lot of chemistry between you, and a lot of it is coming from your side."

The whole conversation with Morgan really upset me. Was I heading into a romance that would end in disaster? Someone was bound to get hurt. It would never work out. I asked her what I should do.

"Well," she said slowly, "you could consider being 'friends with benefits.'"

What? Honestly, I had never even heard that expression before. Morgan explained what it meant. She added, "You could suggest that to him. No strings attached."

I was stunned. Friends with benefits—what did I think of that? I considered it for a long time. I felt things were about to get out of control for Joe and me.

In December, I attended a three-day conference on melanomas in Albuquerque, New Mexico. It was an excellent conference, and I was excited about how much information was shared.

As I was relaxing in my hotel room one evening, I read that the new *Harry Potter* movie had just come out. Joe and I had talked about how much Kell had loved all the *Harry Potter* books, as well as the movies. I spontaneously called Joe and told him about the upcoming movie.

He responded, "Would you like to see it?"

I said I would.

Joe and I went to see the new *Harry Potter* movie the next weekend. Before the movie, we walked around the Pacific Science Center grounds. I felt my heart racing. Joe took my hand, and I let him. *Is this a mistake?* I wondered.

In the theater, we sat very close to each other, still holding hands. I thought to myself, *I'm afraid this is a really big mistake.* But after the movie, Joe drove me home, and I gave him the usual peck on the cheek, and that was all.

The next weekend, Joe and I planned to have dinner together in West Seattle. Toward the end of the dinner, I turned to face him in the booth. My palms were sweaty, and I was slightly lightheaded. I reached within myself for some courage. I quietly asked him what he would think about us being "friends with benefits."

His eyes widened, and he looked a little surprised. He held my hand and replied, "Well, Lynne, we can talk about this."

"You have to promise that no matter what happens, we will still be friends," I said.

"Yes, Lynne, of course," he replied.

I didn't believe him; I was a complete emotional wreck.

As crazy as it may seem, Joe and I planned it all out. The next weekend, we went back to the same restaurant for dinner and then back to my house. What can I say? It was a night like none I had ever had in my life. It was as if all this friendship, caring, and love that had been percolating between us for 15 years just bloomed into the most unforgettable night.

Four months later, on July 5, 2011, Joe and I were married just before sunset on Ke'e Beach on the island of Kauai. It was a beautiful wedding, just the two of us. A Hawaiian Kahu (minister) married us. At the end of the ceremony, there was a little sprinkling of rain. The Kahu said it was a blessing on our marriage to have that sprinkling of rain on our wedding day. All these years later, we feel that blessing every day.

The sunset was magnificent.

Married at sunset on July 5, 2011,
at Ke'e Beach on the island of Kauai

Epilogue

Just before I turned 70, I retired from nursing and healthcare. It seemed like the right time. Joe and I had plans for more adventures.

I encouraged Joe to stop accepting more clients and instead work full-time remodeling his own house near the beach on Puget Sound. He gutted most of the inside and remodeled it for just the two of us. After both Max and Kell died while I was living there, it was hard to go back to my old house. Joe and I now had our own house together.

We are no longer able to carry heavy backpacks, but now we have a 20-foot Lance travel trailer that we pull with our Ford F150 truck. We have traveled all over the western United States and hiked in many national parks. We have also made several trips to Europe for more hiking and exploring.

Kell is buried here in Seattle. Every few months, I visit his grave, so thankful for the 24 years I had with him. I miss him so much, but I'm grateful he is no longer suffering from depression.

Eric, Kye, and Soren also live in Seattle. Soren is a sophomore in high school. The three of them remain a huge part of my life.

Joe and I have been married for 14 years, which have been some of the happiest I have ever had. I feel so fortunate.

I hope you've enjoyed the book, finding it both useful and fun. I have a favor to ask you.

Would you consider giving it a rating wherever you bought the book? Online book stores are more likely to promote a book when they feel good about its content, and reader reviews are a great barometer for a book's quality.

Lynne Barber Vigesaa

Get this book for a friend, associate, or family member!

If you have found this book valuable and know others who would find it useful, consider buying them a copy as a gift. Just contact Lynne Vigesaa at lynnevigesaa@me.com.

About the Author

Born when women faced limited expectations beyond marriage and motherhood, Lynne Barber Vigesaa revolutionized nursing practice in Washington State. Growing up in northern New Jersey, she discovered her calling at age 12 while caring for her Grandma Nellie during her final illness.

After graduating from Columbia University School of Nursing in 1968, Lynne moved to Seattle and fell in love with the Pacific Northwest's mountains. Her passion for hiking evolved into serious mountaineering, leading her to summit Mt. Rainier, Mt. Baker, Glacier Peak, and many others. She completed the challenging Ptarmigan Traverse twice. She traveled for extended trips to China, Mongolia, and Pakistan with her second husband, Max, who was a skilled mountaineer and climber. In Mongolia, they traveled for a week across the Gobi Desert. They spent an exciting but harrowing trip toward the basecamp of K2 on the Concordia Glacier.

Professionally, Lynne pioneered the nurse practitioner role by establishing Washington State's first independent nurse practitioner clinic in rural Darrington. Governor Dan Evans appointed her to the Washington

State Board of Nursing for five years, where she helped define independent prescriptive authority for nurse practitioners—legislation that
transformed the profession. She later served 13 years as medical director at Pacific Medical Center and became the first nurse practitioner to
receive hospital privileges at Evergreen Hospital Medical Center.

Her adventurous spirit extended to endurance cycling, successfully
completing the grueling 750-mile Paris-Brest-Paris race in 2003 after an
initial failed attempt in 1999. Now approaching 80, Lynne lives in Seattle
with her much-loved husband, Joe. Her son, Eric, daughter-in-law, Kye,
and amazing grandson, Soren, live nearby and continue to be a large part
of her life.

Lynne can be reached at: lynnevigesaa@me.com

www.ingramcontent.com/pod-product-compliance
Lightning Source LLC
Chambersburg PA
CBHW060411130626
46555CB00005B/2028